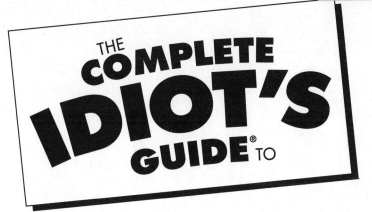

THE
COMPLETE
IDIOT'S
GUIDE® TO

Choosing a
College Major

by Randall S. Hansen, Ph.D.

ALPHA

A member of Penguin Group (

This book is dedicated to everyone searching for a meaningful career, searching for a college major and career that will lead to a successful and fulfilling life.

ALPHA BOOKS

Published by the Penguin Group

Penguin Group (USA) Inc., 375 Hudson Street, New York, New York 10014, USA

Penguin Group (Canada), 90 Eglinton Avenue East, Suite 700, Toronto, Ontario M4P 2Y3, Canada (a division of Pearson Penguin Canada Inc.)

Penguin Books Ltd, 80 Strand, London WC2R 0RL, England

Penguin Ireland, 25 St. Stephen's Green, Dublin 2, Ireland (a division of Penguin Books Ltd.)

Penguin Group (Australia), 250 Camberwell Road, Camberwell, Victoria 3124, Australia (a division of Pearson Australia Group Pty. Ltd.)

Penguin Books India Pvt. Ltd., 11 Community Centre, Panchsheel Park, New Delhi—110 017, India

Penguin Group (NZ), 67 Apollo Drive, Rosedale, North Shore, Auckland 1311, New Zealand (a division of Pearson New Zealand Ltd.)

Penguin Books (South Africa) (Pty.) Ltd, 24 Sturdee Avenue, Rosebank, Johannesburg 2196, South Africa

Penguin Books Ltd., Registered Offices: 80 Strand, London WC2R 0RL, England

Most Alpha books are available at special quantity discounts for bulk purchases for sales promotions, premiums, fundraising, or educational use. Special books, or book excerpts, can also be created to fit specific needs.

For details, write: Special Markets, Alpha Books, 375 Hudson Street, New York, NY 10014.

Publisher: *Marie Butler-Knight*
Editorial Director: *Mike Sanders*
Managing Editor: *Billy Fields*
Acquisitions Editor: *Tom Stevens*
Development Editor: *Julie Bess*
Production Editor: *Kayla Dugger*
Copy Editor: *Jeff Rose*

Cartoonist: *Richard King*
Cover Designer: *Bill Thomas*
Book Designer: *Trina Wurst*
Indexer: *Brad Herriman*
Layout: *Ayanna Lacey*
Proofreaders: *Mary Hunt and Donna Martin*

Contents at a Glance

Contents

Appendix

Introduction

You'll find that you'll make many, many important decisions while you attend college, but certainly one of the most important of those is choosing your major(s) and possible minor(s), along with a clear career direction.

Let me start with taking some pressure off of you. Choosing a major is a journey—a journey that takes time and considerable research and reflection. In most cases, you have no reason to rush into a decision … so, as I love to say to all who will listen: Don't panic! Take a deep breath and let this book be your guide.

Besides being an author and career expert, I am also a college professor, and I can assure you I had no idea about being any of these things when I was a teen—or even when I was in my twenties! But then again, I also did not have a book like this one to help guide and direct me, and I might have found these careers sooner if I had.

My agenda? I want you to be happy. I want you to be able to let go of outside influences, outdated stereotypes, and misconceptions, and find the career and major that will make you happy and fulfilled. Unless you are independently wealthy, you will spend more time at work than anywhere else, so shouldn't you have the right to find a career that you love?

This is the type of book that will continue to serve you, even after you have chosen your major, so I encourage you to read it and keep it nearby.

What's in It for Me?

Not to sound overly dramatic, but this book will have a significant impact on your life, perhaps even change your life. Some people say a college major is not important; it's getting the degree that matters. In my view, both are important. Yes, you need the college degree to get your foot in the door for most jobs, but choosing the right major gives you a much bigger advantage in moving ahead in your career—whether getting a better job upon graduation or getting into the graduate program you desire.

A final comment for both genders, though it's especially for the female students reading this right now. Please do not let anyone or anything discourage you from pursuing your career passion. Years ago, certain careers were gender-specific, but no more. You have the opportunity to find a job in any career you choose—as long as you have the skills and ability to succeed in it.

How This Book Is Organized

This book is organized into six parts.

Part 1, "Choosing a Major and a Career," provides you with insights into finding your career passion, discovering more about yourself and possible careers and majors, researching potential careers, and learning more about college majors and minors.

Part 2, "Careers in the Arts Using a Major in …," focuses on a wide variety of career options if you decide to major in the arts, which are defined broadly to include everything from the performing arts to the fine arts and English and foreign languages.

Part 3, "Careers in Business Using a Major in …," stresses the types of career paths you can pursue with various majors in business, including accounting, finance, international business, management, marketing, and real estate.

Part 4, "Careers in the Sciences Using a Major in …," highlights the wide variety of careers available to you if you choose to major in one of the "hard" sciences, such as chemistry or biology, as well as engineering or physics.

Part 5, "Careers in Service to People Using a Major in …," invites you to learn more about careers that have a direct impact on helping people—with majors in education, health care, exercise science, and pre-med and pre-pharmacy.

Part 6, "Careers in the Social Sciences Using a Major in …," spotlights a wide variety of career paths you could follow if you major in one of the social sciences, including history, psychology, and sociology, as well as criminology and pre-law.

Extras

As you work your way through the book, you'll encounter some extra bits of information that I believe you will find helpful as you make the journey in choosing a major and career.

Here's what you can expect:

This little chart-and-arrow icon indicates job growth potential.

And this little dollar icon indicates high earnings potential.

The Professor Says

These tips are intended to give you more details, insight, and insider information.

Major Pitfalls

Occasionally, I will warn you of some typical problems or issues that you'll want to avoid or minimize.

A Day in the Life

These career snapshots are designed to give you some insights into a typical day in a specific career.

profiles

My hope is that you'll be inspired and empowered by these real career stories.

Acknowledgments

No book today is written in a vacuum, and this book owes its content to a bunch of people and sources—all of whom I owe a debt of gratitude. First, to my agent, Marilyn Allen, for bringing me this book project. Second, to my loving and amazingly talented partner and spouse, Katharine Hansen, for her insights, reflections, and careful edits, without which this book would not be nearly as good as it is. Third, to my business experience class at Stetson University (where I teach), who while learning more about their own majors and careers, also compiled some of my preliminary research. Finally, to my current and former deans at the School of Business Administration, Stetson University, Dr. James Scheiner and Dr. Paul Dascher, for their continued personal and professional support in encouraging me to pursue my career passions.

In terms of content, this book pulls together information from many, many sources—from government, industry, and business—to provide you with the best and most useful information possible about careers, jobs, and salaries. For career outlook information, the best source will always be the U.S. Department of Labor's Bureau of Labor Statistics, which publishes the *Occupational Outlook Handbook* (in print and online). For salary information, the two best sources are Salary.com and PayScale.com, as well as various professionals and industry sources.

Special Thanks to the Technical Reviewer

The Complete Idiot's Guide to Choosing a College Major was reviewed by an expert who double-checked the accuracy of what you'll learn here, to help us ensure that this book gives you everything you need to know about career and major selection. Special thanks are extended to Kelly Cleary, a wonderful person and dedicated career professional, for her detailed comments and suggestions in making this a better book for you.

Trademarks

All terms mentioned in this book that are known to be or are suspected of being trademarks or service marks have been appropriately capitalized. Alpha Books and Penguin Group (USA) Inc. cannot attest to the accuracy of this information. Use of a term in this book should not be regarded as affecting the validity of any trademark or service mark.

Part 1

Choosing a Major and a Career

This part provides you with insights into finding your career passion, discovering more about yourself and possible careers and majors, researching potential careers, and learning more about college majors and minors. While it might be natural to jump ahead to the chapters whose subjects interest you the most, I encourage you to read through these first three chapters. You'll learn about the importance of finding your career passion for success in college—and in life. You'll also find some great information about how to learn more about specific career paths, and I'll walk you through the basics of what college is all about.

The following chapters will give yout the tools to not only discover the future you envision, but to develop the skills to succeed in it.

"I need advice on a major."

Chapter 1

Planning Your Future

In This Chapter

◆ Learn the importance of career planning

◆ Begin to see the connection between passion and career

◆ Take the leap to learning more about yourself

◆ Conduct some self-assessment exercises

Congratulations! By opening this book and reading this first chapter, you are already on your way to a more rewarding, enjoyable, and successful future—in college and in your career. Didn't know it was that easy, huh? Well, it's not really, but making the commitment to start thinking about your future is a very, very important first step.

If you're like the typical college-bound teen, you may know you want to go to college—maybe it's even expected of you. However, you probably have no solid idea of what you should—or want to—major in once you get there. And even if you think you know for sure what you want to major in, this chapter will still help you learn more about yourself and perhaps open up some new doors and other possibilities. The same holds true if you have way too many ideas about what you might want to major in; this chapter will help narrow your focus.

This chapter is all about helping you do some initial planning for your future. Don't worry; you don't have to make a decision today that you have to stick to for the rest of your life. The work you do in this chapter, however, will give you a solid foundation for learning more about yourself.

And no jumping ahead! Before you even think about looking to see how an art major compares to a marketing major, you should take the time to look at yourself—your interests, talents, and ambitions—because that's what career planning is all about.

Career Planning 101

Have you been asked this question yet by your parents or other family members: "So what are you planning to do with your life?" If you have, and you're like most of us, your typical answer is some sort of mumbled response. And that's okay; it's a scary question, especially for a teen. Imagine the idea of having to choose just one thing to do for the rest of your life! Heck, it's a scary question to ask someone of almost any age.

You might not be aware of this fact, but people of all ages struggle with career planning, and a lot of people choose a career for all the wrong reasons. For example, some people choose their career based on family pressure to do so, while others do it for the expected financial rewards. Your goal should be choosing a career for the right reason—because it's something you are passionate about, something you can see yourself doing for a long time.

Major Pitfalls

Don't let anyone convince you that your career dream is unattainable. Most people mean well in trying to steer your career search in a certain direction, but only you know yourself—and until all the doors are shut in your face, there is always the possibility that the next one you try will open to the career of your dreams.

Because of advances that enable people to live longer and changes in retirement requirements, some of you will work for perhaps 50 years once you finish college. That's a long time to be in one career! And guess what? If you're like most people, you won't stay in one career all that time; studies show that people change careers (not *jobs* but *careers*) about five or six times over their life. So choosing a career path in college is important, but over the next 50 years your tastes and interests may change—and new careers that do not even exist today are bound to emerge, some of which may appeal to you.

Finding Your Career Passion

"Passion" may seem an odd word choice when paired with "career," but rest assured that one of the most important elements of personal happiness is being passionate about your career and your job. You do not want to be one of those people who live for the weekends and dread Sunday evenings. Life is too short—though you may not believe that just now—to not love the work you do.

Will you love your work and your career as much as you love other things and people? Why not? It is completely possible to not only find the career that is a perfect match for your skills and interests, but also one that inspires you and fuels your desire to perform better and work harder.

At this point in your life, you may not have much—if any—work experience, but if you have worked one or more part-time jobs while in high school or college, you know how many of these positions are just dreadful. These are dead-end, low-paying, low-respect jobs that help you pay the bills or save for a new car or trip but give you very little personal fulfillment.

Finding a career that you have a passion for is all about obtaining fulfillment. Some of these jobs may also not be the highest-paying jobs in the world, but career passion is not about the money; it's about how the job makes you feel inside. So as you look at some of the starting salaries listed later in this book, don't let a lower-paying job stop you from considering a career in that field.

Loving your job and career will go a long way toward loving your life, so take the time to find your career passion. The ideal scenario is one where you find a career that combines what you love to do with what you're great at doing.

The Professor Says

Can you get a good job after college without putting forth all this effort? Sure, but it is a lot less likely that you'll find a job you love without doing so. And if you're okay stocking shelves or waitressing until you can get into graduate school, then feel free to put off making any decisions about your college major and career until then.

Paper and Online Assessments

An easy place to start looking at majors and careers—and perhaps learning more about yourself—is to take one or more self-assessments. So go ahead and take some of them.

You may be surprised about how much you learn about yourself and your preferences. While no single assessment will give you all the answers you may seek, they are a great place to begin your self-analysis.

Your high school guidance office or college career center should be able to provide you with at least one assessment. Books of self-assessments are widely available, as are plenty of assessment tests online.

Remember, though, that assessments cannot predict the future, and the results you get are only as good as how well you respond to the questions. In other words, if you plan to take the time to complete one or more assessments, take the time to do them thoughtfully so you get as much useful information as possible.

The two most common types of assessments are personality and type indicators and interest inventories.

Personality and Type Indicators

Your personality is a combination of a number of traits—behavioral, temperamental, emotional, and mental—and these assessments attempt to measure them.

Myers-Briggs Type Indicator (MBTI). This very popular tool measures your preferences along four dimensions and places you into 1 of 16 different "types." Much research has examined type and value structures, communication styles, and career choice.

Keirsey Temperament Sorter. Similar to MBTI, this tool places you in one of four temperaments—or personalities—defined as long-term patterns of behavior. Within each of the four temperaments are an additional four subsets of more specific personality types.

The Big Five Personality Test. This tool measures what many psychologists consider to be the five fundamental dimensions of personality—extroversion, agreeableness, conscientiousness, emotional stability, and intellect/openness.

Interest Inventories

As their name implies, these tests attempt to assess the things that most interest you and then match those interests to possible careers.

Campbell Interest & Skill Survey. This assessment, which focuses on careers that require post-secondary education, measures self-reported vocational interests and skills and confidence in your ability to perform various occupational activities.

CareerKey. This tool is based on Dr. John Holland's personality types and is designed to help you discover which Holland personality types you are most like, identify the careers that are most promising, and learn detailed information about each one.

FOCUS. This popular tool for high school and college students assesses your interests, skills, work values, personality, and preferences and helps you explore occupations, career paths, and educational programs that match your personality.

Motivational Appraisal of Personal Potential (MAPP). This assessment attempts to identify your true motivations toward work, allowing you to match yourself to job categories to see where you best fit. It also identifies your learning, communication, and management styles, as well as your leadership preferences.

Strong Interest Inventory. This assessment, widely used in college career centers, also uses Holland's types, providing you with a rating for each of the six Holland Codes. However, it also provides you with results on basic interests, occupations (211 in the current inventory), and personal style.

The Professor Says

Don't get too caught up in the results of these assessments; they are simply designed to give you some insights into your personality and highlight some of your interests and strengths. So if you don't like the results from one of the assessments, simply toss them aside and move on with your career exploration.

Ask Yourself These Questions

One of the best tools for clarifying your underlying interests, passions, and possible career paths is to sit down and reflect on a series of questions about how you have lived your life thus far. These questions are designed to really make you think and reflect on who you are as a person and what you want to become.

So find a place where you can sit down for a while, grab a pen and some paper, and start the process. You don't have to respond to all of these questions in one sitting … and it might be best, once you have answered all the questions, to take a break before you try to determine what your answers mean for your future. The only real rule for this exercise is to be honest with yourself.

Your favorite activities. What do you love to do in your free time? Try to brainstorm five to eight activities. Don't count activities you have to do or are doing to make yourself look better to college admissions folks. Identify the activities that you truly enjoy. Once you're done writing them down, look for a theme.

Skills that come naturally to you. What are the skills that come to you without thought and effort? Are you a math whiz who can easily add and subtract large numbers in your head? Can you hear a foreign language and immediately be able to replicate the inflections? What are some of the things at which you are a "natural"? Brainstorm three to five of these skills.

Your favorite classes and subjects. Looking back through your school years, what were the classes—or specific subjects—that you enjoyed the most, that inspired you to learn more? These do not need to be the classes in which you received the highest grades; rather, these are the classes that you actively attended because you loved the course material. Make a list of your favorite classes and subjects and look for some themes.

Your dream jobs and careers. If you could do any job in your life, what would you choose? You may have done this exercise in elementary school, but it's time to do it again; however, you can keep the same jobs you chose then and any others that interest you now. The key is to ignore any roadblocks and simply choose dream careers. So for example, even if you always wanted to be a fighter pilot but are not eligible because of health reasons, still put it on your list. Write down at least five careers that you think you would enjoy.

Types of things that energize you. What types of things energize you? Think about people, places, and activities. For example, if you are a diehard competitor that rises to the occasion no matter how tired you are, then competition should be on your list. If visiting the zoo is still something that gets you excited, put it on your list. Try to develop three to five examples.

Your lifelong interests. Examine the past 5 or 10 years for activities, subjects, or causes that you have been deeply involved with at a personal level. What are some of your long-term interests? For example, if you have always loved bicycling, have a poster of Lance Armstrong (or wear one of his wristbands), or ride your bike as often as you can, put biking on your list. Record your list of interests—and then look for themes and connections.

Areas where you are already perceived as an expert. What are a couple of areas where your friends and family see you as an expert—or at least as someone who is knowledgeable about the issue? Are you the person in your family that everyone finds when they are having a problem with their computers? Are you an expert on all things related to baseball? Write down as many examples as you can think of where you are an expert.

Outside influences and pressures about what others think should be your career. Sometimes we think we want a career in a certain career field simply because we have been told so many times that we're perfect for it (even if we hate the thought of ever doing it). So try and separate true interests from ones where you have been influenced by others—or ones you are pursuing because you want to please someone else. Write down your *true* career interests (if you have not done so already).

Values you most cherish. What are the values you hold dear and that help guide how you live your life? Make a list of them. This one may be the toughest for you to tackle, but think about the core values and principles by which you live your life. Typically, these are most influenced by your upbringing—your family's values and your religious beliefs. This question is critical because you will never be able to work in a career that does not offer the same values that you possess.

Subject areas you most enjoy reading about. When you are in a bookstore or the library, what are the subjects of the books and magazines that you are drawn to? What websites do you visit the most and devote the most time to? These subjects can be related to your classes and schoolwork but should not be ones that you are required to read; rather, these are subjects you enjoy reading for your own pleasure and knowledge. Develop a list of your favorite subjects.

Best type of work environment for your personality. What type of work environment fits you best—the fast-paced, always-changing, or the slow-paced, predictable? This question might be a little premature for you to answer, but you could also think about the various classroom or teaching styles you have experienced in the past and see if you prefer one style over all others.

Your volunteering and community service experience. What types of volunteering have you done or wish you could do? Again, as you make this list, think about experiences you would participate in even if you were not using them for college applications. What types of community service appeal to you? Look for a theme in terms of the types of organizations, types of people, or types of service you perform.

Majors and prospective career paths taken by your friends. Make a list of the careers that your closest friends work in (or plan to work in). See anything that really grabs your interest? Write it down. Please note that this examination is not about copying what your friends are doing; rather, because friendships are formed around common interests and bonds, examining their plans may provide some insight into your interests.

Your deeply rooted beliefs—your life's calling. Have your friends and family told you repeatedly that you would be excellent in a particular job or career? Do you have a deeply held desire for a particular career? Do you think about your calling in life? It sounds corny—or maybe even sacrilegious—but some people are born for certain careers. For me, it's about being a teacher, about empowering people and making a difference in their lives. What's your calling? Write it down.

Types of things you currently do to help people. When your friends or family ask you for help, what are the types of things they ask you to help with? What are the types of things you wish people would ask you to do? If you're still struggling with this one, use this prompt: people I know often ask me for help with .... Make a list.

Goals in life you want to achieve. What are some of the big goals you want to achieve in life? Do you want to save lives? Makes lots of money? Be a movie star? Live in a big house? Save Earth? Become president? Think big here—and think about the top couple of goals that mean the most to you right now. (Note, of all your answers, these will probably change the most as you move through life.) What types of careers might help you accomplish these goals? Write down answers for both goals and careers.

Your self-discovery results. Gather your assessments, preliminary research, and answers to the questions and see if you can find a couple of obvious themes running through them. Don't rush this process ... contemplate. Make a final list of potential jobs and career paths.

We'll spend the next two chapters first looking at how you can learn more about careers, and then at how majors fit into the whole picture. So if you need more time to think about your passions, take your time—the following chapters will wait until you are ready to proceed.

The Least You Need to Know

- Choosing a career is a big decision for you, and one that does not need to be—and should not be—rushed.

- The happiest and most successful people are those who are passionate about their careers.

- Career planning is all about self-discovery—learning more about who you are, what you're good at, and what you want to accomplish in your life.

- There are multiple tools and methods for self-assessment and self-discovery—and the more of these you use, the more you'll learn about yourself.

Conducting Career Research

In This Chapter

- ◆ Discover the importance of a career-fitting major
- ◆ Use your network of contacts to learn about careers
- ◆ Acquire useful tools for conducting career research
- ◆ Find out how to go about gaining real-world experience

After completing some self-assessment in the previous chapter, now knowing yourself better than perhaps ever before, how can you leverage this new-found knowledge about yourself to find the ideal career? What are some of the best methods for conducting the same depth of research on careers as you did on yourself? Why is it even important to spend the time researching careers?

This chapter will provide you with the tools you need to make informed choices about your future—in your choice of college major and in career paths.

Looking for Fit

Some experts believe there should be very little connection between major and career—that students should choose a major for the value of learning, not to help with a career. But both are intimately related and should ideally focus around your career interests, skills, and passions.

For example, if you have a passion for history, and that's what you major in while attending college, then it would be odd for you to then go into sales rather than pursue a career in a field that uses those same passions, such as becoming an archivist or working for a museum or historic site.

That's the value of this book—it links hundreds of real career paths and jobs with 26 academic areas (comprising 58 majors). You can see what types of jobs and careers are available for someone with a passion for design or psychology or the sciences.

Once you have chosen a major and one or more potential career paths, how do you know they're right for you? Let me recommend four ways to test whether you have chosen the right major and career. If possible, start this process as early as possible in your college career—or better, while still in high school.

Before you begin the process, organize some research on the major. What are some typical jobs and career paths of graduates? Spend some time examining in detail the lives of people in these jobs. Research what typical days at their jobs look like.

All this research and all these experiences should give you enough information to help you decide if you have chosen the right field. By the way, if you find you really do not like any of the career paths for your major, then you'll need to consider if you have time to change your major or make other changes to find your correct career path.

Finally, remember that for many of us, it takes years and years to truly find our career passion. We may work in or around it for years before we truly find it. Others make dramatic career changes later in life. The sooner you start this process, the sooner you'll achieve success.

Using Your Network

Probably the best way to conduct research on careers is by sitting down and asking people about their jobs, and this section and the next describe how you can find the people to interview and what the process might be like for you.

Perhaps one of the most overused and misunderstood words in career development is "networking." Your network—more formally called your network of contacts—is simply everyone you and your family and friends know. So your network includes your family, friends, neighbors, teachers, classmates—and their family, friends, neighbors, teachers, classmates, and so on.

The Professor Says _____

Here are some questions you could ask people about their careers:

- ◆ How did you choose your career?
- ◆ Would you choose it again if given a second chance?
- ◆ How did you prepare for this career?
- ◆ What was your first job after college?
- ◆ What's a typical day like for you?
- ◆ What's the best part of being in this career?
- ◆ What's the worst part of being in this career?
- ◆ What was your major in college?

People in your network have a vested interest in helping you because they are either directly or indirectly connected to you, so they are more likely to agree to sit down with you and chat about their careers.

Thinking about becoming a lawyer? It's pretty likely that there are several lawyers within your network of contacts—and all it takes is asking around. And obviously, the bigger your network, the more likely you'll find several people you can talk with.

Once you've tracked down people with the careers you are considering, the only thing you need to decide is how to best approach them—and whether you want to chat with them in person, by phone, or by e-mail.

Once you're done meeting with them, keep a record of what you learned so that you can add it to your career research. Finally, a nice touch to help you be remembered for the future is to send each person you talked with a thank-you note, because everyone likes to be appreciated.

The Professor Says _____

More questions you could ask people about their careers:

- ◆ What are the various jobs in this field?
- ◆ Why did you decide to work for this company?
- ◆ What do you like most about this company?
- ◆ Do you find your job exciting or boring? Why?
- ◆ How has your job affected your lifestyle?
- ◆ Are you happy with the salary you make?
- ◆ What are the problems you see working in this field?
- ◆ What are the major frustrations of this job?

Informational Interviews

What do you do if you have a really small family or live in a small town? How can you conduct career research if no one in your network or extended network is in the career you are trying to research? The answer lies in a great tool called informational interviewing.

Informational interviewing is exactly what it sounds like—interviewing designed to yield the information you need to choose a career path, learn how to break in, and find out if you have what it takes to succeed. It's a highly focused conversation with someone in your career field who can provide you with key information you need.

So how do you get started conducting some informational interviews? It's basically a five-step process.

First, you need to find people to interview. Literally anyone is a candidate for an informational interview, from an entry-level employee right up to the top management. And the Internet gives you the tools to find people in just about any job within just about any organization. Some good places to start are with professional organizations, organizational directories, and company websites. If you're currently in college, ask your adviser or professors for current students or recent graduates to interview; you also should check with the alumni office to find graduates currently doing what you want to do. Another great source is speakers brought in to your classes. You can literally contact any organization and ask for the name of the person by job title. There's no one in the world whom you can't try contacting.

Second, you need to contact the person and politely request an interview. Typically, you ask for no more than 30 minutes of the person's time. You can make the request by mail, e-mail, or phone. If someone referred you to this person, be sure to mention that early in the invitation. For example, if your primary-care physician recommended a surgeon to interview because surgery is what you are considering as a career, make certain you mention your doctor's name in the first sentence of the conversation, letter, or e-mail. When setting up the interview, you always want to introduce yourself and explain why you are contacting the person; indicate where you got the person's name; and ask if the person would be available for a short meeting to discuss his or her occupation. You may also want to explain a little about your own background and why you are asking for the interview. Be sure that the prospective interviewee does not get the impression that you are asking them for a job.

Third, you'll want to prepare for the interview by developing a list of questions like the ones mentioned in the tips earlier in this chapter. Gather paper and pen, laptop, or tape-recorder so you can document the interview.

Fourth, conduct the interview as professionally as possible. Arrive on time, dressed as professionally as possible, and never go beyond the 30-minute timeframe unless the person you are interviewing initiates an extended interview. At the end of the interview, thank the person and ask him or her for the names and contact information of people who are in the same career but have had different experiences.

Fifth, always send a thank-you note shortly after the interview. The person gave up part of his or her day for you, so the least you can do is show your appreciation.

Job Shadowing

What do the groundhog seeing his shadow (or not) and career research have in common? About 10 years ago, the National Job Shadow Coalition (comprising America's Promise, Junior Achievement, the U.S. Department of Education, and the U.S. Department of Labor) named February 2—Groundhog Day—as the national kick-off for connecting students from across the country with workplace mentors, with the idea of placing students side-by-side with a professional as he or she goes through a normal day on the job.

Job shadowing, which you can initiate on your own, allows you to see firsthand the work environment, employability and occupational skills in practice, the value of professional training, and potential career options. While job shadowing is a bit more intrusive than an informational interview, it's common enough that you should be able to find several people who will allow you to spend the day with them.

The people to ask about a possible job shadow would be people in your network of contacts or people with whom you had a successful and pleasant informational interview. And certainly check to see if your school has a job-shadowing program already in place.

Here's how to get the most from your job-shadowing experience:

- Dress professionally.

- Arrive on time and be polite, courteous, and enthusiastic.

- Don't be afraid to ask questions, but don't bombard the professional with so many questions that he or she can't get any work done.

- If your professional attends a meeting on your shadow day, by all means ask if you can sit in.

- While your aim is to observe a typical work day, be open to unexpected opportunities such as attending a trade show or meeting of a professional organization with your professional.

- Be open to meeting as many people as possible during the experience.

- Observe everything!

- Be aware of the professional's and the organization's needs as you're shadowing, and do your best not to interfere with the normal workflow.

Finally, remember to always send a heartfelt thank-you to the person you shadowed. While the person probably got a big kick out of showing you the ropes, he or she still gave up a lot of time and energy to show you around, so write a polite thank-you letter.

Internships

Internships—short work experiences—used to be the sole domain of college students, but as more high schools and middle schools have increased career planning and preparation, some very smart and connected high school students are obtaining internships before they even start college. Your goal, now that you are thinking about majors and careers, should be to obtain as many internships as possible before you graduate from college.

Internships are situations where you work for an employer for a specified length of time to learn about a particular industry or occupation. An internship can last anywhere from one week to several months. You can do an internship over the summer (probably the most common), during the school year, or even over school breaks and holidays.

Actually gaining experience in your career field before even taking your first college class is a major coup and one you should consider. And the internship experience will not only provide you with firsthand knowledge of what it is like to work in your prospective career field, it also gives you valuable work experience (whether you decide to change majors and career paths or not) that will help you get your first job after college—and perhaps even help you with your college applications.

The best places to start in tracking down one or more internships are your high school and your network. Ask your guidance counselor about the school's internship program because there may be some local employers who are already hiring high school students. (And here's an idea: if your school does not have an internship program, you might consider working with student government and school administrators to develop one!) If the high school search is fruitless, it's time once again to go back to your network and ask about the possibility of obtaining help in landing an internship.

Finally, one of the other major benefits of internships is that many employers often hire their interns into entry-level positions. Therefore, besides gaining valuable experience, you may actually get one or more job offers from the organizations you intern with while in college.

Major Pitfalls

Unfortunately, most internships are unpaid, so while the experience could be priceless in helping you choose your ideal career and major, if you were hoping to also collect some spending money for prom, a car, etc., you may be out of luck.

The Least You Need to Know

- ◆ One of the most important things you can do to have a successful career is to find a career field that best fits you—your interests, skills, and abilities.

- ◆ The best way to learn if a career is right for you is to spend time researching all aspects of it.

◆ Whenever possible, the best method for researching a career is to take it for a "test-drive" through experiential activities such as job shadowing or internships.

◆ One of the key sources of people—people who will be extremely helpful to you now and throughout the rest of your life—is your network of contacts.

Deciding on Majors and Minors

In This Chapter

◆ Learn the basics of college majors and minors

◆ Begin the process of taking charge of your future

◆ Realize that college is just the beginning

◆ Pursue a major (and minor) that makes you happy

Now that you have learned more about yourself and conducted some research on possible career paths, it's time to examine the paths you might take once you're in college—the correct mix of majors and minors to help you achieve your career goals.

This chapter is about giving you an inside look at what college is all about, helping you deal with outside pressures, and providing advice about always following your passion.

A College Primer

Students in college take a series of courses, some required and some elective, in a variety of fields—but to graduate and earn a degree, you typically need to complete a concentration of studies in at least one area in what is called a major. You may also complete a less-intensive study of one or more areas in what is called a minor.

Degrees

Here's a quick overview of the types of degrees you can earn when attending college:

Degree: An award conferred by a college, university, or some other educational institution as official recognition for the successful completion of an academic or vocational program.

Associate's degree: The standard degree awarded by two-year colleges and institutes that normally requires at least two but less than four years of full-time equivalent college work. The Associate's degree prepares graduates for the workforce or for progression toward a Bachelor's degree.

Bachelor's degree: The traditional degree given by American colleges and universities. It normally requires at least four years but not more than five years of full-time equivalent college-level work. The Bachelor's degree prepares graduates for entrance into the workforce or for progression toward a higher degree or certification.

Master's degree: A post-Bachelor's degree program that requires completion of a program of study of at least the full-time equivalent of one academic year, but not more than two academic years of work. The best-known degrees are Master of Arts (M.A.) and Master of Science (M.S.), but there are a huge variety of others in most industry fields. Some Master's degrees are designed to lead to an eventual Doctoral degree. Many other Master's candidates are in professional programs, preparing for a special kind of work, such as Master of Business Administration (MBA), Master of Social Work (MSW), or Master of Architecture (MArch).

Doctoral degree: The highest degree you can earn for graduate study. The Doctoral degree classification includes such degrees as Doctor of Education (Ed.D.), Doctor of Public Health, Doctor of Nursing Science (D. NSc.), Doctor of Psychology (Psy.D.), and the Doctor of Philosophy (Ph.D.) degree in any field (agronomy, arts, business, food technology, education, engineering, humanities, public administration, ophthalmology, radiology, sciences, etc.).

Post-baccalaureate certificate: A focused and professionally oriented program of study that requires completion of additional credit hours beyond the Bachelor's degree. These programs are designed for persons who have completed a baccalaureate degree but do not meet the requirements of Master's degree programs. Examples include refresher courses or additional units of study in a specialty or subspecialty.

Post-master's certificate: A focused program of study that requires completion of additional credit hours beyond the Master's degree, but does not meet the requirements of academic degrees at the Doctoral level. Examples include refresher courses or additional units of study in a specialty or subspecialty.

Professional degree: An earned degree in one of the following fields: chiropractic medicine (DC, DCM), dentistry (DDS, DMD), medicine (MD), optometry (OD), osteopathic medicine (DO), pharmacy (Pharm.D), podiatry (PodD, DP, DPM), divinity/ministry (BD, MDiv), law (LLB, JD), rabbinical and Talmudic studies (MHL, Rav), or veterinary medicine (DVM).

Majors and Minors

A college major is an organized collection of classes focused on a specific academic discipline (subject, professional field). When completed, a major makes you knowledgeable in that discipline, preparing you for either a career or further studies in graduate school. Most colleges will offer the same core classes with each major, but additional courses taught within the major are often different from college to college because of the specific interests or backgrounds of the faculty teaching at each academic institution.

Do you need to choose a major today? Not unless you are a junior in college still struggling to find one. In fact, staying undeclared your first year of college might be your best choice—especially if you still have no idea what you want to do with your life—because you can take a variety of courses, dabbling in a variety of fields until you find ones that appeal to you.

On the other hand, keep in mind that if you plan your four years of college well, you can often major or minor in multiple fields—making you a stronger candidate for employers or graduate schools—and still graduate in four years. Once you have chosen your major, become an expert on it—on

The Professor Says

If you have enough electives and are searching for a second major or minor, you should seriously consider one in business. Think about it. No matter what your career path, whether working for a big corporation or starting your own business, you will need business skills to be successful.

the classes that are required for it, the sequences in which the classes must be taken, and the elective classes you wish to take. You should be able to find all the details you need in your college or university's bulletin or catalog, as well as in your major's fact sheet or website.

Changing majors is typically more paperwork than anything else, so do not let the process stop you from changing to your new major. Keep in mind that some majors require prerequisites—courses you'll have to take before you can declare the new major. And you won't be alone in changing your major, as some students change their majors multiple times over the course of their college careers.

Professors and Advisers

No matter what type or size of college you attend, some of your best resources for major and career advice will be your professors. Obviously, small colleges and universities, which tout small class sizes and availability of their faculty, have an advantage here, but even if you decide to attend your state's massive public university, you should always have access to your faculty—it will just be easier in smaller schools than larger ones.

Your professors are there to guide you, direct you, and empower you. They are experts in their fields, and as such, they can provide you with all sorts of advice about the major, about graduate programs, and about careers. The catch? You'll need to be proactive and ask them for help. Most faculty are required to hold office hours to meet with students, so track down the information and show up during office hours to ask for guidance.

What do you do if you are thinking of a major or career path, but have not taken a class in that area yet? You can still easily find a professor who teaches in that area and schedule an appointment. If you're unsure, ask some upper-level students who have taken courses in that major which professor is the most approachable.

The Professor Says

While this book focuses more on majors, jobs, and careers, it is important to note that while your college degree is the most important element to obtaining a job upon graduation, the grades you earn while in college are also important. Besides the fact that some employers screen college job-seekers by their grade point average (GPA), more and more, many fields are requiring graduate studies for career advancement—and one of the key admissions criteria used by graduate schools is your undergraduate GPA.

In most schools, you'll also be assigned an academic adviser. Sometimes these folks are professors in your chosen major and sometimes they are professional staff—like your high school guidance counselor. These people are also good sources for you in your exploration of majors and careers—start with them even if you are considering changing your major because they can give you direction on where you can go to get the information you need.

Career Center and Alumni Office

If you remember nothing else from this book, please remember this advice: as early as possible in your college career, find the career services office and make friends with the wonderful folks who work there. Every university has a career center (sometimes called a Career Development Center or Career Resources Center, and so on), and some larger universities may have multiple career centers. By visiting the center, you'll gain access to a vast amount of resources—from self-assessment tests to major and career information to job-hunting advice.

Most career centers have professional staff whose mission is to help all students find successful and rewarding lives—through guidance in choosing a major, gaining work experience, and finding a job at graduation. The centers also have libraries full of resources to guide you through your four years of college. So whether you are totally undecided about your major or crystal clear about your future plans—or anywhere in between—the career services office will be your ally and trusted friend in helping you live the future you see for yourself.

The other extremely useful office on campus that you should find early on is the alumni office. These are the folks who keep tabs on all the previous graduates of the university. Why would you want to go to this office? Some of the best resources for researching potential majors and careers, finding internships, or learning about graduate schools are your college's past graduates—its alumni. These folks were where you are now a few years back and are almost always willing to lend a helping hand to a student at their alma mater—and you make connections with these folks through the alumni office.

Special Programs

This book is focused on traditional four-year degree programs that result in a Bachelor's degree—and lead to interesting and rewarding jobs and careers—but there are also some colleges and universities that offer special programs that might interest you. These programs are typically five- or six-year programs that lead to a graduate degree in a career field that requires a graduate degree to work professionally. You'll most often find these special programs in the sciences and professional studies, such as architecture, engineering, physical and occupational therapy, medicine, and law.

The advantages of these programs include acceptance into the graduate program (assuming you meet all the requirements) and a slightly shortened timeframe for completing your graduate studies. In some cases, students can complete the two-year Master's program in one year beyond the usual Bachelor's degree.

What's Best for You

Choosing your college major and prospective career path can be a daunting experience, but it's really just a continuation of the journey you have been taking since the first time someone asked you what you wanted to do when you grew up. The response you gave to that question—perhaps doctor, firefighter, lawyer—was your first encounter with thinking about what is best for you, even though you probably did it without much thought or introspection.

The key thing to remember is that it's your future—your college experience, your career, your life. As best you can, you should remove the stresses you may feel—from family, friends, teachers—who may constantly ask you about what you plan to major in while you are in college, because the stress can cloud your judgment and make you rush into something that usually does not have to be rushed.

The Professor Says

Regardless of your major, you should be developing and building a set of transferable skills so that you will be more marketable to employers at graduation. Transferable skills are often called the "soft" skills and include such things as communications, research and planning, interpersonal, decision-making, adaptability, and teamwork and leadership skills.

And while you are removing the stress, also wash away any envy you feel about your friends who seem so confident about what they want to do with their lives and already know their college major and career plans.

On the other hand, don't ignore the issue of choosing a major either. It's okay to feel overwhelmed by the decision at times—as long as you also start sorting out the basics about your future, which is probably why you are reading this book!

Never Be Afraid to Change Direction

Finally, remember that choosing a career—and a major—is a process, and that you may change course several times as you go through the exercises in this book and as you take various courses and encounter new experiences while in college. And don't be afraid to change—many, many college students change their majors at least once before they graduate, and quite a few change their majors several times before they settle on the one for them.

And this process will not stop at college. Finding the best career for you is a lifelong process that just happens to start in college and with choosing a college major. There are career fields that have not even been discovered yet.

The Professor Says

College is about attaining an education while gaining some amount of training for a future career, but don't let major, minor, or general education requirements stop you from also dabbling in courses that interest you. Take as many eclectic electives as you like—that's what college is all about.

The Least You Need to Know

- There's nothing mysterious about a college major or minor—each is simply a concentration of courses within a specific academic discipline, with a major having a higher concentration than a minor.

- Some of the most useful resources for major and career advice are the professors who teach classes in your particular field, so seek out their advice early in your college career.

- Find your college's career center and take advantage of all the tools and resources it offers to help you learn more about yourself, as well as about majors and careers.

- Above all else, remember that choosing a college major and pursuing a career path are choices only you can make for yourself; it's your life and future, not anyone else's.

- Never be afraid to change your major or career plans—many, many college students do. It's far better to change and find fulfillment than not and be miserable in a career that does not fit you.

Part 2

Careers in the Arts Using a Major in ...

This part focuses on the wide variety of career options created if you decide to major in the arts, which are defined broadly to include everything from the performing arts to the fine arts and foreign languages. The chapters that follow focus on careers for people with a talent and a passion for the arts, whether as an artist or musician, an actor or designer, or someone with a talent for communicating in your native tongue or with one or more foreign languages. You'll also find information about majoring in perhaps the most versatile major of them all—humanities.

So if you are a naturally creative person, then you'll enjoy exploring the following chapters, which examine majors in the visual arts, humanities, design, English, foreign languages, and the performing arts.

"Well, check out Mr. Architecture Major ..."

Chapter 4

Visual Arts: Art, Art History, Photography, and Film Studies

In This Chapter

- ◆ Discover careers that use your passion for visual arts
- ◆ Learn the typical classes a visual arts major requires
- ◆ Expected top jobs for a visual arts major

What do you do if you love creating or studying works of art, photography, or film? How can you use your gifts of artistic ability or critical vision in a successful and rewarding career?

This chapter reveals rewarding careers for students majoring in some aspect of the visual arts—art, art history, photography, and film.

About the Majors

Students majoring in the visual arts have a unique talent and appreciation for how people view and perceive works of art, whether the works are paintings, sculpture, pottery, sketchings, photography, or film.

Art/Art Studio

The art major helps students formulate and develop their personal vision. To accomplish this goal, courses teach skills that allow students to express themselves successfully through multiple media. Upon declaring the art major, students designate an area of concentration for advanced-level work. This area could include drawing, painting, sculpture, ceramics, photography, digital art, or a combination of any of these media.

Many colleges and universities offer a major in art. Following are some courses you might expect to find.

Designing for Visual Art	Ceramics: Hand Building
Introduction to Drawing	Ceramics: Wheel Throwing
Introduction to Painting	Sculpture Studio
Photography as Art	Advanced Drawing
Introduction to Sculpture	Advanced Ceramics
Digital Imaging Basics	Printmaking
Drawing Studio	Art in Elementary School
Painting Studio	Art in Secondary School

Art History

Students majoring in art history learn the many ways that cultures express themselves through the arts. Classes focus on the traditional "fine" arts (paintings, sculpture, architecture, prints, and the decorative arts) to more contemporary art forms (advertisements, billboards, commercial signs, and visual culture). In studying art history, students acquire the tools for both visual analysis and historical understanding, learning to analyze individual works of art while becoming proficient in cultural analysis and historical interpretation.

Most colleges and universities have an art history major. Typical courses include:

Introduction to Art History	Topics in Art History
American Art	Art Theory
Ancient and Medieval Art	Introduction to Art Museology
European Art	Art Criticism
African American Art	Comic Art
Modern Art	Art and Business

Photography

Technology has made photography a changing field, so students should look for majors that offer traditional film and darkroom study as well as offering the latest advances in digital photography. A good curriculum should allow students to explore and experiment, combining traditional techniques with cutting-edge digital technology to achieve hybrid results.

Photography is fairly specialized, so you will need to seek out universities that offer this major.

Typical courses include:

Basic Photography	Large Format Photography
Intermediate Photography	Photojournalism
Color Photography	Digital Imaging
Color Processes	Advanced Digital Imaging
Lighting Techniques	Pinhole Cameras
Studio Lighting	Manipulative Photography

Film Studies

Film studies majors learn the impact film has on culture as an art form and a social medium by studying film history, theory, and production. Most curricula typically apply this theoretical knowledge to the experience of filmmaking and exhibition through programs in script writing, photography, production, and digital editing.

Sometimes part of a broader visual arts major and sometimes as a specific major, film studies can be found at a number of larger universities. Typical courses include:

Introduction to Film	Women and Film
Film Theory	Experimental Film
History of Film to 1940	Art and Digital Technology
Film Styles	Film Editing
History of Film Since 1940	Film Criticism and Theory
Screenwriting	World Cinema
Film Production	The Business of Film
Film and Literature	Computer Animation

Background on Careers

Artists generally fall into one of four categories: fine artists, who create original work using a variety of media and techniques; craft artists, who create or reproduce hand-made objects; multimedia artists and animators, who use electronic media to create visual images; and art directors, who manage the art creation and distribution process. Almost two thirds of artists are self-employed. (For those interested in graphic design, see Chapter 6.)

Art historians typically specialize in a specific time period or region of a country and become experts in their field or teachers. Some art history majors go into art administration, where they handle the business end of arts exhibitions and arts programming.

Photographers shoot pictures that tell a story or record a significant event. Some photographers specialize in a certain area of photography, such as portrait, fashion, commercial, corporate, scientific, news/editorial, architectural, or fine arts. More than half of photographers are self-employed.

Film study majors typically take one of two paths—producing original work (whether commercial or documentary) or analyzing film in the context of film criticism.

Some top jobs and careers for students who earn a Bachelor's degree with a major in the visual arts include …

Curator Assistant. As an assistant curator, you'll work with the art museum curator to administer all aspects of the museum's permanent and visiting collections, and deal with all aspects of new collection acquisitions. Some curators specialize in particular media, eras, or locations. Aspects of the work include deciding how to best display, catalog, and safeguard the art collections. You'll also help create supporting materials, such as guidebooks and informational plaques.

Design Assistant. In this job, you'll work with the design director and other members of the design staff in any number of industries, including fashion, architecture, the arts, and marketing. Your daily work assignments may require drafting, model building, and fabrication skills, as well as an understanding of conservation issues. You'll also work with multiple outside vendors and handle general office duties.

Illustrator. As an illustrator, you'll create drawings and pictures that portray your own or other people's ideas. You may work in any number of diverse fields that require illustrations, including textbooks, storybooks, cartoons, advertisements, commercial packaging, or company annual reports. Successful illustrators determine the nature and subject of their work by consulting with clients, editors, writers, and art directors for creative direction.

Animator. In this job, you'll find yourself designing and producing computer-generated images or cell animations for advertisements, television stations, video games, films, and the Internet, as well as for product-design, medical-imaging, architecture, and interior-design firms. And within each of these industries, you might perform a variety of roles, including 2-D animator, 3-D animator, character designer, color specialist, inker, background painter, prop designer, storyboard artist, layout artist, special effects specialist, or compositor.

Production Assistant (Film/Television). As a production assistant, you will find yourself performing a variety of different jobs. This position is a foot in the door to the film or television industries. You may find yourself working on the set, in the production office, with the art department, at the costume department, for the transportation division, or on location—most of the time running errands and assisting in the smooth operation of production.

Art Educator/Education Assistant. In this job, you'll work in a museum or gallery playing a vital role in the educational experience of the organization's patrons. This position often designs and arranges various educational activities and programs for all current and incoming exhibits, including classes, workshops, lectures, tours, and community outreach programs. You'll often also serve as liaison to all the area schools and teachers, and should have some interest in curriculum development.

Other Career Possibilities. Here are some other job and career paths for visual arts majors:

Antiques Dealer	Art Instructor
Art Acquisition Specialist	Art Librarian

Camera Operator

Film Critic

Filmmaker

Film Restoration Artist

Greeting Card Designer

Painter

Photographer Assistant

Potter/Ceramicist

Program Assistant

Script Editorial Assistant

Sculptor

Sound and Special Effects Specialist

Story Editor

Talent Agent

The Professor Says _____

Some of the more lucrative and prestigious career paths that art majors follow require additional education at the graduate level. These careers include:

◆ College Professor (Master's degree or higher)

◆ Art Lawyer (Juris Doctor)

◆ Art Therapist (Master's degree or higher)

◆ Arts Administrator (Master's degree)

Skills Needed/Developed

Visual arts majors develop valuable and transferable skills. The following skills are the most critical to graduates:

Creativity and Vision. Artists and critics use intuition and innovation to understand and extract ideas while generating and analyzing visual concepts.

Communications. A career in the arts requires strong speaking, interpersonal, and writing skills to effectively express the concepts behind the art created or analyzed in individual or broader contexts.

Cultural Analysis. A sense of aesthetics and the cultural value of art, from both a historic and current perspective, is vital for a career in the arts.

Technical/Computer Skills. As careers in the arts continue to evolve, there is a growing need for the use of computers in creating and analyzing art.

The Professor Says _____

Other transferable skills you gain from these majors include:

◆ Attention to detail

◆ Flexibility

◆ Time management

◆ Project management

Expected Growth

Jobs in the arts, whether for artists who create works of art or film critics who analyze the work, will always be available—but growth in new jobs is expected to be moderate.

Artists

Job growth for artists is expected to be about as fast as the average (10 to 15 percent) for all jobs, but competition remains strong as the number of artists exceeds the number of available openings.

Sources of additional information:

◆ Alliance for the Arts (www.allianceforarts.org)

◆ Americans for the Arts (www.artsusa.org)

◆ Arts Resource Network (www.artsresourcenetwork.org)

◆ College Art Association (www.collegeart.org)

Art Historians

Job growth for art historians is expected to be about as fast as the average (10 to 15 percent) for all jobs, but job placement will be competitive.

Sources of additional information:

◆ Association of Art Historians (www.aah.org.uk)

◆ Art History Network (www.arthistory.net)

Photographers

Job growth for photographers, while expected to be about as fast as the average (10 to 15 percent) for all occupations through the next decade, is highly competitive, with many people attracted to the field.

Sources of additional information:

◆ Professional Photographers of America (www.ppa.com)

◆ National Press Photographers Association (www.nppa.org)

Wondering what employers look for in a staff photographer? Here's a sample photographer job description:

> We have an opening for a staff photographer for our magazine publications and tabloid life section. Potential candidates should be skilled in portraiture, feature and fashion photography, and have a solid knowledge of both studio and on-location lighting. Two years experience is preferred, but recent graduates will be considered. You must have a degree in photography from an accredited four-year college or university. Our Life Section and magazine publications combine lively, engaging images on display covers, with the best reporting and visual storytelling, both still and video. The monthly magazines are glossy and compete with several other rack publications throughout the city. Our photographers are expected to be full contributors to the idea process that drives our publications' coverage.

profiles

Photographer/Filmmaker Lauren Greenfield

Lauren Greenfield is known for her work in documenting the youth culture of the United States, especially female youth culture, with her work gaining international exposure in newspapers and magazines, books, and museum exhibitions. She graduated with a Bachelor's degree in visual environmental studies from Harvard University and began a career in photography, interning for *National Geographic* magazine. In 2005, *American Photo* named her one of the 25 most influential photographers working today. She has authored two books, *Girl Culture* and *Fast Forward*, and recently completed her first feature-length documentary film, *THIN*, which premiered at the Sundance Film Festival. Her firm, Lauren Greenfield Photography, is based in Los Angeles.

Film Studies/Filmmakers

There will always be a demand for filmmakers and the critics who critique them, but job growth is expected to be about average.

Sources of additional information:

◆ American Film Institute (www.afi.com)

◆ Society for Cinema & Media Studies (www.cmstudies.org)

Museum/Gallery Curators

Demand for museum and art gallery curators is expected to be slower than average (under 8 percent) over the next decade.

Sources of additional information:

◆ Art Museum Network (www.amn.org)

◆ Association of Art Museum Directors (www.aamd.org)

Design Assistants

The need for design assistance—in architecture, fashion, and the arts—should continue to spur employment growth.

A source of additional information is the Association of Professional Design Firms at www.apdf.org.

Illustrators

Employment for illustrators is expected to grow about as fast as the average (10 to 15 percent) for all jobs over the next decade. Expect a great deal of competition for jobs.

A source of additional information is the Society of Illustrators found at www.societyillustrators.org.

Animators

Some job growth is expected—about as fast as the average (10 to 15 percent) for all careers—but expect strong competition for available jobs, because qualified applicants generally outnumber job openings.

profiles

Illustrator Edward Gorey

Edward Gorey (1925–2000) was a well-received and well-loved illustrator, writer, and set and costume designer. He studied art at the Chicago Art Institute and French at Harvard University (where he roomed with future poet Frank O'Hara). He started his career as an illustrator in the art department of Doubleday Anchor, illustrating book covers. He later created numerous illustrations for publications such as *The New Yorker* and *The New York Times*, and in books by a wide array of authors from Charles Dickens to John Updike, Virginia Woolf, and many others. He authored many classic works under a variety of pen names. His well-known animated credits for the PBS *Mystery* series introduced him to millions of television viewers. He won a Tony Award for Best Costume Design for his 1977 Broadway production of *Dracula*.

Production Assistants (Film/Television)

Production assistant jobs are expected to grow about as fast as the average (10 to 15 percent) for all careers over the next decade.

Wondering what employers look for in a film production assistant? Here's a sample production assistant job:

> We are looking for a highly organized individual with the ability to manage multiple projects at a time to be the assistant for a small film and video production company. You will report directly to the president of the company whose main responsibilities are directing/producing projects as well as bringing in new projects. You will also work with the marketing department, production teams, and others as needed. Tasks will vary from day to day, but general responsibilities will be managing correspondence, managing and tracking tasks, creating/updating databases, and organizing files and paperwork. More interesting tasks will include assisting on the production of film/video projects, writing for projects, creative input, and much more depending on your interests/skills. It is essential this individual have excellent time-management skills, a sense of urgency to get things done, and an ability to prioritize what is important each day in the office.

Art Educators/Education Assistants

Job growth is expected to be about as fast as the average (10 to 15 percent) of all careers over the next decade.

A source of additional information is The National Art Education Association found at www.naea-reston.org.

Wondering what employers look for in an educational assistant? Here's a sample art education assistant job description:

> We seek an energetic art historian to play a critical role as part of the team in both initiating and implementing the museum's educational programming. In tandem with regularly scheduled gallery and garden lectures, the educator holding this position is responsible for all weekend programming, including family workshops, adult courses, and the Saturday lecture series. In addition, the successful candidate will specifically serve as a liaison and resource for teachers and high school students, including coordinating the high school/staff mentoring internship. We prefer a candidate that has previous art education or museum experience, with a strong knowledge of modern and contemporary art. We require an undergraduate or Master's degree in art history, fine arts, or art education.

The Professor Says

Not sure about these career choices? These are just some of the career possibilities for a major in the visual arts. Remember that it is always important to learn more about prospective careers by going online, talking with professors, conducting informational interviews, and job-shadowing.

Earnings Potential $

While there is great variability in the earning potential of jobs in the arts, overall, visual arts graduates earn about $29,000 per year—much less than the average annual salary for all college graduates, which is currently around $38,000.

This section provides some general guidelines of salaries to expect upon graduation. Remember, salaries vary by employer, industry, and region.

Photographer. Median annual salary of an entry-level photographer is approximately $26,000. Freelancer salaries vary widely.

Curator Assistant. Beginning salary for a curator assistant is $33,300.

Design Assistant. Median annual earnings of a design assistant is about $35,500.

Major Pitfalls

Ever heard the comment about starving artists? You better believe it, as the vast majority of artists are self-employed and often eke out a career as an artist by supplementing their income in some other work or profession.

Illustrator. The median annual salary of an entry-level illustrator is about $34,500. Freelancer salaries vary widely.

Animator. The median annual salary of an entry-level animator is $40,000. Freelancer salaries vary widely.

Production Assistant. The average salary for a production assistant is $26,000 a year.

Art Educator. The median annual salary for an entry-level position as an art educator is $34,000.

The Professor Says

What is your next step after choosing your major? You need work experience. Just about all "entry-level" jobs for college graduates require some work experience outside the classroom. Seek out internships, volunteer, and figure out other ways to gain the experience you need.

The Least You Need to Know

◆ Many career paths are open to students who have a passion for the visual arts.

◆ If you love the visual arts, you will be able to find a rewarding career no matter what your artistic talents.

◆ Jobs with a Bachelor's degree in one of the visual arts generally pay much lower than the national average.

◆ Job growth in the visual arts should be moderate, but you should also expect a lot of competition for the jobs that are available.

Chapter 5

Humanities

In This Chapter

◆ Discover careers that use your cultural awareness

◆ Use your varied talents in jobs that demand them

◆ See what a typical humanities major is all about

◆ Learn what jobs you can anticipate as a humanities major

Do you have a lot of different interests? A passion more for learning—for an extensive education—than a career? Do you have talents in the arts and writing? Do you desire a major that provides you a breadth of knowledge about people and culture? This chapter reveals rewarding careers for students who major in the humanities.

About the Major

Students majoring in humanities focus on the study of human culture. Some of these areas, such as art, history, language, literature, music, philosophy, and religion, date back to ancient times. Other fields, such as American studies, film, or digital publishing, study the most recent forms of human culture.

While just about all colleges offer courses in the humanities (and all the related disciplines), humanities itself is actually a fairly specialized major, with a limited number of schools offering a major.

The Professor Says

Why humanities? Here's what one employer has to say:

"Teach kids the humanities, and give them a broad liberal education, and I'll teach them business skills. The ones who will end up in the top 20 jobs in the organization are the people who can stand back and examine the context in which business operates and connect the dots in creative ways."

—Matthew W. Barrett, CEO, Barclays

Of the colleges that do offer a humanities major, the most common method of organizing it is as an interdisciplinary degree program consisting of courses drawn from a number of academic disciplines.

Here are some course requirements you might expect to find if you major in humanities.

Introduction to Humanities	Modern European Heritage
Literature and the Arts	French Civilization
Music and the Visual Arts	German Civilization
Mythology	Russian Civilization
Cross-Cultural Encounters	Italian Civilization
Humanities in America	Modernization and Modernism
Cultural Expression of Gender	Utopia/Dystopia
Medieval Heritage	Twentieth Century Culture
The Renaissance	The Idea of the Self

With additional courses from these academic disciplines:

American Studies	Communications Studies
Art	Comparative Literature
Asian Studies	English
Classics	Latin American Studies

History

Music

Philosophy and Ethics

Religious Studies

Theatre

Women's Studies

Background on Careers

By choosing to major in humanities, you will be preparing yourself for a career that emphasizes creativity, communication, and analysis, and developing the skills sought after by many employers. But unlike other majors that offer very specific career paths, very few careers use the subject knowledge you learn from humanities directly.

Some top jobs and careers for graduates with a Bachelor's degree with a major in humanities include:

Acquisitions Editor, Assistant. In this job, you'll assist the senior staff in working with a book publishing company's current authors, finding and recruiting new authors, arranging for reviews of selected manuscripts by experts in the field, monitoring and coordinating manuscripts through the various stages of acquisition, determining the financial feasibility of new projects, setting book pricing and print runs, presenting projects at marketing launch meetings, and suggesting opportunities for sales and marketing efforts. You'll also handle basic clerical duties and maintain editorial files.

 Major Pitfalls

While a humanities major provides you with many of the skills employers seek, more than any other major, humanities graduates are more likely to go on to graduate school than find a job.

Advertising Copywriter. As an advertising copywriter, you will work with the account-management team and an art director to conceive, develop, and produce effective advertisements that meet client demands. You will write persuasive advertising copy for display in all types of media—including magazines and newspapers, billboards, television and radio, and the web—as well as for catalogs, posters, leaflets, and brochures. You'll also often act as a liaison with production companies, photographers, typographers, designers, and printers.

Art Library Assistant. As an art library assistant, you'll likely work in a museum and gallery library or an academic library, though some larger public libraries also contain an arts collection. The materials typically found include slides, videos, graphic materials, and artist books. As an assistant, you'll work with senior staff in advising and supporting library users; handling reference inquiries; identifying, acquiring, and cataloging art materials; and keeping daily statistics of the library's traffic, usage, and transactions.

Historic Site Tour Guide. In this job, your primary function is historical interpretation of a historic structure or site. You'll also lend a hand in managing operations, conduct informational tours (explaining key points of interest and answering visitor questions), assist in developing interpretive programming, help schedule volunteer staff, assist in planning publicity, and help with writing and developing informational literature and signage.

Retail Management Trainee. As a retail management trainee, you'll work with retail managers, the people charged with making a store, group of stores, or a retail company profitable; they thrive on making it all click week after week and year after year. Through a management-training program, you'll learn all aspects of store management, and usually combine on-the-job training with short courses in special aspects of retail. In some companies, you'll have the title of assistant store manager while in training.

Special Events Assistant. In this job, you'll play a supporting role in coordinating and executing marketing programs, events, and conferences for a particular organization or industry. Events can include business-related sponsorships, trade shows, conferences, and large signature/corporate events. You may be involved with hotel/conference reservations, list management, banquet/food reservations, speaker recruitment, gifts and giveaways, and tracking follow-up activities to measure results of the event.

Writer. There are all sorts of writers, but typically you'll either work for an employer or client and have specific topics assigned to you, or you'll work on subjects that interest you and develop documents (articles, short stories, book manuscripts) that you will then pitch to potential buyers (as a freelance writer). Writers gather and interpret information from a variety of sources, often adding their interpretation of the material as they develop their finished product.

Other Career Possibilities. Here are some other job and career paths for humanities majors:

Bibliographer

Book Reviewer

Community Relations Specialist

Fact Checker

Historian

Legislative Aide

Narrator

Playwright

Poet

Politician

Public Information Officer

Publishing Assistant

Speech Writer

Storyteller

Technical Writer

The Professor Says _____

Some of the more lucrative and prestigious career paths that humanities majors follow require additional education at the graduate level. These careers include:

♦ Arts Critic (Master's degree or higher)

♦ Clergy/Religious Leader (Master's degree or higher)

♦ College Professor (Master's degree or higher)

♦ Lawyer (Juris Doctor)

♦ Therapist (Master's degree or higher)

Skills Needed/Developed

Students majoring in the humanities develop numerous valuable and transferable skills, but the following are the most critical to graduates:

Writing. The written word is essential in the humanities. Majors must develop the ability to string together words in a clear, compelling, and persuasive manner; review and modify their work after writing it; and rewrite elements.

Oral Communications. Almost as important as the written word is the ability to express your thoughts in a clear and understandable manner. Humanities majors must learn this important skill.

Critical Thinking and Synthesizing Information. This is perhaps the most important skill humanities majors must master. It includes the process of actively and skillfully conceptualizing, applying, analyzing, and drawing inferences; synthesizing and integrating information; distinguishing between fact and opinion; and/or evaluating information gathered from or generated by observation, experience, reflection, reasoning, or communication.

Research. Simply the ability to conduct, analyze, and report on research using various techniques and sources. Development of these research skills allows deeper investigation into other cultures and cultural artifacts.

The Professor Says

Other transferable skills you gain from these majors include:

- Attention to detail
- Interpersonal communications
- Planning and organizing
- Working independently

Expected Growth

Because of the plethora of careers a humanities major can choose, it isn't possible to provide any general advice about job growth except to stress that the skills developed in this major will never go out of style.

Acquisitions Editors, Assistant

Job growth for acquisitions editorial staff is expected to be about as fast as the average (10 to 15 percent) for all jobs.

Sources of additional information:

- Association of American Book Publishers (www.publishers.org)
- Publishers Marketing Association (www.pma-online.org)

Wondering what employers look for in an acquisitions assistant editor? Here's a sample acquisitions assistant editor job:

> The successful applicant will be responsible for assisting in developing plans for growth; working on-campus and attending conferences to commission new works; soliciting projects from potential authors; and preparing projects for transmittal to production. You must have excellent communications and networking skills, exceptional follow-through skills, strong analytical and business skills, and be familiar with all stages of the publishing process. A Bachelor's degree is required; some acquisitions editorial experience ideal but not required. Travel of 12+ weeks per year for campus visits and conventions will be required.

Advertising Copywriters

Job growth for advertising copywriters is expected to be about as fast as the average (10 to 15 percent) for all jobs.

Sources of additional information:

- ◆ American Advertising Federation (www.aaf.org)
- ◆ Advertising Educational Foundation (www.aef.com)
- ◆ International Advertising Association (www.iaaglobal.org)

profiles

Direct Mail Copywriter Ben Hart

Ben Hart, a pioneer in direct marketing, is a true master of direct mail copywriting. His gift for persuasive communication has generated hundreds of millions of dollars in donations and sales for scores of nonprofit organizations and businesses. Hart graduated cum laude from Dartmouth College in 1982. He has written several books about direct marketing, including *How to Write Blockbuster Sales Letters*, *Automatic Marketing*, and *Fund Your Cause With Direct Mail*. Hart's work has been highlighted in *Direct Marketing* magazine, *DM News*, *Who's Mailing What!* and several books and textbooks on direct mail marketing.

Art Library Assistants

The combination of a large number of retirements and the increase in the use of digital information should spur moderate to high job growth (15 to 19 percent) over the next decade, especially in specialized libraries.

A source of additional information is the Art Libraries Society of America found at www.arlisna.org.

Historic Site Tour Guides

Job growth for historic site guides and administrators is expected to be the same as the average (10 to 15 percent) for all jobs over the next decade.

Sources of additional information:

- ◆ National Trust for Historic Preservation (www.nationaltrust.org)
- ◆ World Federation of Tour Guide Associations (www.wftga.org)

Retail Management Trainees

There will always be a demand for retail managers, but job growth is expected to be slower than average (under 8 percent) over the next decade.

Sources of additional information:

◆ National Association for Retail Marketing Services (www.narms.com)

◆ National Retail Federation (www.nrf.com)

◆ Retail Industry Leaders Association (www.retail-leaders.org)

Wondering what employers look for in a retail management trainee? Here's a sample retail management trainee job description:

> As a store manager you will be running a multimillion-dollar enterprise. In order to prepare you for this role, this position is designed to provide extensive training, both on-the-job and through company training programs, to give you the management and technical skills necessary to become a store manager. Each management trainee works one-on-one with experienced store managers, spending time in each department learning to manage the day-to-day store operations. Management trainees will learn management responsibilities, merchandising, advertising, inventory, bookkeeping, and human resources. Promotion is based on performance and productivity without regard to seniority. College degree and retail experience preferred.

Special Events Assistants

Demand for special events assistants and coordinators is expected to grow faster than average (18 to 25 percent) over the next decade.

Sources of additional information:

◆ Convention Industry Council (www.conventionindustry.org)

◆ International Special Events Society (www.ises.com)

Wondering what employers look for in a special-events assistant? Here's a sample special events assistant job description:

> Interfaces with agencies, personnel, and participants in the execution of special events. Must be flexible and able to work long hours during events, promotions, and concerts. Assists in the production and dissemination of promotional information and signage needed for special events. Provides for and coordinates media coverage of special promotions through television, radio, newspaper, and trade publications. Provides necessary information to enable appropriate departments to evaluate the success of special events and promotions on the basis of media coverage generated or other qualitative and quantitative measures. Required to work on multiple projects. Must be detail-oriented and have excellent organizational and communication skills.

A Day in the Life ... of a Special Events Assistant

8:00 A.M.	Arrive early for work to send out some last-minute e-mails before we hit the road. We're actually doing a week's worth of events, each day at a different venue.
9:00 A.M.	I grab the trip binder and rush out of the office. While traveling, I call my contact at today's venue to make sure everything is ready for us.
10:30 A.M.	Arriving on the scene, it's time to help with final setup.
11:00 A.M.	Because of a snag in the plans, I need to make a quick run to an office supply store to make some additional copies of materials.
12:00 P.M.	The event begins, and my main job now is working the information booth, inviting people up to the table, chatting with them about our services, and making sure they leave with some company goodies.
4:00 P.M.	With the event over, it's now time to help with packing up all our materials and ensuring we know how to get to tonight's hotel.
4:30 P.M.	I call my contact from tomorrow's venue to check on final preparations and learn the media will be at the event.
5:30 P.M.	I arrive at the hotel and check and send e-mails regarding the other events for this week.
6:30 P.M.	Dinner with the crew. We break down the events of today and strategize how tomorrow's event can be better. I mention the media. Media coverage is a great tool for bringing more attention to the event—and ideally better attendance.
8:00 P.M.	Free time at the hotel to relax before tomorrow's busy day.

Major Pitfalls

While graduates in many other majors can search for jobs that specifically list their degree, it's unlikely you will ever see a job posting or want ad that specifically requests a degree in humanities ... but don't let that bother you!

Writers/Authors

Job growth for writers is expected to be about as fast as the average (10 to 15 percent) for all jobs, but competition remains strong, as many people are attracted to writing.

Sources of additional information:

◆ The American Society of Journalists & Authors (www.asja.org)

◆ The Authors Guild (www.authorsguild.org)

◆ National Association of Women Writers (www.naww.org)

◆ Poets & Writers (www.pw.org)

◆ Writers Guild of America (www.wga.org)

profiles

Writer, Scholar Katharine Hansen

Katharine Hansen is a published author, creative director of a major website, and college professor. (She is also the wife and partner of this author.) She graduated with honors with a Bachelor's degree in humanities from Stetson University and is a member of Phi Beta Kappa, one of the oldest honor societies. She teaches business communication at Stetson University, leads the creative charge for Quintessential Careers (the leading career-development site on the web), and has authored many articles and several books, including: *Dynamic Cover Letters*, *Dynamic Cover Letters for New Grads*, and *A Foot in the Door*. She is currently working on two new book projects, both the result of her doctoral studies.

Earnings Potential $

While there is great variability in the earning potential of jobs using your broad humanities skills, overall, humanities majors—at $31,000—earn less than the average annual salary for all college graduates, which is currently around $38,000.

This section provides some general guidelines of salaries to expect upon graduation. Remember, salaries vary by employer, industry, and region.

Acquisitions Editor, Assistant. The average salary for an assistant acquisitions editor is $29,000.

Advertising Copywriter. The average salary for a beginning advertising copywriter is $38,000 a year.

Art Library Assistants. Beginning salary for art library assistants is about $29,000.

Historic Site Tour Guide. Median annual earnings of an entry-level historic site tour guide are $28,000.

Retail Management Trainee. Beginning salary for a retail management trainee is about $40,000.

Special Events Assistant. The median annual salary of a special events assistant is $40,000.

Writer/Author. Salaries for writers and authors vary widely.

The Professor Says

The career possibilities for a humanities major extend beyond the ones featured here. Remember that it is always important to learn more about prospective careers by going online, talking with professors, conducting informational interviews, and job-shadowing.

The Professor Says

Remember that you're not done once you pick your college major—in fact, it's just begun because the next thing you need to do is gain work experience. Just about all "entry-level" jobs for college graduates require some work experience outside the classroom. Seek out internships, volunteer, and figure out other ways to gain the experience you need.

The Least You Need to Know

◆ As a humanities major, your career choices are almost limitless, which is great, but some time and planning are required so you find one right for you.

◆ When you make your career choice, it's best to try and minor or specialize in an area that is career-oriented.

◆ There will always be jobs for people who have a strong understanding and value of culture.

◆ As a humanities major, you'll gain a breadth of knowledge unparalleled by any other major.

6

Design: Digital, Graphic, Fashion, Interior, and Architecture

In This Chapter

◆ Discover careers that use your passion for design

◆ Use your creativity in jobs that demand them

◆ Learn the typical classes a design major requires

◆ Learn the kind of salaries to expect in design

What do you do if you love planning, creating, and building stuff? What can you do with your life if your true passion is design? How can you make a living using the skills of spatial relations, creativity, creation, manipulation, and imaging?

This chapter reveals rewarding careers for students majoring in some aspect of design—digital, graphic, fashion, interior, or architecture.

About the Majors

Design majors share a number of common traits, interests, and skills. You just naturally love to draw, design, and create things—whether art, logos, fashion, furniture, web pages, or more. Design is so much more than a major for most students—it's a lifelong interest. When someone tells you to go back to the drawing board, it's a request you enjoy complying with.

Design is used every day for products, packaging, or clothing; inside our school and office buildings; in the landscaping of our parks; or on our favorite websites and in other publications.

Digital Design

Digital design majors use multimedia technology to assemble graphics, text, sound, and video into meaningful productions. The major includes work in graphic design, art theory, typography, digital image manipulation, animation, and other multimedia applications. Digital designers might work in a variety of fields.

Digital design (sometimes referred to as digital arts) is a pretty specialized major and only available at certain colleges and universities. Typical courses include:

- Introduction to Digital Arts
- Computer Art
- Computer Graphic Art and Design
- Image Manipulation
- Principles of Web Design
- Multimedia Authoring
- Multimedia Communications
- Photography
- Advanced Web Design
- Radio Production
- Advanced Graphic Design
- Image Manipulation
- Digital Media Technology
- Editing and Publishing
- Digital Audio and Video Editing
- Set Design and Lighting
- Applied Desktop Publishing
- Music Technology
- Digital Arts Studio
- Principles of Audio Production
- Fundamentals of Digital Animation
- Multimedia Recording Techniques

Graphic Design

Graphic design majors learn how to use words and images to express messages that an organization wishes to communicate to their audience. Graphic designers work in print (producing logos, newsletters, annual reports, packaging, stationery, and more) and electronically (through websites, interactive multimedia, graphic computer interfaces, television, and video).

Graphic design is a fairly specialized major, so you will need to seek out universities with this major. Typical courses include:

Graphic and Industrial Design Fundamentals

Graphic Design Theory and Practice

Imaging for Graphic Design

Illustration Fundamentals

Typography

Photography

Visual Communication

Creative Illustrations

History of Graphic Design

Advanced Graphic Design Studio

Creative Advertising Design Theory

Digital Graphic Design

Introduction to Web Design

Fashion Design

Fashion design majors learn about designing, manufacturing, and merchandising apparel and accessories. Fashion designers communicate ideas three-dimensionally through their knowledge of color, fabric, and silhouette. Today's fashion designer must produce beauty and excellence in design, as well as a marketable product.

Fashion design is a fairly specialized major, so you will need to seek out universities with this major. Typical courses include:

History of Fashion

Design Studio

Fashion Drawing

Design Construction

Fashion Design

Fashion Digital Studio

Fashion Industry Seminar

Design Technology

Themes in Fashion History

CAD (Computer-Aided Design)

Design Communication

Photography

Fashion Portfolio

Fashion Production and Manufacturing

Interior Design

Interior design majors learn how to envision an entire space, working on all aspects of the space—whether residential, retail businesses, corporate offices, public buildings, or other commercial properties—to help balance the aspirations, functional needs, and budgets of clients through a combination of engineering and artistic considerations.

Interior design is a fairly specialized major, thus many colleges and universities will not have this major. Typical courses include:

Interior Design Studio

CAD for Interior Design

Interior Building Technology

Lighting and Acoustics

Color: Theory and Practice

Set Design

History of Architecture and Interiors

Textiles and Materials for Interiors and Architecture

Restoration/Rehabilitation Interiors

Technical Drawing and Graphic Representation

Architecture

Architecture majors learn how to use both the analytical "left brain" and the creative "right brain" in creating or preserving structures and land, and typically specialize in architecture (to prepare for a graduate degree program), architectural studies, or landscape architecture. Majors in these programs appreciate architecture and aesthetics and desire to continue in the field at some level.

Architecture is a specialized major, thus many colleges and universities will not have this major. Typical courses include:

History of Design

History of Architecture

Architectural Design Methods

Structures and Materials

Construction Management

Model Building

Building Preservation

Landscape/Urban Design

History of Landscape Architecture

Architectural Design: Environment

Architectural Design: Form, Natural Systems, and Architecture

Architecture and Landscape Architecture Studio

Landscape Construction Materials and Methods

Background on Careers

Digital designers typically work in advertising and print fields, as well as in multimedia and interactive design. You'll successfully plan and deliver graphic communications solutions across a variety of media, including video, print, and the web.

Graphic designers plan, analyze, and create visual solutions to communications problems. In this job, you use a variety of print, electronic, and film media and computer software to execute a design appropriate to a given context. About a third of all graphic designers are self-employed.

Fashion designers may design clothing and accessories for a manufacturer in New York, Los Angeles, or anywhere in the world. Apparel technology, production, and distribution are global. Textile and pattern companies, theater, television, film, and amusement parks all require designers of costumes and apparel. About one in four fashion designers are self-employed.

Interior designers can specialize in residential design for single or multifamily properties or in commercial and industrial design for corporate offices, meeting facilities, sports complexes, or medical establishments. About a third of all interior designers are self-employed.

Some top jobs and careers for students earning a Bachelor's degree with a major in design include:

Interior Designer. As an interior designer, you may work as an individual consultant, in partnerships, corporations, or with architectural–interior design firms. You'll generally work under deadlines to satisfy the design needs of clients by formulating designs that are practical, aesthetic, and conducive to the intended purposes of the client's space. Successful designs raise productivity, sell merchandise, or improve lifestyle. Some interior designers specialize in a particular field, style, or phase of interior design.

A Day in the Life ... of an Interior Designer

8:00 A.M.	I arrive at the office to check e-mails and review status reports of current projects. Review daily calendar.
9:30 A.M.	Off to one of my newest projects to complete final measurements and imaging.
11:00 A.M.	Back to the office for a design team staff meeting to review current projects and discuss upcoming client meetings.
12:00 P.M.	Lunch out of the office so that I can run by a few of my favorite fabric houses to collect some unique samples for an afternoon appointment.
1:30 P.M.	Back at my computer putting the finishing touches on some 3D mock-ups for the upcoming meeting.
2:30 P.M.	Pitch meeting with new client. I love this part of my job because I enjoy showcasing my ideas for resolving a client's problem.
3:30 P.M.	While it is still fresh in my mind, I make some initial sketches and changes to the design as requested by the client.
4:30 P.M.	As usual, this is my time to catch up on paperwork and phone calls. I need to place some orders for existing projects.
5:00 P.M.	E-mail follow-up notes to prospective clients to make certain they have all the information.
5:30 P.M.	On my way home, I stop by a big office complex where my company has designed the entire interior to observe the construction and see the drawings and plans becoming a reality.

Logo Designer. A logo is a graphically designed symbol or icon set in a specific type-face and arranged in a unique way with distinct colors and shapes—all designed to represent the brand identity of a company, product, organization, or service. As a logo designer, you'll work with a client to develop several logo possibilities. Once the final design is chosen, you'll produce an image that can be used in a variety of contexts and media.

Publication Designer. As a publication designer, you'll plan, design, organize, and produce all types of printed publications and promotional materials such as newspapers, magazines, brochures, annual reports, invitations, posters, postcards, and flyers. You'll proofread and edit copy for accuracy, make and/or recommend revisions, and prepare files for printers.

Furniture Designer. In this job, you'll use a variety of skills in first researching future commercial or residential furniture trends and needs, and then developing, designing, and overseeing manufacturing all types of furniture projects. You may work alone or alongside colleagues creating concepts and designs that balance innovative design, functional requirements, and aesthetic appeal, and may work for a mass manufacturer or a custom design firm.

Exhibit (Trade Show) Designer. Trade shows play a vital role in communicating new products to industry participants. As an exhibit designer, you'll plan, design, fabricate, and install exhibits and displays. You'll collaborate with organizations, museums, and trade show sponsors to determine how to best create an exhibit in the space provided. Some designers also create sets for movie, television, or theatre productions.

Landscape Architect. As a landscape architect, you'll design, plan, and arrange natural and synthetic elements on the land. You'll deal with a wide range of external spaces from public parks and tourist areas to industrial parks and commercial developments. Some landscape architects specialize in one or more areas, such as residential development, shopping center development, environmental preservation and restoration, park and recreation development, and waterfront improvement.

Multimedia Designer. In this job, you'll focus on incorporating multimedia features—such as text, animation, sound, and images—into television or film production, animation, audio production, and set design, as well as several other multimedia, and production design fields. With a degree in multimedia design, you will be prepared to pursue entry-level positions with film studios, television stations, advertising agencies, and video production houses. You may also work with live productions, such as live theater and live concerts.

Web Designer. As a website designer, you are responsible for everything from creating a site's navigation, color scheme, and overall design to incorporating features such as e-commerce, online community, search engine optimization, animations, interactive applications, and advertising hosting. These designers also ensure that the site's design is optimized for the specific technologies supporting it. Web designers need traditional design skills as well as competency with web-specific design factors.

Other Career Possibilities. Some other job and career paths for design majors include:

Brand Identity Designer	Costume Designer
Cartoonist	Exhibit/Display Staff
Catalog Page Designer	Fashion Illustrator
Cinematographer	Fashion Reporter
Communication Specialist	Greeting Card Designer
Contractor	Jewelry Designer

Layout Artist

Patternmaker

Retail Store Designer

Video Game Designer

The Professor Says _____

One of the best ways to prepare to major in the visual arts in college is to take as many art and design courses as you possibly can while still in high school.

Skills Needed/Developed

Students majoring in some area of design develop numerous valuable and transferable skills. The following are the most critical to graduates:

Creativity. This is perhaps the most essential skill that any designer possesses—you'll develop, design, and create new applications, ideas, systems, or products to solve a need or problem.

Communications (in writing, visually, and verbally). Speaking, writing, and listening skills are essential to a design career. You must be able to listen to the needs of clients, ask appropriate questions, and respond. Designers also make presentations to clients, so good presentation skills are essential.

Problem-Solving. This skill involves the ability to identify complex problems, review existing conditions and restrictions, and develop and evaluate alternative solutions to solve the client's problem.

Time Management. You'll often work on multiple projects under varying time pressures, which requires the essential skills of organizing, planning, prioritizing, and meeting deadlines.

Technical/Computer Skills. As a designer, you'll need to have a solid understanding of and competence with computer-based design tools and software.

The Professor Says _____

Other transferable skills gained from these majors include:

- ◆ Teamwork
- ◆ Research and planning
- ◆ Analytical and spatial
- ◆ Decision implementation
- ◆ Recordkeeping/ handling details

Expected Growth

About a third of all designers are self-employed—freelancers who work with multiple customers and clients—but this section focuses on full-time positions and careers, all of which are generally expected to grow about as fast as average (10 to 15 percent) over the next decade.

Digital Designers

Job growth for digital designers is expected to be faster than the average (18 to 25 percent) for all careers over the next decade as technology drives new job creation.

A source of additional information is the International Digital Media and Arts Association (www.idmaa.org).

Graphic Designers

Among design specialists, it has been projected that graphic designers will find the most new jobs. Demand will increase with the rapidly expanding market for web-based information and expansion of the video entertainment market.

Sources of additional information:

- American Institute of Graphic Arts (www.aiga.org)
- International Council of Graphic Design Associations (www.icograda.org)

profiles

Graphic Designer David Carson

David Carson is the principal and chief designer of David Carson Design, Inc. He attended college at San Diego State University, where he graduated with a Bachelor's degree with honors and distinction. Numerous groups have honored his studio's work with a wide range of clients in both the business and arts worlds. Carson, whose work has received worldwide attention through hundreds of magazine and newspaper articles, was named "Designer of the Year" by the International Center for Photography (NY) for his use of photography and design. Carson's book, *The End of Print*, is now in its fifth printing and has sold more than 125,000 copies worldwide, making it the biggest-selling graphic design book of all time. His company has offices in New York City and Charleston, South Carolina.

Fashion Designers

Demand for fashion designers should remain strong over the next decade, though declines in the fashion industry could hurt demand for designers.

Sources of additional information:

◆ Council of Fashion Designers of America (www.cfda.com)

◆ Costume Designers Guild (www.costumedesignersguild.com)

◆ International Association of Clothing Designers & Executives (www.iacde.com)

Interior Designers

Rising demand for interior spaces (new and remodeled) of private homes, offices, and other institutions should continue to spur employment growth (10 to 15 percent) and keep demand high for interior designers.

Sources of additional information:

◆ American Society of Interior Designers (www.asid.org)

◆ International Interior Design Association (www.iida.org)

◆ Foundation for Design Integrity (ffdl.org)

Architects

Employment is expected to grow about as fast as the average (10 to 15 percent) for all jobs over the next decade. Expect much competition for jobs, although retirement of veteran architects will open up opportunities.

Sources of additional information:

◆ The American Institute of Architects (www.aia.org)

◆ Association for Women in Architecture (www.awa-la.org)

Logo Designers

Some job growth is expected, about as fast as the average (10 to 15 percent) for all careers, but expect strong competition for available jobs because qualified applicants generally outnumber job openings.

Architect and Designer Michael Graves

Michael Graves is an award-winning architect and designer. He received a Bachelor of Science in architecture from the University of Cincinnati and earned a Master of Architecture degree the following year from Harvard University's Graduate School of Design. Graves is often recognized with moving American architectural thought from abstract modernism to post-modernism. Cited as one of the most unique visionaries in modern American architecture, Graves has received more than 160 design awards, including the 1999 National Medal of Arts and the 2001 Gold Medal from the American Institute of Architects. His firm, Michael Graves & Associates, with more than 100 employees in offices in Princeton, New Jersey, and New York City, has a highly diverse, international practice in architecture, interior design, product design, and graphic design.

Publication Designers

Job growth is expected to be about the same as the average over the next decade, but opportunities will always be available for people with strong design skills.

A source of additional information is the Society of Publication Designers (www.spd.org).

Furniture Designers

As more Americans turn their focus inward to their homes, the need for all types of furniture designs—and thus designers—is expected to be relatively strong (10 to 15 percent) over the next decade.

Sources of additional information:

◆ American Society of Furniture Designers (www.asfd.org)

◆ International Furnishings and Design Association (www.ifda.com)

Exhibit (Trade Show) Designers

A mixed job forecast, with most predicting about average job growth (10 to 15 percent) over the next decade as market competition results in bigger trade shows.

A source of additional information is the Exhibit Designers and Producers Association (www.edpa.com).

Wondering what employers look for in an exhibit designer? Here's a sample exhibit designer job description:

> If you have lots of crazy ideas and no outlet for them, come join us in a fun, creative environment. This position is responsible for the design of mid-size tradeshow projects. This includes preparing, attending, and driving the creative portion of mid-size projects. You'll oversee the preparation of artwork, construction of exhibit components by outside contractors, and placement of collections to ensure intended interpretation of concepts. Candidates must have working knowledge of FormZ & Adobe Creative Suite and possess strong presentation skills. The employee must be able to handle multiple jobs, meet deadlines, and work within budgets. This is an entry-level position and a great opportunity for a new graduate.

Landscape Architects

Job growth is expected to increase faster than average (18 to 25 percent) over the next decade as properties continue to be developed and current workers retire.

A source of additional information is the American Society of Landscape Architects (www.asla.org).

Multimedia Designers

Job growth is expected to be much faster than average (25 percent or higher) over the next decade. A source of additional information is Association for Multimedia Communications (www.amcomm.org).

Wondering what employers look for in a multimedia designer? Here's a sample multimedia designer job description:

> Design and develop electronic and traditional collateral to support specific marketing communications initiatives. Technical activities will include, but not be limited to, creating web portals and micro-sites, graphics and icons, electronic demos, online surveys, electronic newsletters, and e-mail campaigns. Activities may also include graphic design, page layout, and print process support for traditional marketing initiatives. A qualified candidate will possess the ability to translate complex and abstract concepts into highly effective communications. You should be able to work in a collaborative environment, meet deadlines, and juggle multiple assignments.

Web Designers

As the Internet continues to grow rapidly and as more and more companies need to have an online presence, this job is expected to continue to grow (18 to 25 percent) over the next decade.

Sources of additional information:

◆ International Webmasters Association (www.iwanet.org)

◆ Web Design & Developers Association (www.wdda.org)

The Professor Says

Your next step? Pick the couple of careers that most fit your interests with a design major and dig more deeply into them. Remember that it is always important to learn more about prospective careers by going online, talking with professors, conducting informational interviews, and job-shadowing.

Earnings Potential 💲

Design graduates earn less than the average annual salary for all college graduates, which is currently around $38,000. Graphic designers average about $32,000, fashion designers around $35,000, and interior designers about $30,000. For an architect (with professional degree beyond undergrad), starting salary is about $36,000.

This section provides some general guidelines of salaries to expect upon graduation. Remember, salaries vary by employer, industry, and region.

Logo Designer. Median annual salary of a logo designer is approximately $32,000. Freelancer salaries vary widely.

Publication Designer. Beginning salaries for a publication designer range from $32,000 to $40,000.

Furniture Designer. Median annual earnings of a corporate furniture designer is about $30,000. Freelancer salaries vary widely.

Major Pitfalls

Many designers are self-employed, and while working as a freelance designer gives you a lot of flexibility, it does not give you a steady paycheck or fringe benefits (like health care).

Exhibit (Trade Show) Designer. The median annual salary of an exhibit designer is about $34,000.

Landscape Architect. The median annual salary of an entry-level landscape architect is $38,000.

Multimedia Designer. The average salary for multimedia designers is between $35,000 and $60,000 a year.

Web Designer. The median annual salary for a typical corporate web designer is $49,500. Freelancer salaries vary widely.

The Professor Says _____

Your next step after choosing your major? Gaining work experience. Just about all "entry-level" jobs for college graduates require some work experience outside the classroom. Seek out internships, volunteer, and figure out other ways to gain the experience you need.

The Least You Need to Know

- If you love creating and building stuff, then a major in design should fit you perfectly.

- Multiple career paths and multiple majors exist for people with a passion and eye for design.

- Salaries in design are close to the average for all college graduates, though multimedia and web designers earn much higher salaries.

- If you want steady employment as a designer, you probably will have to start with a lower-paying entry-level position, but you could also consider becoming a freelance designer.

Chapter 7

English, Journalism, and Communications Studies

In This Chapter

- ◆ Discover careers that use your passion for writing
- ◆ Use your communication skills in jobs that demand them
- ◆ Learn the typical classes a language arts major requires
- ◆ Find out what jobs and salaries to expect

Do you have a passion for writing? Do you enjoy words? Have you always been a keen communicator or persuader? Consider yourself a wordsmith? This chapter reveals rewarding careers for students majoring in some aspect of language arts—English, journalism, or communications studies.

About the Majors

Students who major in English, journalism, or communications have a unique talent and appreciation for how people communicate, along with a desire to use the power of the written or spoken word in their careers.

English

The English major strengthens your reading, writing, and critical-thinking skills as you learn to appreciate the persuasive power and aesthetic pleasures of language. These skills prepare you for a plethora of careers. As a major, you can survey literature, study and write prose, or strengthen your verbal communication skills for a professional career outside English.

Almost all colleges and universities offer a major in English. Some courses that you might expect to find include:

English Composition

Research and Argumentation

Introduction to Literature

American Literature

English Literature

World Literature

Literature and Film

College Grammar

History of the Language

Creative Non-Fiction

Poetry Workshop

Dramatic Writing

Advanced Creative Writing

Shakespeare

Women and Literature

Language and Culture

Introduction to Linguistics

Sociolinguistics

Journalism

Journalism majors learn to report, write, and edit articles for publication (newspaper, magazine, or web) or broadcast (radio and television). Many colleges and universities offer journalism courses, but a smaller number of schools actually offer a major in journalism.

Typical courses include:

Introduction to Print Media

News Reporting and Writing

History of American Press

Feature Writing

Copyediting

Advanced Reporting

Media Law and Ethics

Magazine Article Writing

Web Writing and Reporting

Editing Procedures

Broadcast Journalism

Investigative Journalism

Science and Health Reporting

Business Reporting

Narrative Journalism

Sports Reporting

Editorial, Column, and Review Writing

Communications

A communications major integrates courses in speech; interpersonal, intercultural, organizational, and mass communication; and technical writing and public relations. You'll learn the dynamics of communication among individuals, groups, and cultures and their application to the media.

Communications is a fairly common major that just about all colleges and universities offer. Typical courses include:

Interpersonal Communications

Public Speaking

Intercultural Communications

Mass Communications

Ethics in Communications

Classical Rhetoric

Rhetorical Theory and Criticism

Argumentation

Small Group Communications

Gender and Communications

Philosophy of Communications

Technical Writing

Writing for Public Relations

Public Relations Theory

Communication and the Aging

Nonverbal Communications

Background on Careers

The communications skills you develop with a major in any of these fields provide you with some of the tools most demanded by organizations today.

English majors, through their studies, acquire a broad-based understanding of social, cultural, and literary perspectives. They develop the tools necessary to write, teach, or work in any career that requires strong writing and editing skills.

Journalism majors perfect the researching, writing, and editing skills they need to prepare for careers working in the media—newspapers, magazines, radio, television, and web publications—or working in corporate communications.

Communications studies majors learn and apply communications theories to various situations and contexts, understand the role media and mass communications plays in society, use tools and technology to gather information, and describe and use various communications styles in a variety of contexts. These majors prepare to enter business, industry, nonprofit, or government service.

Some top jobs and careers for students earning a Bachelor's degree with a major in English, journalism, or communications include:

Author/Writer. All sorts of writers exist. Typically you'll either work for an employer or client and be assigned to write about specific topics, or you'll work on subjects that interest you and develop documents (articles, short stories, book manuscripts) that you pitch to potential buyers. As a writer, you'll gather and interpret information from a variety of sources, often adding your interpretation of the material as you develop your finished product.

Reporter. In this job, you'll collect and analyze information about newsworthy events to write news stories for publication. Reporters educate and inform their readers, so a key part of the job requires finding and verifying factual information from various sources. You'll receive story assignments from your editor and evaluate news leads and news tips to develop story ideas. Finally, you'll organize your research, determine your angle, and write the story according to prescribed editorial style and format standards.

Broadcast Journalist. As a broadcast journalist, you'll contribute to the researching, writing, editing, reporting, and recording of news and feature material for broadcast on a variety of news and current affairs programs on television and radio and, increasingly, the web. Work can include generating stories, interviewing people, attending press conferences, gathering images and sounds, packaging stories and reports, and reporting from a studio or on location.

Editorial Assistant. As an editorial assistant, you'll play a critical role in assuring the production quality of a publication by reviewing and editing copy; verifying facts, dates, and statistics using standard reference sources; coordinating photography, illustrations, and graphics; securing copyrights and permissions for copyrighted materials; conferring with authors regarding changes made to their manuscripts; and preparing page layouts to position and space articles and illustrations.

Publicity/Public Relations Specialist. In this job, you'll assist in planning, developing, and implementing communication strategies that generate positive media coverage for your employer (corporation, nonprofit, or person). The job also requires time spent building relationships with the media; managing special projects and events; handling general administrative duties such as filing, faxing, and photocopying; and being a spokesperson.

Advertising Copywriter. As an advertising copywriter, you will work with the account management team and an art director to conceive, develop, and produce effective advertisements. The advertisements must meet client demands through persuasive advertising copy for display in all types of media—including magazines, newspapers, billboards, television, radio, and the web—as well as for catalogs, posters, leaflets, and brochures. The job also often includes acting as a liaison with production companies, photographers, typographers, designers, and printers.

Proofreader. In this job, you'll play an essential role in assuring the accuracy and quality of the final published materials by reading copy or page proofs to find and mark errors in one of two ways. Sometimes you'll compare proofs to the original copy and mark any differences you find, while at other times you simply check the proof for errors in grammar, spelling, punctuation, and style. Proofreaders work in all industries that publish documents, including newspapers, magazines, publishing houses, and commercial organizations.

Other Career Possibilities. Some other job and career paths for English, journalism, and communications majors include:

Acquisitions Editor	Playwright
Bibliographer	Poet
Book Reviewer	Public Information Officer
Community Relations Specialist	Publishing Assistant
Fact Checker	Speech Writer
Greeting Card Writer	Storyteller
Lexicographer/Linguist	Teacher, English or ESOL
Narrator	Technical Writer

The Professor Says

Some of the more lucrative and prestigious career paths that language arts majors follow require additional education at the graduate level. These careers include:
- ◆ College Professor (Master's degree or higher)
- ◆ Communications/Media Lawyer (Juris Doctor)
- ◆ Speech Therapist (Master's degree or higher)

Skills Needed/Developed

Students majoring in some area of communications develop numerous valuable and transferable skills, but the following are the most critical to graduates.

Writing and Editing. The written word is the essential building block in any form of communications. Language arts majors develop the key skills of using words in a clear, compelling, persuasive manner; reviewing and modifying work after writing it; and rewriting elements as needed.

Oral Communications. Speaking skills are essential for those pursuing a career in communications. You'll need to express yourself clearly, concisely, and confidently, as well as ask intelligent questions.

The Professor Says

Other transferable skills gained from these majors include:

- ◆ Synthesizing information
- ◆ Critical thinking
- ◆ Attention to detail
- ◆ Planning and organizing
- ◆ Working independently

Interpersonal Communications. Most communications careers involve working with people, therefore requiring the ability to talk and listen in one-on-one and small-group situations.

Time Management/Meeting Deadlines. Being able to set priorities, manage multiple projects and assignments, and meet deadlines are essential skills for a career in communications.

Research. Simply, the ability to conduct, analyze, and report on research using various techniques and sources. Whether working as a reporter, writer, or copywriter, these tools help gather the necessary information.

Expected Growth

Jobs will always be available for good writers—whether working for traditional media such as newspapers and magazines; emerging media, such as the web; or working in related fields, such as in public relations or advertising—but growth in new jobs is expected to be moderate (10 to 15 percent).

Authors/Writers

Job growth for writers is expected to be about as fast as the average (10 to 15 percent) for all jobs, but competition remains strong, as many people are attracted to writing.

Sources of additional information:

- The American Society of Journalists & Authors (www.asja.org)

- The Authors Guild (www.authorsguild.org)

- National Association of Women Writers (www.naww.org)

- Poets & Writers (www.pw.org)

- Writers Guild of America (www.wga.org)

profiles

Writer/Storyteller Amy Tan

Amy Tan is the author of many short stories and books. Her most famous (and first full-length novel) is *The Joy Luck Club*, which, upon its publication in 1989, won several awards (including the National Book Award and the *L.A. Times* Book Award) and spent eight months on *The New York Times* best-seller list. She graduated with honors from San Jose State University, earning a Bachelor's degree with dual majors in English and linguistics, before attaining her Master's degree in linguistics, also from San Jose State University. Her first job was as a language development consultant before starting a business-writing firm, providing speeches for executives of large corporations. She later became a full-time freelance writer before eventually tiring of that and moving into writing fiction. Tan's short stories and essays have appeared in *The Atlantic*, *Harper's*, and *The New Yorker*.

Reporters

Job growth for reporters is expected to be slower than average (under 8 percent) for all occupations over the next decade because of continuing media consolidations. The one bright spot for reporters is in new media (including websites, blogs, etc.).

Sources of additional information:

- Society of Professional Journalists (www.spj.org)

- Association of Young Journalists (www.youngjournos.org)

- Investigative Reporters & Editors (www.ire.org)

- Unity: Journalists of Color (www.unityjournalists.org)

Wondering what employers look for in a staff reporter? Here's a sample reporter job description:

> We are seeking a full-time, aggressive reporter for a group of weekly newspapers. Candidate should have a journalism background, with a degree in journalism or a related field; must demonstrate good news judgment, language skills, and accuracy; be organized and work independently. The successful applicant will be proficient at general assignment work, hard news, and features. Successful candidate will have reporting experience, some of it ideally as a city, county, or state government reporter; a solid understanding of local governments and of community journalism; and the ability to craft clean, lively copy that effectively communicates issues that affect our readers' daily lives.

A Day in the Life ... of a Reporter	
8:00 A.M.	Watch the local news to see what they are covering while getting ready for work. Also check the competition to see what stories we missed.
9:00 A.M.	Arrive at work and check the overnights to see what else has happened since I left yesterday.
9:30 A.M.	Track down sources for a couple of stories I am working on; this is the hardest (and sometimes most tedious part) of my job.
11:00 A.M.	With enough research and source information for one of my stories, I begin writing. The thing I love about journalism, about being a reporter, is that we document the world around us.
1:00 P.M.	Head out for a quick lunch. I always try and talk with people when I am out because you just never know where story ideas are going to come from.
2:30 P.M.	A quick chat with my editor about where I am with one of his pet projects about mismanaged growth by the county government. This is going to be a big story, so there's a lot at stake, and I have to be especially careful with this story.
3:00 P.M.	Finish writing my story from earlier in the day.
4:00 P.M.	It's back on the phone (and yes, I am on the phone a lot during the day) attempting to talk to additional sources.
5:00 P.M.	Chat with some of my colleagues who are basically starting their days as I am finishing mine. There's the sports writer and photographer heading off to a local game, the government beat reporter heading to a long night of covering a council meeting, and the copy editors preparing to tackle putting together another paper.
6:00 P.M.	Home for dinner and the local news.

Broadcast Journalists

Job growth for broadcast journalists is expected to be slower than the average (under 8 percent) for all jobs over the next decade, as traditional media consolidation reduces demand.

Sources of additional information:

◆ National Association of Broadcasters (www.nab.org)

◆ NewsLab (www.newslab.org)

Major Pitfalls

Writing and reporting used to be one of the most highly respected and glamorous careers, but over the last decade the public's views have changed dramatically and journalists are often viewed as having an established agenda.

profiles

Broadcast Journalist Barbara Walters

Barbara Walters is a broadcast pioneer, making history in 1976 as the first female to anchor a news broadcast when she co-anchored the *ABC Evening News* with Harry Reasoner. She is a graduate of Sarah Lawrence College with a Bachelor's degree in English. She currently co-hosts (as well as co-owns and co-executive produces) the daytime talk show *The View*, and she continues to appear on the news magazine *20/20*, as well as hosts highly rated celebrity interview specials. She has interviewed every American president and first lady since Richard and Pat Nixon. Over the years, she has received national recognition for her work and has received numerous prestigious honors and awards, including several honorary Doctorate degrees.

Editorial Assistants

There will always be a demand for editorial assistants, but job growth is expected to be about average (10 to 15 percent) over the next decade.

Wondering what employers look for in an editorial assistant? Here's a sample editorial assistant job description:

> This entry-level position has wide-ranging duties, including assisting the editors and reporters of the business news division, monitoring incoming business news stories from bureaus worldwide, preparing business news calendars, and performing miscellaneous clerical tasks. Editorial assistants typically have also found some opportunities to write stories and to advance to a writing or editing

position. Good communications skills, an attention to detail and an ability to juggle multiple tasks are required. Some experience with business news is preferred.

The Professor Says

You don't need a career in the communications field if you choose this major—you could easily combine your passion for writing with another interest, such as career development, and become a career counselor. Communications skills are always in top demand by employers.

Publicity/Public Relations Assistants

Demand for publicity and public relations assistants is expected to grow faster than average (18 to 25 percent) over the next decade.

Sources of additional information:

◆ Public Relations Society of America (www.prsa.org)

◆ Public Relations Student Society of America (www.prssa.org)

◆ International Public Relations Association (www.ipra.org)

Wondering what employers look for in a publicity assistant? Here's a sample publicity assistant job description:

Fast-growing publishing group seeks a publicity assistant to assist senior staff members to implement book publicity campaigns and attain maximum publicity for the division's titles. Responsibilities include preparing mailings to reviewers, helping to coordinate authors' tour schedules, and maintaining databases. You will also handle general administrative duties such as filing, faxing, and photocopying. Duties will also grow to include creating and writing materials such as press releases and press kits, and booking media for authors on tour. This is an extremely fast-paced, telephone-heavy position that requires someone with good phone manners and the ability to work well under pressure and meet tight deadlines. Exceptional writing, organizational skills, and attention to detail are an absolute must.

Advertising Copywriters

Job growth for advertising copywriters is expected to be about as fast as the average (10 to 15 percent) for all jobs.

Sources of additional information:

◆ American Advertising Federation (www.aaf.org)

◆ Advertising Educational Foundation (www.aef.com)

◆ International Advertising Association (www.iaaglobal.org)

Proofreaders

There will always be a demand for proofreaders, but because of the changing publication process, job growth is expected to be slightly below average (5 to 10 percent) over the next decade.

A source of additional information is Proofreading Jobs (www.proofreadingjobs.org).

Wondering what employers look for in a proofreader? Here's a sample proofreader job description:

We are looking for someone who has impeccable grammar and English skills; excellent editing, proofing, and writing skills; and knowledge of AP Style and use of standard proofreader marks (knowledge of Chicago Style a plus), as well as extensive knowledge of office software, including spreadsheet, word processing programs, and Adobe Acrobat. You'll also have the ability to plan and coordinate schedules and deadlines, manage multiple projects at a time, meet tight deadlines, and manage a network of independent writers and content creators.

The Professor Says

Not sure about these career choices? These are just some of the career possibilities for a major in English, journalism, or communications studies. Remember that it is always important to learn more about prospective careers by going online, talking with professors, conducting informational interviews, and job-shadowing.

Earnings Potential $

While there is great variability in the earnings potential of jobs using communications skills, overall, all three of these majors earn less than the average annual salary for all college graduates, which is currently around $38,000. English and communications graduates earn about $31,000 per year, while journalism grads earn about $30,000 annually.

This section provides some general guidelines of salaries to expect upon graduation. Remember, salaries vary by employer, industry, and region.

Writer/Author. Salaries for writers and authors vary widely.

Reporter. Beginning salary for a print news reporter is about $29,000.

Broadcast Journalist. Median annual earnings of an entry-level broadcast journalist is $29,158.

Editorial Assistant. The median annual salary of an editorial assistant is about $32,000.

Publicity Assistant. The median annual salary of a publicity assistant is $38,000.

Advertising Copywriter. The average salary for a beginning advertising copywriter is $38,000 a year.

Proofreader. The median annual salary for an entry-level proofreader is almost $30,000.

> **The Professor Says**
>
> Remember that you're not done once you pick your college major—in fact, it's just begun, because the next thing you need to do is gain work experience. Just about all "entry-level" jobs for college graduates require some work experience outside the classroom. Seek out internships, volunteer, and figure out other ways to gain the experience you need.

The Least You Need to Know

- Good communicators will always be in demand, so if you have a passion and a gift for communicating, you should have little trouble finding a job.

- The communications field offers myriad career paths—in print, broadcasting, multimedia, and marketing.

- If communications is just one of your passions, consider using those skills in a different career combined with one of your other passions, such as business or education.

- Entry-level salaries in communications tend to be much lower than the average for all college grads.

Chapter 8

Foreign Languages

In This Chapter

- ◆ Discover careers that use your love of languages
- ◆ Use your passion for other cultures in jobs that demand them
- ◆ Learn the typical classes foreign language majors require
- ◆ Find key job and salary information

Do you have the ability to hear someone speaking a language and immediately be able to mimic it? Enjoy learning new languages and learning about different cultures? Do you already speak multiple languages? Do you desire to use your passion for languages in your life? Love to travel?

This chapter reveals rewarding careers for students who major in one or more foreign languages.

About the Major

Students majoring in a foreign language not only learn both the written and spoken language—developing a proficiency in reading, listening, writing, and speaking—but also study the history, culture, philosophy, literature, politics, and business of the countries or regions of the world in which

The Professor Says _____

Here are just a few of the languages you'll probably only find at larger colleges and universities: Danish, Hindi, Farsi, Chinese, Greek, Latin, Italian, Portuguese, Finnish, Hebrew, Thai, Russian, Arabic, Swedish, and Japanese.

the language is used. Typically, majors will also spend at least one semester abroad, immersed in the life and culture of a foreign country.

Just about all colleges and universities offer a handful of foreign language majors, and we'll cover the common ones here—French, German, and Spanish—but if you are looking for a specific language, it makes sense to do your research and find the schools that offer it.

Here are some course requirements you might expect to find if you major in foreign languages.

Typical courses include:

Elementary French (or German, Spanish)

French (or German, Spanish) Conversation

Intermediate French (or German, Spanish)

French (or German, Spanish) Civilization

Advanced French (or German, Spanish)

French (or German, Spanish) Literature

French (or German, Spanish) Grammar

French (or German, Spanish) Cinema

French (or German, Spanish) Culture

French (or German, Spanish) Business

French (or German, Spanish) Composition

French (or German, Spanish) Study Abroad

The Professor Says _____

Many students who major in a foreign language plan ahead and double major, choosing a second major that is related to a career objective, such as political science (foreign service career; see Chapter 26), international business (business career; see Chapter 11), or education (teaching career; see Chapter 22).

Background on Careers

Of course, you could easily become a teacher or professor of foreign languages at the secondary school or college level (although additional education and certifications are typically required) as some majors do, but what about other career paths for people who do not want to teach? In today's globally competitive world, where knowing at least one other language gives you a competitive edge, foreign language specialists also find work in government, libraries, nonprofit organizations, and small and large corporations.

More specifically, here are some top jobs and careers for students who earn a Bachelor's degree with a major in foreign languages.

Flight Attendant. If you have a strong interest in travel, then working as a flight attendant right after you graduate might be ideal for you. In this job, you'll promote the safety of the traveling public by ensuring that travelers adhere to safety regulations. You'll also try to make flights comfortable and enjoyable for passengers by providing adequate supplies of food, beverages, and any other provided amenities. You'll also answer questions about the flight; distribute reading material, pillows, and blankets; and help small children, elderly or disabled persons, and any others needing assistance.

Foreign Service Agent/Officer. The Federal government hires you as a foreign language major because of your immersion into the language, culture, history, and politics of foreign countries. When you work as a foreign service agent or protocol specialist (also referred to as a diplomat), you'll work at various locations around the world (including in the United States) promoting the interests of the U.S. government and businesses. Numerous governmental agencies need workers to provide critical insight and context for potential policy decisions.

Foreign Trade Analyst. In this job, you'll play a key role in a company's international department or division, researching, evaluating, and reporting on the company's foreign trades. You'll be responsible for making certain the company complies with international regulations and policies, evaluating the best methods of market distribution and sales, analyzing domestic warehousing and

The Professor Says

When considering employment outside the United States—whether for an international company or a world aid organization—remember that you'll face much stronger competition for available jobs, often from college graduates from other parts of the world who know multiple languages. If possible, you should try to pick up some exposure to additional foreign languages outside your major.

supply channel logistics, maintaining oversight of foreign factory operations, building collaborative relationships with trading partners and suppliers, and assisting in the development or modification of the internal trade policy and procedure manuals.

Immigration Information Officer/Immigration Specialist. As an immigration information officer, you will work for the Homeland Security's Bureau of Citizenship and Immigration Services, answering questions about immigration applications as well as determining eligibility for some benefits and providing services such as processing applications for U.S. citizenship, processing asylum and refugee cases, administering the visa program, and issuing work authorizations. Immigration specialists can typically be found in the human resources departments of organizations that employ foreign nationals, and typically require a business background in addition to the language training.

Import/Export Administrator/Specialist. As an import/export administrator, you'll work under the supervision of the import/export manager and typically be responsible for the movement of merchandise and/or material in or out of the country in compliance with federal, state, and local regulations. You'll work with both domestic and international shippers, oversee the completion of all paperwork and required documentation, monitor monetary transactions associated with international distribution to ensure efficient movement of products in and out of the country in a timely manner, and perhaps negotiate with clients or handle issues with customs officials.

International Aid/Development Worker. For people who want to make a difference in the world, your work in this job will take you to war-torn or high-poverty countries where you will assist an aid organization (such as the U.N., Red Cross, Peace Corps, or World Health Organization) in meeting the needs of the people who live there, often developing educational or training programs to help communities build a sustainable future. You may be involved in managing one or more projects, training or supervising volunteers, coordinating efforts with other aid organizations, and soliciting additional funding to continue on-going programs. As an international aid worker, you'll work long hours in sometimes harsh conditions for minimal pay, but with great personal satisfaction.

International Financial Manager/Banking Officer. In this job, you could work in one of several departments for a local, national, or international financial institution and oversee a functional area, such as lending, trusts, mortgages, and investments, or a program area, such as sales, operations, or electronic financial services. You may be involved in soliciting new business, authorizing loans, or managing the investment of funds. As a new graduate, you'll typically start in a low-level management position.

Interpreter. As an interpreter, you'll make intercultural communication possible through language, idea, and concept translation—often translating during pauses in a monologue or immediately as the words are spoken. By possessing a special language aptitude in two different languages, you usually translate into their best-known, or "active," language from your secondary, or "passive," language, converting languages into others. You'll need to have a good understanding of what is communicated and be able to make clear and accurate verbal articulations/expressions. You'll typically find work in such areas as social service, entertainment, and business.

Translator. As a translator, you'll make intercultural communication possible through language, idea, and concept translation by writing, analyzing, and editing written material to convert it into another language. You may undertake work that varies in style, subject matter, and length in a process that usually entails making an initial review to get a general understanding of the material, researching any unknown words, and conducting additional research on subjects that may be unclear. You'll also correspond with original source providers or organizations that issue the documents to confirm correct translation.

Other Career Possibilities. Here are some other job and career paths for foreign language majors:

Archivist	Foreign Language Tutor
Bilingual Counselor	Human Resources Specialist
CIA/FBI Agent	Marketing Analyst
Communications Specialist	Proofreader
Court Interpreter	Public Relations Assistant
Cultural Officer	Teacher, Foreign Language
Foreign Correspondent	Tour Guide
Foreign Credit Manager	Travel Agent

The Professor Says

What languages will be most in demand in the future by business, governments, and other organizations? Experts suggest the need is greatest for Arabic, Chinese (and other Asian languages), and Russian, as China and the Pacific Rim gain additional market power and Russia and the Middle East continue to play dominant roles in world trade and politics.

Skills Needed/Developed

Students majoring in foreign languages develop numerous valuable and transferable skills. The following are the most critical to graduates.

Cultural Sensitivity/Language Skills. Among the most important skills international business majors learn are valuing and appreciating other societies and cultures, as well as becoming fluent in multiple languages.

Interpersonal Communications. This skill deals with your ability to talk and listen in one-on-one and small-group situations, one of the core elements of communications.

The Professor Says

Other transferable skills you gain from these majors include:

◆ Researching

◆ Attention to detail

◆ Ability to work independently

Communications. You'll need to possess strong speaking, writing, and listening skills (in two or more languages) for a successful career.

Organizational Skills. This skill deals with your ability to manage large amounts of information and demands through task analysis, time management, and goal-setting.

Teamwork. Your appreciation of other cultures should assist you in your ability to work with other people—whether they are similar or different.

Expected Growth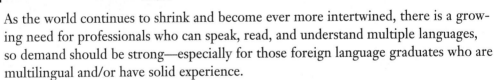

As the world continues to shrink and become ever more intertwined, there is a growing need for professionals who can speak, read, and understand multiple languages, so demand should be strong—especially for those foreign language graduates who are multilingual and/or have solid experience.

Flight Attendants

Job growth is expected to be as fast as the average (10 to 15 percent) for all jobs over the next decade.

Sources of additional information:

◆ Association of Flight Attendants (www.afanet.org)

◆ Association of Professional Flight Attendants (www.apfa.org)

Wondering what employers look for in a flight attendant? Here's a sample flight attendant job description:

> With our rapid growth, both in fleet size and network, we are looking for exceptional people to build their careers with us. We currently employ people from more than 120 different nationalities who speak more than 80 different languages to cater for the truly multicultural clientele on our network of over 88 destinations. The diversity and mix of nationalities, cultures, religions, and ethnic backgrounds has contributed positively to the success we have achieved as an international airline. Every new cabin crew will be provided with comprehensive training in our state-of-the-art training college. However, to qualify for this opportunity, you will need to meet the following criteria: minimum age 21 years at the time of application; educated to at least high school standard, but college degree preferred; medically fit to meet air crew requirements; and fluent in written and spoken English (fluency in another language is a strong asset). Finally, you should be the sort of person who has the natural ability to work in teams that have a focus on customer safety and satisfaction.

Foreign Service Agents/Officers

Job growth is expected to be better than average (20+ percent) as older diplomats retire and diplomatic opportunities around the world increase.

Sources of additional information:

- American Foreign Service Association (www.afsa.org)

- Association for Diplomatic Studies and Training (adst.org)

- U.S. Department of State (www.state.gov)

Foreign Trade Analysts

Demand for foreign trade analysts is expected to be about as fast as the average (10 to 15 percent) over the next decade.

Wondering what employers look for in a foreign trade analyst? Here's a sample foreign trade analyst job description:

> Working with the global marketing team, you'll be responsible for the daily tactical activities of corporate import and export compliance programs, ensuring that compliance requirements and business objectives are achieved along with

assisting with special projects as required. Establish and maintain an export and import control infrastructure, which includes developing and maintaining export and import compliance manuals; export classification/licensing; and employee education and training. Involves auditing of core business functions and international locations; responding to customs inquiries; managing brokers; ensuring compliance with export laws and regulations, including transfer of technical data; monitoring regulatory changes and revising compliance policies and practices in accordance with changing legal framework and business models; executing internal processes for problem resolution; and providing diplomatic guidance to employees. Must have strong focus on customer service for internal customers; be prepared for diplomatic interaction with all levels. Bachelor's degree is preferred.

Immigration Information Officers/Immigration Specialists

Job growth for immigration specialists is expected to be about as fast as the average (10 to 15 percent) for all jobs.

Wondering what employers look for in an immigration information specialist? Here's a sample immigration information specialist job description:

Immigration information officers provide technical counsel to the public about immigration and nationality laws and regulations and elicit information to serve as the foundation for administrative and/or legal action. They screen applications and petitions filed for benefits under the Immigration and Nationality Act for completeness, appropriate fees, and proper supporting documents; determine prima facie eligibility for applications; and dissuade aliens from filing for benefits for which they are not eligible. Exploring all avenues of assistance available to clients, the immigration information officer determines the more advantageous benefits and assists clients in completing the required forms while questioning clients to determine if they are attempting to submit applications under fraudulent situations and reasons. Successful completion of a Bachelor's degree or a full four-year course of study from an accredited college or university in any field leading to a Bachelor's degree may be substituted for the required experience at the GS-5 level. Candidates selected for the position who have not already graduated from the Immigration Information Officer Basic Training Course (IIOBTC) will be required to attend this course and to achieve a cumulative passing grade on the examinations.

Import/Export Administrators

Job growth is expected to be about as fast as average (10 to 15 percent) over the next decade.

Sources of additional information:

◆ Federation of International Trade Associations (www.fita.org)

◆ Professional Association of Exporters & Importers (www.paei.org)

Wondering what employers look for in an import/export specialist? Here's a sample import/export specialist job description:

> An import/export specialist coordinates shipping arrangements, prepares/ provides shipping documentation, and acts as a customer liaison for international and military customers for the consumer, after-market, and capital divisions. Requirements include obtaining freight quotes and making the best business decision based on service and cost; communicating directly with international customers regarding timely shipment of their orders; communicating directly with freight forwarders and international transportation carriers to assure on-time departure and delivery; communicating directly with U.S. custom brokers to ensure accurate customs declarations and timely deliveries; obtaining freight quotes to make the best financial decision for the business as well as for service performance; invoicing all international and military orders while tracking fixed and variable freight costs of international shipments, including duties, taxes, and fees to be sure that all expenses are billed back to the customer when possible; and implementing improved cost/time saving processes/procedures. Must have excellent communication skills and ability to work well with others, as well as being organized, flexible to change, and understanding of the needs of the business and customer service.

International Aid/Development Workers

Job growth for international aid and development workers is expected to be about the same as the average for all jobs over the next decade (10 to 15 percent growth), although higher demand is expected for workers with a health-care background.

Sources of additional information:

◆ Idealist.org (www.idealist.org)

◆ OneWorld.net (us.oneworld.net)

International Financial Managers/Banking Officers

Job growth for international financial managers and banking officers is expected to be the same as the average (10 to 15 percent) for all jobs over the next decade.

Sources of additional information:

◆ American Bankers Association (www.aba.com)

◆ Association for Financial Professionals (www.afponline.org)

◆ Financial Women International (www.fwi.org)

Interpreters

Demand for interpreters is expected to grow faster than average (18 to 25 percent) over the next decade.

A source of additional information can be found at American Translators Association (www.atanet.org).

Wondering what employers look for in an interpreter? Here's a sample interpreter job description:

> Provides oral and written translation services for non–English-speaking patients and families throughout the hospital, as it relates to medical care. Provides written translation and sight translation of relevant materials to enhance patients' and families' comprehension of medical procedures, treatment, discharge instructions, patient and family education, and follow-up care. Conducts training for hospital staff on cross-cultural communication and related subjects. Requires completion of state approved Basic Medical Interpreters Certification or willingness to take such course with satisfactory results. Bachelor's degree or equivalent experience in education and experience are required. Bilingual with full proficiency in Spanish and English a must.

Translators

Job growth for translators is expected to be faster than the average (18 to 25 percent) for all jobs over the next decade.

Additional information can be found at American Translators Association (www. atanet.org).

Wondering what employers look for in a translator? Here's a sample translator job description:

> We are seeking a bilingual individual fluent in reading and writing English and Spanish to research, write, translate, interpret, edit, proofread, and produce material for our publications, pamphlets, brochures, website, manuals, technical documents, and correspondence. You'll also be expected to provide interpretation services in various settings (for example, at conferences, hearings, or interviews). Successful candidate will have a Bachelor's degree in Spanish or equivalent, be fluent in reading, writing, and speaking Spanish, have some translation and interpretation experience, be computer-proficient, and have knowledge of the computer industry. You must possess strong written and verbal communication skills and exhibit excellent attention to detail, and be able to communicate and translate complex technical language to a wide audience. Candidates will be asked to demonstrate translating skills and must complete and pass background and drug testing.

Earnings Potential $

While there is a lot of variability in the earning potential of jobs using your foreign language skills (depending on how you choose to use your language skills), overall, foreign language majors—at $32,500—earn less than the average annual salary for all college graduates, which is currently around $38,000.

This section provides some general guidelines of salaries to expect upon graduation. Remember, salaries vary by employer, industry, and region.

Flight Attendant. Starting salary for a flight attendant is about $30,000.

Foreign Service Agent/Officer. Starting salary for a foreign service agent is about $40,000.

Foreign Trade Analyst. The average salary for a beginning foreign trade analyst is $42,000 a year.

Immigration Information Officer/ Immigration Specialist. Beginning salary for immigration specialists is about $31,000.

The Professor Says

There are lots of career possibilities for a major in foreign languages beyond the ones featured here. Remember that it is always important to learn more about prospective careers by going online, talking with professors, conducting informational interviews, and job-shadowing.

Import/Export Administrator/Specialist. The average salary for an entry-level import/export specialist is about $43,000.

The Professor Says ____

Your next step after choosing your major? Gaining work experience. Just about all "entry-level" jobs for college graduates require some work experience outside the classroom. Seek out internships, volunteer, and figure out other ways to gain the experience you need.

International Aid/Development Worker. Starting salaries vary based on job and location, but the typical salary for a college graduate is $30,000.

International Financial Manager/Banking Officer. Beginning salary for a banking officer is about $32,000.

Interpreter. The median annual salary of an interpreter is $31,000.

Translator. Beginning salary for a translator is $38,000.

The Least You Need to Know

◆ Having a passion for other cultures and the ability to learn multiple languages are solid foundations for a wide variety of jobs.

◆ Whenever possible, it's best to combine your foreign language major with a minor or major in an area that is a bit more career-oriented.

◆ As the world gets smaller, there will always be good jobs for people who can speak multiple languages.

◆ Most jobs that use a major in a foreign language pay fairly well, though many pay below the average of all college graduates.

Performing Arts

In This Chapter

- ◆ Discover majors that use your passion for performance
- ◆ Learn the typical classes a performing arts major requires
- ◆ Find out what jobs and salaries to expect

Do you have a passion for the performing arts? Do you enjoy acting, dancing, singing, or playing a musical instrument? Do you have a gift for some type of performance art? Love performing for an audience?

This chapter reveals rewarding careers for students who major in some aspect of the performing arts—theatre, music, or dance.

About the Majors

Students majoring in theatre, music, or dance have a unique artistic talent and a passion for sharing that gift with an appreciative audience.

Theatre/Theatre Production

The theatre major offers numerous advantages, even for those who do not see themselves working in the theatre after they graduate. Students typically learn the inner workings of all aspects of the theatre and theatre management as well as actually performing in theatre productions. And it's not just about acting, as students also learn set, lighting, and costume designing, as well as directing, playwriting, and producing.

Many colleges and universities offer a major in theatre or theatre arts. Some courses you might expect to find at most schools include:

Introduction to Theatre	Acting II
Theatre Workshops	Directing II
Acting I	Scene Design and Painting
Directing I	Production Management
Performance Studies	Summer Theatre
Stagecraft	Musical Theatre
Stage Lighting	Theories of the Theatre
Creative Dramatics	Playwriting
Voice and Diction	Theatre History
Costume and Makeup	The Business of Theatre

Music

Students majoring in music prepare for either professional careers in music or for continued study in a graduate program. They typically receive advanced training in basic musical disciplines and become proficient in applied and theoretical areas—while also receiving an education in other areas outside of music.

Many colleges and universities offer music courses, but a much smaller number of schools actually offer one or more majors in music.

Typical courses include:

Music as a Profession	Advanced Performance
Music Theory	Introduction to Music Analysis
Diction for Singing	Analysis of World Music
Aural Training	Music in the Arts
Instrument Performance	History of Popular Music

Advanced Aural Training

Careers in Music

Basic Conducting

Advanced Conducting

Introduction to Composition

Orchestra

Choral Arranging

Symphonic Literature

Music History

Music and Technology

Music Genres

Music Pedagogy

Instrument Lessons

Advanced Lessons

Dance

Students majoring in dance usually follow one of two avenues. In the first, you'll receive a well-rounded dance education in both technique and theory courses that can lead to a variety of dance-related careers. In the second, you'll take courses designed to meet the needs of highly talented students interested in preparing for a professional dance career.

Dance is a fairly specialized major (sometimes housed in the department or college of theatre or music), so only a select number of colleges and universities offer a major.

Typical courses include:

Introduction to Modern Dance

Dance Production

Dance Theory

Movement Analysis

Dance History and Philosophy

Improvisation

Dance in the 20th Century

World Dance

Ballet

Advanced Ballet

Jazz Dance Technique

Advanced Jazz

Modern Dance

Advanced Modern Dance

Dance Composition

Choreography

Advanced Dance Composition

Dance Administration

Methods of Teaching Dance

Pointe and Variation

Creative Dance for Children

Dance Repertory

Background on Careers

The skills you develop through a major in any of these fields are some of the most in-demand by performing arts organizations today.

Theatre majors go into acting, directing, children's theatre, drama ministry, stage management, designing costumes, sets, or lights, publicity, theatre management, business, or film. Students with a theatre major learn to work collaboratively and creatively and become effective listeners and perceptive thinkers.

Music majors, through the study of music composition, theory, history, education, conducting, technology, and performance, prepare for careers in the performing arts, as well as in the fields of recording, writing, teaching, composing, and researching.

Dance majors pursue a course of study to acquire a firm intellectual grasp of the theoretical, historical, and creative forces that shape dance as an art form, as well as take courses that help perfect their craft through both instruction and performance, leading to careers as professional dancers, as well as in dance education and arts management.

Some top jobs and careers for students earning a Bachelor's degree with a major in theatre, music, or dance include:

Actor. As an actor, you'll perform in stage, radio, television, or film productions, as well as cabarets, nightclubs, theme parks, cruise ships, commercials, and industrial/training films. You may struggle to find steady work, and it's unlikely that you'll ever reach superstar status. You may also find work behind the scenes, doing narration or voiceovers for commercials, animated productions, and books on tape.

Musician/Singer. In this job, you'll play musical instruments; sing, compose, or arrange music; and perform in music, theatre, and dance productions and at nightclubs, theme parks, cruise ships, concert halls, and other venues. You may perform for live audiences or work for recording or production studios producing music for musical recordings, commercials, television, and film.

Dancer. As a dancer, you'll perform in a variety of settings, such as dance productions, opera performances, musical theatre, television, movies, music videos, commercials, theme parks, and cruise ships. Mostly dancers work as part of a group, although top artists do perform solo. Dance specialties include ballroom, folk, ethnic, tap, jazz, modern, and others.

> **The Professor Says**
>
> If you have a passion for the performing arts, but know you do not want a career as a performer, you should consider additional courses outside your major—such as business, design, and education—to give you the additional skills you'll need for your career.

Arts Management Specialist. As an arts management specialist, you'll work in a performing arts organization, which typically has all sorts of needs in the areas of programming, business, management, and administration. These positions require candidates with both a passion and understanding of the arts, as well as specific skills in marketing, management, and education. You'll work with outside vendors, develop educational programs, aid in the production of promotional efforts, and assist with fundraising and donor management. You'll assist the manager/administrator, who controls the finances of the center, with the goal of producing exciting and profitable performances.

Designer, Assistant. This position (sometimes called production designers, particularly in the film and television industry) creates the overall visual style of a theatre, television, or film production. You'll work closely with the director and production team to plan the design style for sets, locations, costumes, and props and lighting, while taking into account the available budget and any logistical problems caused by outdoor locations or complex scenery changes. You can specialize in sets, costumes, or lighting.

Event Planner, Assistant. As an event planner, you'll either work within an organization, helping manage corporate events (such as meetings, retreats, and conferences), or within an event-planning business, managing events for all types of clients. You'll offer advice for all aspects of the event, often developing the schedule, including speakers, food, and location. You may also handle all logistics, from booking speakers to purchasing awards and gifts, to arranging travel, lodging, and catering. A popular and growing subset of event planners is wedding planners.

Promoter. As a promoter, you'll function as the marketing and selling arm by developing marketing strategies to promote events ranging from rock concerts to arts festivals to international chess tournaments in a variety of venues—including arenas, clubs, festivals, churches, and auditoriums. You'll work with artists and performers (the talent), as well as with television, radio, special-events coordinators, ticket sellers, media reviewers, bulk mailers, and local merchants to market an event.

Stage Manager, Assistant. In this job, you'll synchronize everything that happens during any type of stage performance, bringing all the elements of a performance together at the right time. You'll coordinate an actor's movements; manage props, scenery movements, and lighting and sound effects; and organize rehearsals and schedule artistic and technical operations. The stage management team consists of a stage manager, a deputy stage manager, and an assistant stage manager. You ensure that props are correctly set and scene changes run smoothly.

Talent Agent, Associate. In this job, as the name implies, you'll represent talent—musicians, dancers, actors, comedians, magicians, illusionists, clowns, models, artists, hypnotists, ventriloquists, and others—helping them move forward in their careers by providing motivation and securing jobs (called "bookings") and auditions. You may work by yourself or as part of a talent agency. You must be self-motivated, be able to multi-task, have great organizational skills, and enjoy talking on the phone. Typically, you'll have to start with relatively unknown clients and build your reputation.

The Professor Says

Some of the more lucrative and prestigious career paths that performing arts majors follow require additional education at the graduate level. These careers include:

◆ College Professor (Master's degree or higher)

◆ Dance Therapist (Master's degree or higher)

◆ Music Attorney (Juris Doctor)

◆ Music (Master's degree or higher)

Teacher, Performing Arts (Acting, Dance, Music). As a performing arts teacher, you will share your artistic knowledge with students so that they can express themselves through some aspect of the performing arts. Teachers in schools work regular school hours, but often work outside of these hours planning lessons or attending meetings. You may also may be involved in extra-curricular activities (rehearsals and performances) during weekends, school holidays, or after school. A Bachelor's degree and a teaching certificate are required to teach at the elementary through high school levels. To teach at the college level, a postgraduate degree may be required, as well as some work experience.

Other Career Possibilities. Some other job and career paths for performing arts majors include:

Casting Specialist

Choreographer

Composer/Arranger

Community Affairs Liaison

Dance Therapist

Disc Jockey

Music Attorney

Music Librarian

Musical Instrument Maker/Repairperson

Performing Arts Critic/Writer/Editor

Playwright

Publicist/Press Agent

Recording Technician

Royalties Broadcast Monitor

Scriptwriter/Screenwriter

Tour Coordinator

Skills Needed/Developed

Students majoring in some area of the performing arts develop numerous valuable and transferable skills. The following are the most critical to graduates.

Oral Communications. Speaking skills are essential to those pursuing a career in the performing arts. You'll need to be able to express yourself clearly, concisely, and confidently, whether acting on stage or explaining a musical or dance movement.

Interpersonal Communications. Most performing arts careers require working with people, so you must be able to talk and listen in one-on-one and small-group situations.

Listening. Active listening is essential to a career in the performing arts, as it aids in taking direction and cues from directors, managers, and peer performers.

Teamwork. The ability to work with other people—whether they are similar or different. Actors, dancers, and musicians often work as parts of teams or troupes, so this skill is essential for you to learn.

The Professor Says

Other transferable skills you gain from these majors include:

◆ Creativity
◆ Observation
◆ Critical thinking
◆ Planning and organizing
◆ Working independently

Expected Growth

There will always be jobs for performers—whether working on stage or behind the scenes—but growth in new jobs is expected to be moderate (about 10 percent).

Actors

Job growth for actors is expected to be about as fast as the average (10 to 15 percent) for all jobs, but competition remains strong as many people are attracted to acting.

Sources of additional information:

◆ Actors' Equity (www.actorsequity.org)
◆ American Federation of Television & Radio Artists (www.aftra.com)
◆ Screen Actors Guild (www.sag.org)

Musicians/Singers

Job growth for musicians and singers is expected to be about as fast as the average (10 to 15 percent) for all jobs, but competition is expected to remain strong.

Sources of additional information:

◆ American Federation of Musicians (www.afm.com)

◆ American Guild of Music (www.americanguild.org)

Dancers

Job growth for dancers and choreographers is expected to be about as fast as the average (10 to 15 percent) for all jobs, but competition is expected to remain strong.

Sources of additional information:

◆ American Dance Guild (www.americandanceguild.org)

◆ American Guild of Musical Artists (www.musicalartists.org)

Arts Management Specialists

Job growth is expected to be about as fast as the average (10 to 15 percent) for all jobs.

Wondering what employers look for in an arts management specialist? Here's a sample program specialist job description:

> The cultural arts program specialist will assist in the demonstration of the vitality of Native communities and cultures through the performing arts and literature. The incumbent conceives, develops, and produces a variety of public programs. The incumbent will be responsible for the coordination of a variety of the museum's public programs and productions, including programs featuring native music, dance, theater, storytelling, author events, and related demonstrations, as well as special program events and projects that relate to native cultural arts. The incumbent identifies, plans, and produces public programs in the museum's theater and other program spaces; develops, tracks, and administers program budgets; and schedules all materials to maintain smooth workflow between the department and outside parties. The incumbent contacts performers, presenters, and authors to arrange their programs; develops the conceptual frameworks of presentations, performances, and related program activities; and develops and

implements outreach plans to inform the general public and special targeted audiences of these programs. The incumbent writes notes for programs, press releases, and other material to inform the public, media, staff, and targeted communities.

Designers, Assistant

Job growth for design assistants is expected to be about the same as for all occupations over the next decade (about 10 to 15 percent).

Sources of additional information:

◆ Costume Designer Guild (www.costumedesignersguild.com)

◆ Set Decorators Society of America (www.setdecorators.org)

◆ International Association of Lighting Designers (www.iald.org)

Event Planners

Demand for events planners and coordinators is expected to grow faster than average (18 to 25 percent) over the next decade.

Sources of additional information:

◆ Convention Industry Council (www.conventionindustry.org)

◆ International Special Events Society (www.ises.com)

Wondering what employers look for in an event planner? Here's a sample event planner specialist job description:

> The event planner specialist is responsible for the internal coordination and planning of our annual gala and is responsible for all corporate oversight and will act as the liaison to external event planning consultants. You'll help manage aspects of assigned events including site selection, hotel contract, food and beverage menus, air and ground transportation (if applicable), agenda development and review, registrations, on-site supervision of event, and budgeting; review all meeting invoices/accounts payable and forward for appropriate signature and payment. Ensure timely processing; manage working relationships with external consultants assisting in the administration of various events; and maintain quality customer service and work professionally with the event consultant. Requires a Bachelor's degree in area of specialty.

Promoters

There will always be a demand for promoters, but job growth is expected to be about average (10 to 15 percent) over the next decade.

---

profiles

Promoter Bill Graham

Bill Graham (born Wolfgang Grajonca) is one of the most famous and beloved rock promoters. He managed the San Francisco Mime Troupe before moving on to present entertainment in his own clubs, including the Fillmore West and Fillmore East. He later closed his clubs to focus on promoting large-arena concerts and tours, promoting artists like The Rolling Stones, Jimi Hendrix, Neil Young, Bob Dylan, David Bowie, and Elvis Costello. He also devoted much time and energy to a wide range of benefit events, mobilizing musicians on behalf of crucial social issues and helping to raise millions of dollars for causes such as The Live Aid Concert for African Famine Relief and many others. Among his many honors, he received MTV's Lifetime Achievement Award, the Humanitarian Award of B'nai B'rith, the Award of Honor of the San Francisco Arts Commission, and the prestigious Scopus Award of the American Friends of Hebrew University. He was inducted into the Rock & Roll Hall of Fame.

Stage Managers, Assistant

Demand for stage managers is expected to grow about as fast as the average (10 to 15 percent) for all careers over the next decade.

A source of additional information is the Stage Managers Association (www.stagemanagers.org).

Wondering what employers look for in an assistant stage manager? Here's a sample assistant stage manager job description:

> To serve as one of two assistant stage managers for a four-show rotating repertory season that will include *Othello, Much Ado About Nothing, Amadeus, Godspell,* and the children's show. Will be assigned to one stage manager for each show assigned; assist the stage manager in the running and organization of daily rehearsals; assist in scheduling and posting rehearsal and production calls and any other stage management duties that are deemed necessary and appropriate while working within the parameters of the festival's production schedule; responsible for running backstage during production for the two shows assigned; attend all scheduled rehearsals, paper techs, dry techs, and technical rehearsals.

Looking for someone with previous experience and who has worked with children, but will train the right person. Theatre degree preferred.

Talent Agents, Associate

Job growth for talent agents is expected to be about as fast as the average (10 to 15 percent) for all jobs.

Sources of additional information:

◆ The Association of Talent Agents (www.agentassociation.com)

◆ North American Performing Arts Managers & Agents (www.napama.org)

Teachers, Performing Arts

Teachers will always be in demand, and while overall job growth for teachers is expected to be about as fast as average (10 to 15 percent), because of cuts in the funding of arts education, new jobs will be harder to find.

Sources of additional information:

◆ American Alliance for Theatre & Education (www.aate.com)

◆ Educational Theatre Association (www.edta.org)

◆ National Center for Alternative Certification (www.teach-now.org)

◆ Music Teachers National Association (www.mtna.org)

◆ National Dance Education Association (www.ndeo.org)

◆ National Educational Association (www.nea.org)

The Professor Says _____

Your next step? Pick the couple of careers that most fit your interests with a major in performing arts and dig more deeply into them. Remember that it is always important to learn more about prospective careers by going online, talking with professors, conducting informational interviews, and job-shadowing.

Earnings Potential $

While there is great variability in the earning potential of jobs using your performing arts skills, overall, all three of these majors, at an average of $29,000, earn less than the average annual salary for all college graduates, which is currently around $38,000.

This section provides some general guidelines of salaries to expect upon graduation. Remember, salaries vary by employer, industry, and region.

Arts Management Specialist. The median annual salary of an arts management specialist ranges from about $25,000 to $30,000.

Designer, Assistant. Beginning salary for a design assistant is about $30,000.

Event Planner. The median annual salary of an entry-level events planner is $40,000.

Promoter. The median annual salary of a promoter varies widely.

Stage Manager, Assistant. The median annual salary of a publicity assistant is $26,000.

Talent Agent, Associate. The median annual salary of an associate talent agent varies widely, partly based on the size of the agency, quality of the talent, and commission schedule.

Teacher, Performing Arts. The median annual salary for an entry-level teacher is about $32,000.

> **The Professor Says**
>
> Remember that you're not done once you pick your college major—in fact, it's just begun, because the next thing you need to do is gain work experience. Just about all "entry-level" jobs for college graduates require some work experience outside the classroom. Seek out internships, volunteer, and figure out other ways to gain the experience you need.

The Least You Need to Know

◆ The performing arts field offers myriad career paths for creative and talented individuals—on and off stage.

◆ Even if you know you will not become a professional actor, dancer, or musician, you can still find other career paths to take to follow your passion.

◆ Good communicators and public speakers will always be in demand, so if you have strong communications skills, you should have little trouble finding a job.

◆ Entry-level salaries in the performing arts tend to be much lower than the average for all college grads.

Careers in Business Using a Major in ...

This part stresses the different types of careers and majors in business, from being the next real estate mogul to solving corporate crimes or creating the next big idea. People who have a passion for business typically are a bit more career-focused than other majors, but that does not mean you can't learn more about the major—or the types of careers you can find within each of them.

The following chapters show you the types of career paths you can pursue with various majors in business, including accounting, finance, international business, management, marketing, and real estate.

"I'm thinking international finance."

10

Accounting, Finance, and Economics

In This Chapter

- ◆ Discover careers that use your passion for numbers
- ◆ Use your analytical skills in jobs that demand them
- ◆ Learn the typical classes accounting, finance, and economics majors require
- ◆ Find out what kind of jobs and salaries to expect

What do you do for a career if you love numbers? Do spreadsheets and financial models excite you? Do you love charting and graphing stock prices, income levels, or inflation? What if you only review the financial section of the newspaper of your favorite news site?

This chapter reveals rewarding careers for students majoring in accounting, finance, or economics.

About the Majors

All three of these majors depend on strong analytical skills as the tools used in these majors help us understand the financial well-being of a company or industry—even the whole economy. Number-crunching and bottom-line analysis is something that is performed everyday, all over the world, as financial centers open and close.

Accounting

Accounting majors learn all the business basics while developing the analytical skills they need for professional careers in public accounting, business, and government. Additionally, accounting provides students with the ability to understand the elements of the audit process, analyze financial statements, and apply critical accounting information to facilitate better management decisions.

Accounting is a fairly common major, especially at colleges that have a school of business. Typical courses include:

Financial Accounting Basics	Financial Reporting
Management Accounting	Business Law for Accountants
Financial Accounting I	Business Valuation
Financial Accounting II	Accounting Information Systems
Managerial Cost Accounting	Government and Nonprofit Accounting
Auditing I	
Federal Taxation of Entities	

Finance

Finance majors acquire the tools they need for a wide range of careers, including those in the financial service sector, such as banking, brokerage, insurance, and financial analysis. The major is also excellent training for commerce and government.

Finance is a fairly common major, especially for universities that have a college of business. Typical courses include:

Money and Financial Institutions	Real Estate Principles
Business Finance	Investments

Financial Management I

Financial Management II

Multinational Finance

Bank Management

Financial Risk Management

Equity Fund Management

Fixed Income Fund Management

Corporate Finance

Principles of Insurance and Risk Management

Economics

Economics majors obtain a thorough understanding of economics and business behavior through the study of how effectively a society meets its human and material needs. Students gain insights into what motivates people to behave as they do and how different groups with different behaviors interact when they come together, making it both an analytical and broad-based major.

Economics is the most common of these three majors, and can be found at just about every college and university (although the major is sometimes housed in the business school and other times within arts and sciences—often with very different requirements, so do your research). Typical courses include:

Macro Economics

Micro Economics

Exploring Foreign Economies

Humane Economics

Intermediate Macro Economics

Financial Institutions

Intermediate Micro Economics

Economies of Europe

Economics of Race and Gender

Research Economics

International Economics

Ecometrics

Energy, Environment, and Economics

Economic Principles, Policies, and Issues

Background on Careers

Accounting graduates advise the management of an organization on profits and losses, develop and review accounting systems, and ensure that the organization adheres to government laws and regulations. Accountant career paths can be divided into four areas: public accountants, management accountants, government accountants, and auditors and internal auditors.

The Professor Says

Many accountants—close to 40 percent—further their credentials on the job market by taking additional accounting coursework, obtaining experience, and passing a certification exam to gain the title of Certified Public Account (CPA).

Finance graduates can specialize in banking, where you work for a financial institution; corporate finance, where you work for a business and help it find the money to operate, grow, and make acquisitions, as well as plan its financial future and manage any cash on hand; investment banking, where you work within companies or governments to issue securities, help investors trade securities, manage financial assets, and provide financial advice; money management, where you hold stocks and bonds for clients; or financial planning, where you assist individuals with their investment portfolios and financial futures.

Economics graduates typically specialize in business, government, or academic economics. Business economists work in manufacturing, mining, transportation, communications, banking, insurance, retailing, investment, and other types of organizations.

The Professor Says

For finance graduates going into the sale of stocks, bonds, mutual funds, insurance, or real estate, additional professional licenses are required.

Government economists work in national, state, and local governments, serving in a wide variety of positions involving analysis and policymaking. Some economics majors graduate and go on to Master's and doctoral studies in economics to become academic economists.

Some top jobs and careers for students earning a Bachelor's degree with a major in accounting, finance, or economics include:

Actuary. In this job, you'll conduct analyses, pricing, and risk assessment to estimate financial outcomes; apply knowledge of mathematics, probability, statistics, principles of finance and business to calculations in life, health, social, and casualty insurance, annuities, and pensions; and develop probability tables regarding fire, natural disasters, death, unemployment, etc., based on analysis of statistical data and other pertinent information.

Budget Analyst. As a budget analyst, you develop and manage an organization's financial plans, typically seeking to find ways to improve efficiency and use of financial resources. You'll collaborate with department heads and other managers to provide advice and technical assistance for the preparation of annual budgets and budget forecasting, as well as monitor budgets, conduct cost-benefit analyses to review financial requests, assess program tradeoffs, and explore alternative funding methods. Budget analysts work in private industry, nonprofit organizations, and the public sector (governments).

Commodities Broker/Trader. In this job, you'll buy and sell physical commodities such as coffee, grain, sugar, crude oil, gas, and nonferrous metals at stock exchanges on behalf of investors, product producers, and buyers. You'll also deal in derivatives (futures and options), which are based on physical commodities. You may also offer financial advice on the purchase of particular commodities, analyze or assess stock market behavior and legal trading practices, and provide critical input into an individual client's financial portfolio. Commodity brokers work at commodity broking companies, investment banks, and exchanges/clearing houses.

Forensic Accountant. As a forensic accountant, you'll examine white-collar crimes such as securities fraud and embezzlement, bankruptcies and contract disputes, and other complex and possibly criminal financial transactions, including money laundering. You'll combine knowledge of accounting and finance with law and investigative techniques, investigating and determining whether an activity is illegal. Many forensic accountants work closely with law enforcement personnel and lawyers during investigations and often appear as expert witnesses during trials.

Internal Auditor. In this job, you'll conduct compliance audits, develop internal controls, and manage accounting information systems to verify the accuracy of an organization's internal records and to check for mismanagement, waste, or fraud. You'll participate in every aspect of the company's business, from evaluating efficiency and effectiveness to mergers and acquisitions to compliance with federal and corporate policies to providing recommendations to improve risk-management practices. Many types of highly specialized auditors exist, such as electronic data-processing, environmental, engineering, legal, insurance premium, bank, and health-care auditors.

Management Accountant. As a management accountant (sometimes also called industrial, corporate, or private accountant), you'll often start your career with an organization as a cost accountant, junior internal auditor, or trainee. You'll work with top management in deciding how money should be spent and participate in decisions about capital budgeting, lines of business, and development of new products—analyzing and interpreting the financial information that corporate executives need in order to make sound business decisions. You'll also prepare financial reports for other groups, including stockholders, creditors, regulatory agencies, and tax authorities. Within accounting departments, management accountants may work in financial analysis, planning and budgeting, and cost accounting.

Underwriter Trainee/Assistant. Aided by computer models and working under the supervision of an experienced risk analyst, you'll analyze information in insurance applications in order to determine risk factors for insurance applicants and assess the likelihood of a claim being made, with the goal of minimizing losses for the company. Pulling information from numerous sources, such as medical records, statistical models, and actuarial studies, you'll decide whether the insurance company will issue an insurance policy, and if so, how much the policy should cost. Many underwriters specialize in either personal or commercial insurance, and then further by type of risk insured, such as homeowners, automobile, fire, liability, workers' compensation, or marine.

Other Career Possibilities. Some other job and career paths for accounting, finance, and economics majors include:

Appraiser	Insurance Agent/Broker
Bank Research Analyst	IRS Investigator
Bond Manager	Pension Fund Manager
Business Forecaster	Portfolio Analyst
Consumer Credit/Loan Officer	Public Accountant (CPA)
Financial Planner	Securities Analyst
Financial Representative	Tax Accountant

Skills Needed/Developed

Students majoring in accounting, finance, and economics develop numerous valuable and transferable skills. The following are the most critical to graduates.

Analytical Skills. You must possess the ability to organize, analyze, and interpret numerical data, ensure the information's accuracy, and make sound recommendations.

Quantitative/Math. Perhaps the most essential skill for any of these majors is having extremely strong math, quantitative, and computational abilities.

Organizational Skills. This skill is the ability to manage large amounts of information and demands through task analysis, time management, and goal-setting.

Recordkeeping/Handling Details. These majors require extreme attention to detail. You must track and record numerical information and records and be able to retrieve them easily.

The Professor Says _____

Other transferable skills gained from these majors include:

- Decision-making
- Written communications
- Interpersonal communications
- Teamwork
- Technical/computer

Expected Growth

Graduates with a solid foundation in business will always be in demand, especially in the coming decade, as many retirements will cause businesses to hire even more business graduates.

Accounting Majors

Job growth for accounting is expected to be faster than the average (18 to 25 percent) for all careers over the next decade.

Sources of additional information:

- American Institute of Certified Public Accountants (www.aicpa.org)
- American Society of Women Accountants (www.aswa.org)
- National Association of Black Accountants (www.nabainc.org)

Finance Majors

Job growth for finance is expected to be faster than the average (18 to 25 percent) for all careers over the next decade.

Sources of additional information:

- American Finance Association (www.afajof.org)
- Association for Financial Professionals (www.afponline.org)

Goldman Sachs CFO David Viniar

David Viniar is an executive vice president and chief financial officer of Goldman Sachs and has been a partner at the investment bank since 1992. He has been labeled as one of the top 10 highest-paid CFOs in the country. He has a Bachelor's degree from Union College. Before serving in his current role, he held numerous titles within the company, including head of the operations, technology and finance division and head of the finance division. He was chief financial officer of The Goldman Sachs Group, L.P., and started with the company in the structured finance department of investment banking. He also serves on the board of trustees of Union College. He was named a CFO Excellence Award Winner by *CFO* magazine.

Economics Majors

Demand for economics majors should remain strong over the next decade because the versatility of the major allows graduates to enter a variety of different but related fields.

eBay President and CEO Meg Whitman

Margaret C. "Meg" Whitman is CEO of one of the most successful Internet companies in the world. Whitman graduated from Princeton University with a degree in economics, but she had started college planning a career in medicine. She became an economics major after holding a summer job selling advertising for a campus publication. Whitman earned an MBA from Harvard Business School. She started her business career with Procter & Gamble in brand management, later working for the consulting firm Bain & Co., Walt Disney, Stride Rite Shoes, FTD, and Hasbro, Inc. Since joining eBay in 1998 as president and CEO, Whitman has helped turn it into a major Internet presence. Numerous publications have acknowledged her power and influence, including *The Wall Street Journal* (one of the 50 women to watch), *Time* (one of the world's 100 most influential people), *Fortune* (the most powerful woman in business), and *Business Week* (list of the 25 most powerful business managers). She sits on the board of directors of Procter & Gamble and DreamWorks Animation.

Actuaries

Demand for actuaries is expected to grow faster than the average (18 to 25 percent) for all jobs over the next decade.

Sources of additional information:

◆ American Academy of Actuaries (www.actuary.org)

◆ International Actuarial Association (www.actuaries.org)

◆ Society of Actuaries (www.soa.org)

Budget Analysts, Junior

Demand for budget analysts is expected to grow about as fast as average (10 to 15 percent) for all jobs over the next decade.

Sources of additional information:

◆ Government Finance Officers Association (www.gfoa.org)

◆ National Association of State Budget Officers (www.nasbo.org)

Wondering what employers look for in a junior budget analyst? Here's a sample budget analyst job description:

> Under supervision, the junior budget analyst assists with and performs professional level work in analyzing operations of city departments and agencies as they relate to the formulation and execution of the annual budget, grants, and financial/fiscal policy. More specifically, duties include: assisting in preparation of budget reports and proposals; assisting in preparation of budget and program delivery calendars; assisting in compilation of budget requests; making budget presentations; performing cost analysis and preparing program reports; preparing, generating, and updating budget documents, contract reports, surveys, and databases; tracking and coordinating revenue and expenditures, grants, program budgets, and other funds; assisting with the preparation and submittal of supplemental budget requests; and assisting with the preparation of quarterly and year-end financial, program and budget, and legislative reports. Possession of a baccalaureate degree from an accredited college or university in accounting, finance, public or business administration, economics, or a related field is required. Some experience in budget analysis and/or financial analysis and reporting is preferred.

Commodities Brokers/Traders

Some job growth is expected—about as fast as the average (10 to 15 percent) for all careers—but expect strong competition for available entry-level jobs.

Sources of additional information:

◆ Commodity Floor Brokers & Traders Association (www.cfbta.org)

◆ National Introducing Brokers Association (www.theniba.com)

Wondering what employers look for in a commodities broker? Here's a sample commodities broker job description:

> We're seeking entry-level candidates for commodity brokers. We are looking for motivated, confident, and trainable individuals who have a burning desire to achieve financial freedom. We work in a fast-moving, high risk/reward, ever-changing environment. If you're hired to work at our firm, you'll be responsible for: monitoring world markets; conducting trades on behalf of our clients; advising clients on the best way to position themselves within markets; seeking and pursuing new business opportunities; and maintaining contact with shipping, transport, and insurance companies. We offer: paid training and sponsorship for the Series 3 license; performance bonuses and incentives; and expert training from senior brokers and management. You must be a self-starter who possesses: outstanding communication skills, with emphasis on telephone skills; high ethical and moral standards; enthusiastic, positive work attitude; and positive customer focus; and be numbers- and detail-oriented.

Forensic Accountants

Job growth is expected to be faster than average (18 to 25 percent) over the next decade, and projects to be the fastest-growing accounting specialty.

A source of additional information is the National Association of Forensic Accountants (www.nafanet.com).

Wondering what employers look for in a forensic accountant? Here's a sample forensic accountant job description:

> Very stable and growing regional CPA firm seeks an accountant for its forensic accounting division, which is composed of a diverse group of practitioners—certified public accountants, certified fraud examiners, statisticians, online and

Internet research professionals, and computer forensic specialists. We also employ former senior law enforcement officials and agents from the FBI, Justice Department, and other government agencies. Successful candidate will have a minimum of a 4-year degree in accounting or finance and some public accounting experience with fraud investigation in divorce, bankruptcy, and commercial cases. Salary is negotiable depending on experience level. Having your CPA—or parts passed—is a plus, as is having CFE certification.

Internal Auditors

Job growth is expected to be faster than the average (18 to 25 percent) for all careers over the next decade.

A source of additional information is the Institute of Internal Auditors (www.theiia.org).

Wondering what employers look for in an internal auditor? Here's a sample internal auditor job description:

> As a staff auditor, you will participate as a team member on audit projects; document processes under review; assess risks, evaluate controls; develop and execute audit tests; summarize and communicate results; and assist in the development of management actions. Qualifications include: an ability to think analytically, communicate complex issues, and develop control recommendations; a B.A. or B.S. in accounting, finance, business, or related field required; professional certification (CIA, CISA, CPA, or equivalent) preferred; effective written and verbal communication; ability to present control analysis and recommendations with clarity and professionalism; demonstrated track record of integrity, effective communication, innovation, and excellence; experience working in teams; and the ability to travel.

Management Accountants

Job growth is expected to be faster than the average (18 to 25 percent) for all occupations over the next decade.

A source of additional information is the Institute of Management Accountants (www.imanet.org).

Underwriter Trainees/Assistants

Job growth is expected to increase about as fast as average (10 to 15 percent) over the next decade for underwriters.

Sources of additional information:

◆ American Institute for Chartered Property Casualty Underwriters (www.aicpcu. org)

◆ Casual and Property Insurance Underwriters (www.cpcusociety.org)

◆ Inland Marine Underwriters Association (www.imua.org)

Wondering what employers look for in an underwriter trainee? Here's a sample underwriter trainee job description:

> We are one of the leading insurance companies in the United States. Our superior financial strength and consistent record of strong operating returns mean security for our customers—and opportunities for our employees. Primary duties: observe and work with underwriters, risk control representatives, and claim representatives to become familiar with the functions of these positions and how they interact and work with one another; develop critical underwriting skills through classroom, independent, and on-the-job training, including analysis of exposures, determination of appropriate insurance coverage and conditions, and the assignment of premium amounts; gather and review information on financial conditions, risk exposures, loss history, and economic trends that may affect the type of insurance coverage provided; establish, support, and maintain effective relationships with customers, agents, and brokers. The ideal candidate for the development program will desire a position that is both analytical and marketing-oriented and possess a Bachelor's degree in risk management and insurance, finance, business administration, or economics. Students with prior related intern experience preferred.

The Professor Says

Not sure about these career choices? These are just some of the career possibilities for a major in accounting, finance, or economics. Remember that it is always important to learn more about prospective careers by going online, talking with professors, conducting informational interviews, and job-shadowing.

Earnings Potential $

Accounting, finance, and economics majors tend to have a higher annual starting salary than the average for all college graduates, which is currently around $38,000. Accounting majors average about $45,000, while finance and economics majors average about $44,500.

This section provides some general guidelines of salaries to expect upon graduation. Remember, salaries vary by employer, industry, and region.

Actuary. Median annual salary of an entry-level actuary is approximately $51,000.

Budget Analyst, Junior. Beginning salary for a junior budget analyst is $44,500.

Commodities Broker/Trader. Median annual earnings of commodities brokers vary widely since the majority of their income is commission-based, but entry-level brokers tend to make anywhere from $50,000 to $100,000.

Forensic Accountant. The average salary for an entry-level forensic accountant is between $40,000 and $60,000 a year.

Internal Auditor. The median annual salary of an entry-level internal auditor is $46,000.

Management Accountant. The average salary for an entry-level management accountant is about $45,000 a year.

Underwriter Trainee/Assistant. Median salaries for underwriter trainees can range from $40,000 for life insurance underwriters to $43,500 for property and casualty insurance underwriters.

> **The Professor Says**
>
> Your next step after choosing your major? Gaining work experience. Just about all "entry-level" jobs for college graduates require some work experience outside the classroom. Seek out internships, volunteer, and figure out other ways to gain the experience you need.

The Least You Need to Know

- Students who have a passion and gift for numbers should find plenty of jobs upon graduation, as increased job growth is expected in most fields.

- Most jobs in accounting, finance, and economics pay well—and better than the average for all college grads.

◆ As is the case with many fields, you can get a good entry-level job with just an undergraduate degree in accounting, finance, or economics, though some careers do require additional courses and certifications.

◆ If you love accounting, but also have a love of investigating and uncovering fraud, then forensic accounting may be the career choice for you; it's also the fastest-growing accounting specialty.

Chapter 11

International Business

In This Chapter

- ◆ Discover careers that use your passion for cultures
- ◆ Use your business skills in jobs that demand them
- ◆ Learn the typical classes an international business major requires
- ◆ Find out what kind of jobs and salaries to expect

What do you do for a career if you love learning and experiencing other cultures and countries? If you're a world traveler—or wish you were? Do you dream of working for a multinational corporation so that you can live and work in diverse parts of the world?

This chapter reveals rewarding careers for students who major in international business.

About the Major

International business is one of the fastest-growing business majors—perhaps one of the fastest-growing of any majors—as students with a broader world view seek out an international major and career. It's also a major from which employers who conduct business in multiple parts of the world demand graduates with both the business and cultural skills to succeed in an ever-shrinking world market. It is hard to imagine that there are any companies—large or small—that are not affected in some way by global events and competition.

International Business

International business majors learn all the business basics (accounting, marketing, management, finance) while developing a sound understanding of international business principles and the languages, cultures, customs, and laws of other regions of the world that are essential for success in today's global economy.

International business is becoming a fairly common major, especially at colleges that have a school of business. Typical courses include:

International Business	Business in Emerging Markets
Global Marketing	International Economics
Global Issues in Management	Import/Export Management
International Accounting	International Business Law
International Real Estate	Managing Global Workforce
Multinational Finance	

The Professor Says

Many international business majors also require students to take at least one foreign language (some require a proficiency in two), and many require some sort of international experience—either studying abroad or an international internship.

Background on Careers

International business graduates are prepared for careers in business, government, and international agencies and organizations in the fields of management, marketing, international trade, and global financial operations and planning. Most international business graduates start their careers in the domestic operations of an organization, with overseas assignments coming after a few years with a company, although they may come faster if the student possesses specialized skills (e.g., language) needed by the company in its foreign operations.

Some top jobs and careers for students earning a Bachelor's degree with a major in international business include:

Export Sales Representative. In this job, you'll typically work for a foreign company in the United States (though you could also represent a U.S. firm overseas), acting as a liaison between a foreign buyer and domestic seller—basically the equivalent of working as a manufacturer's representative. Using the company's product literature and samples, you'll uncover customer needs and wants, conduct sales calls, and sell the product to potential buyers. You may be involved in writing proposals or coordinating bids for competitive tender, as well as coordinating the operations of local distributors.

Foreign Trade Consultant/Analyst. As a foreign trade consultant, you'll work as an independent broker assessing a prospective company's product line and advising on what is exportable. Working with the client company, you'll locate receptive markets, develop market reports, find customers, take care of local registrations and regulatory compliances, arrange deals with local distributors, and help design market entry strategies. You earn a commission by matching buyers with sellers, with the size of the commission based on the volume of sales in the market being managed.

Major Pitfalls

In many ways, this major is sometimes seen as a glorified general business major and it is up to you to take additional courses (and perhaps majors and minors) so that you get the specific skills you need for your international career.

Global Sourcing (Procurement) Specialist. Working under the supervision of the procurement or sourcing manager, you'll seek out sources of products and services that the company requires for its operations, typically comparing domestic and imported products and purchasing from both sources. You will be expected to locate the most suitable goods and services at the best possible price and ensure that they can be delivered where and when they are needed. Some procurement specialists, especially in larger companies, may specialize in logistics or in purchasing specific commodities.

Import/Export Administrator/Specialist. As an import/export administrator, you'll work under the supervision of the import/export manager and typically be responsible for moving merchandise and/or material in or out of the country—in compliance with federal, state, and local regulations. You'll work with both domestic and international shippers, oversee completion of all paperwork and required documents, and monitor monetary transactions associated with international distribution to ensure efficient movement of products in and out of the country in a timely manner, and may negotiate with clients or handle issues with customs officials.

International Business Development Specialist. In this job, you'll work under the supervision of the international business development manager, creating new business opportunities for the company in foreign markets while also maintaining the smooth operation and expansion of existing businesses in those markets. You'll develop plans to proactively work with international customers to meet their sales targets; foster customers' understanding of new products; provide support to the customers, including training and serving as a liaison between the customers and technical staff; collaborate with sales representatives in development of pricing and promotional strategies; and present product-oriented seminars at tradeshows and customer sites.

International Job Analyst. As an international job analysis specialist, you'll collect and examine detailed information about job duties for a company's foreign operations to prepare job descriptions that explain the duties, training, and skills that each job requires—adjusting domestic guidelines to align with local customs. As an entry-level human resources specialist, you may also be called upon to conduct recruitment and selection processes; perform employment and career counseling; analyze issues and data for the purpose of resolving job classification, compensation, performance, and organizational assessment issues; and provide policy guidance and information to management and employees.

Other Career Possibilities. Here are some other job and career paths for international business majors:

Currency Dealer

Customs Broker

Customs Inspector

Export Sales Representative

Foreign Exchange Worker

International Appraiser

International Bank Manager

International Buyer

International Commodities Trader

International Economist

International Finance Writer

International Financial Analyst

International Media Planner

International Real Estate Broker/Agent

International Tax Accountant

International Sales Analyst

The Professor Says _____

Interested in becoming a CEO of a company one day? Studies show the best route to the boardroom is through an international management career, because today's business leaders must have the savvy to understand domestic and foreign markets.

Skills Needed/Developed

Students majoring in international business develop numerous valuable and transferable skills, but the following are the most critical.

Cultural Sensitivity/Language Skills. Among the most important skills international business majors learn are valuing and appreciating other societies and cultures, as well as becoming fluent in multiple languages.

Interpersonal Communications. You'll need to possess the ability to talk and listen in one-on-one and small-group situations, one of the core elements of business decision-making.

Written and Oral Communications. Speaking and writing skills are essential when pursuing an international business career. You'll need the ability to clearly express yourself in at least one language.

Analytical Skills. This skill deals with your ability to manage large amounts of information and demands through task analysis, time management, and goal-setting.

Teamwork. This skill involves your ability to work with other people—whether they are similar or different—and is one of the most important for any career in business.

The Professor Says _____

Other transferable skills you gain from these majors include:

- ◆ Decision-making
- ◆ Problem-solving
- ◆ Leadership
- ◆ Negotiating
- ◆ Technical/computer

Expected Growth

Graduates with a solid foundation in business will always be in demand, especially in the coming decade as many retirements will cause organizations to hire even more business graduates.

International Business Majors

Demand for international business majors should remain strong over the next decade because of the growth of worldwide trade and global markets.

Management Guru Peter Drucker

Peter Drucker (1909–2005) was a management thinker, writer, professor, and consultant. He consulted for nearly every major U.S. corporation, including General Electric, Coca-Cola, Citicorp, IBM, and Intel. He grew up in Vienna, Austria, and earned a doctorate in public and international law at Frankfurt University. He eventually found his way to the United States, where he worked first as a freelance journalist, chiefly for *Harper's*, but also for the *Washington Post*. As a result of his book, *The Future of Industrial Man*, Dr. Drucker was invited by General Motors to conduct a two-year social-scientific analysis of what was at that time the world's largest corporation. He then joined the faculty of New York University's Graduate Business School as professor of management, later becoming the Clarke Professor of Social Science and Management at the Claremont Graduate University in Claremont, California. The university named its management school after him in 1987. He wrote 35 books, including the landmark books *The Practice of Management* and *The Effective Executive*. He received the Presidential Medal of Freedom, the highest civilian honor, and holds 25 honorary doctorates from universities around the world.

Export Sales Representatives

Employment is expected to grow faster than the average for all jobs over the next decade.

Wondering what employers look for in an export sales representative? Here's a sample export sales rep job description:

> An autonomous subsidiary of a U.S. corporation, we are a well-established manufacturer of tertiary, retailer brand, and industrial cleaners. Targeting further growth from export markets, the company has an opportunity for an export sales representative to join its team. Dependent upon the experience of the successful candidate, the role will either focus on building and managing a strong network of distributors worldwide or on opening doors into the mid and major grocery and DIY retailers in Europe. Supported by flexible production capabilities and

a complete in-house R&D expertise covering both product formulation and artwork design, this is a door-knocking role that will excite new business developers. Reporting to the commercial manager, you will be responsible for developing and delivering an export sales plan that will bring profitable growth to the business. Travel is a prerequisite. Candidates will ideally be fluent in French, German, Italian, or Spanish and have either some export sales experience in any industry *or* experience working with European retailers. You should be a good communicator, self-motivated, and a determined character that thrives on "making things happen." Bachelor's degree in business a must.

Foreign Trade Analysts

Employment is expected to grow about as fast as average (10 to 15 percent) for all jobs over the next decade.

Global Sourcing Specialists

Some job growth is expected—about as fast as the average (10 to 15 percent) for all careers.

Wondering what employers look for in a global sourcing specialist? Here's a sample global sourcing specialist job description:

The ideal candidate will have a four-year degree in a business-related field; excellent verbal and written communication skills; excellent organizational skills; must be computer-proficient, especially with Word, Excel, Access, and Outlook; and must possess a high level of accuracy. Must be able to work with minimal supervision and able to meet deadlines. Experience in buying and negotiating with international factories is helpful. The responsibilities of this position include assisting the global sourcing manager and specialist to coordinate the company's global sourcing activities; working with merchandise managers to identify future import opportunities, implement new programs, and maintain global sourcing programs; identifying and qualifying factories for imports; participating in negotiations (terms, packaging, pricing, etc,); coordinating and expediting container shipments (selection, logistics, drop ship orders); and other duties as required. International travel as required.

Strategos Founder Gary Hamel

Gary Hamel is founder and chairman of Strategos, an international management consulting firm based in Chicago, and director of the Woodside Institute, a nonprofit research foundation based in Woodside, California. As a consultant and management educator, Hamel has worked with companies such as General Electric, Nokia, Nestle, Shell, Best Buy, Procter & Gamble, 3M, IBM, and Microsoft. Some of the ideas he's developed have changed how management is practiced around the world—including concepts such as "strategic intent," "core competence," "industry revolution," and "corporate resilience." Hamel earned his Ph.D. from the University of Michigan and has held faculty appointments at his alma mater and Harvard Business School. Since 1983, Dr. Hamel has been on the faculty of the London Business School where he is currently visiting professor of strategic and international management. A frequent contributor to *Harvard Business Review*, *Fortune*, and *The Wall Street Journal*, he is co-author of the best-selling *Competing for the Future* and author of the global best-seller *Leading the Revolution*.

Import/Export Administrators

Job growth is expected to be about as fast as average (10 to 15 percent) over the next decade.

Additional information can be found at the Federation of International Trade Associations (www.fita.org).

International Business Development Specialists

Job growth is expected to be about as fast as the average (10 to 15 percent) for all careers over the next decade.

Wondering what employers look for in an international business development specialist? Here's a sample development specialist job description:

> We seek someone who can conceptualize strategies for profitable penetration into new or existing foreign market segments. You'll champion new program ideas that result in profitable market strategies; help direct execution of account plans to ensure achievement of assigned business goals; monitor market conditions and develop actions to the benefit of the company; coordinate communication between regions to identify market and product design synergies; suggest improvements to current processes; display a high level of critical thinking in

bringing successful resolution to high-impact, complex, and/or cross-functional problems; and demonstrate extensive knowledge of organization's business practices and issues faced and contribute to problem resolution of those issues. Requirements: Experience: Minimum of one-year experience in business development, preferably in international arena (internships acceptable). Education: Bachelor's in international business; advanced degree preferred. Skills: Good written and oral communication skills—must be able to clearly and concisely communicate technical information. Good interpersonal skills—must work well in a team environment. Good organizational skills—must be able to manage several projects efficiently.

International Job Analysts

Job growth is expected to be faster than the average (18 to 25 percent) for all occupations over the next decade.

Wondering what employers look for in an international job analyst? Here's a sample international job analyst job description:

United States-based company with high growth in European market seeks an HR analyst for our international division. You'll perform analytical and technical work in recruitment, examination, classification, and salary administration; advise division on a variety of matters related to human resource management, and play a role in all personnel and administrative policy matters; handle special assignments requiring complex research and analysis; and provide technical assistance and direction to others on assigned projects. Requires Bachelor's degree from an accredited college or university with a major in business administration, public administration, or a closely related field.

The Professor Says

Not sure about these career choices? These are just some of the career possibilities for a major in international business. Remember that it is always important to learn more about prospective careers by researching online, talking with professors, conducting informational interviews, and job-shadowing.

Earnings Potential $

International business majors have a starting salary around $40,000, more than the average for all college graduates, which is currently around $38,000.

This section provides you with some general guidelines of salaries to expect upon graduation. Remember, salaries vary by employer, industry, and region.

Export Sales Representative. Median annual salary of an entry-level export sales representative varies because most of salary is commission-based, but expect an income of at least $50,000.

Foreign Trade Consultant/Analyst. Beginning salary for a foreign trade analyst is $45,000.

Global Sourcing (Procurement) Specialist. Median annual earnings of a global sourcing specialist ranges from $45,000 to $49,000.

Import/Export Administrator/Specialist. The average salary for an entry-level import/export specialist is about $43,000.

International Business Development Specialist. The median annual base salary of an international business development specialist is $45,000, not including bonus/incentive pay for successful market development.

International Job Analyst. The average salary for an entry-level human resources/job analyst is about $43,000 a year.

The Professor Says

Your next step after choosing your major? Gaining work experience. Just about all "entry-level" jobs for college graduates require some work experience outside the classroom. Seek out internships, volunteer, and figure out other ways to gain the experience you need.

The Least You Need to Know

◆ Students with a passion for other cultures and gift for business should find plenty of jobs upon graduation as job growth is expected in most fields.

◆ Most jobs for international business graduates are based in the United States, though some entry-level positions are available abroad.

◆ As is the case with many fields, you can get a good entry-level job with just an undergraduate degree in international business, though the more languages and international exposure you have, the better the job opportunities.

◆ Jobs in international business pay well—better than the average for all college majors.

Management, Entrepreneurship, and Hospitality

In This Chapter

- ◆ Discover careers that use your passion for service
- ◆ Use your entrepreneurial skills in jobs
- ◆ Learn the typical classes management, entrepreneurship, and hospitality majors require
- ◆ Find out key job and salary information

Have you had your own business—whether babysitting, lawncare, or car detailing—for a few years now? Dream of starting your own business? Do you enjoy leading people? Been a leader while in high school? Are you interested in running a hotel or resort?

This chapter reveals rewarding careers for students who major in management, entrepreneurship, or hospitality.

About the Majors

Students who major in one of these "management" majors—management, entrepreneurship, or hospitality—typically prepare for careers as future leaders of organizations.

Management

Management majors learn decision-making, problem-solving, creativity, communications, teamwork, ethics, and change management to prepare for careers as professional managers and administrators in a wide variety of organizations—public or private, product- or service-oriented, profit or not-for-profit. To accomplish this basic objective, management majors typically offer students the opportunity to acquire knowledge about managing human and physical resources and to acquire skills useful in managing any organization.

Most colleges and universities with a business school offer a major in management. In some schools you'll be able to specialize in a particular area of management (such as change management, entrepreneurship, family business enterprise, human resources, international, or leadership).

Typical courses include:

Principles of Management	International Management
Organizational Behavior	Managerial Ethics
Small Business Management	Quality Management
International Business	Organizational Development
Human Resource Management	Leadership
Entrepreneurship	New Venture Creation
Organizational Theory	Problems in Management

Entrepreneurship

The entrepreneurship major provides a solid foundation for students interested in starting their own businesses as well as for leadership roles and project management positions in the corporate and nonprofit worlds, as well as for many other careers in business.

While you will find entrepreneurship courses in most business schools, the entrepreneurship major is typically available only at some larger colleges and universities.

Typical courses include:

Entrepreneurship

Intrapreneurship

Small Business Management

Business Plans

Personal Financial Planning

Accounting and Financial Concepts for Entrepreneurs

Marketing and Management Concepts for Entrepreneurs

Intellectual Property Management and Business

Managing the Small- to Mid-Sized Company

Assessing Early Stage Technologies for Commercial Potential

Hospitality

Hospitality majors, using a combination of a strong business management core with a special focus on the unique challenges in the fields of lodging, foodservice, tourism, and meeting and event management, learn how to run hotels, restaurants, travel agencies, and other businesses that serve business travelers and vacationers. In some majors, you can specialize in hotel and restaurant management or tourism and event management.

While you may find some hospitality courses in most business schools, the hospitality (management) major is typically available only at some larger colleges and universities.

Typical courses include:

Hospitality and Tourism Basics

Lodging Management

Foodservice Management

Hospitality Management

Procurement Management

Casino Management

Club Management and Operations

Franchising

Hospitality and Tourism Law

Beverage Management

Hospitality and Tourism Marketing

Quantity Food Preparation and Service

Human Resource Management for the Service Industry

Cost Controls in Foodservice and Lodging

Resort, Cruise, and Entertainment Operations

Background on Careers

All organizations need managers and leaders, so management, entrepreneurship, and hospitality majors generally find jobs in corporations, government, and nonprofit organizations.

Major Pitfalls

Some critics of management and other business disciplines suggest that the major is too career-focused; thus, while you may find a few grads who decide against working directly in management (such as teaching business at the high school level), most graduates go to work in management-related jobs.

More specifically, here are some top jobs and careers for students who earn a Bachelor's degree with a major in management, entrepreneurship, or hospitality.

Benefits Administrator/Specialist. In this job, working in the human resources department of an organization, you'll administer, process, and maintain company benefits programs (including health insurance, life insurance, and retirement plans), functioning as a liaison between vendors and employees. You'll assist employees with paperwork and forms, as well as monitor claims and contact vendors when necessary. You'll also explain, summarize, and publish material that describes to employees their rights and obligations under their benefit plans.

Entrepreneur. As an entrepreneur, you'll conceptualize, develop, and implement a new business venture based on your ideas for introducing a new product (or service), better servicing an existing market, entering a new market, or some combination of these strategies. You'll assume all the risks for the new venture, but also reap the rewards if successful. If you're like most entrepreneurs, you'll have a strong desire to work for yourself rather than work for some organization—as well as have a driving force for being your own boss. Some entrepreneurs start their own businesses while others become franchisees.

The Professor Says

There are plenty of risks involved in starting your own business, but plenty of rewards, too. If you're like many other high school and college students, you have a strong desire to control your fate and not be stuck working for some large organization; you want ownership of your future rather than having some organization control it for you. Some experts expect your generation to be the most entrepreneurial generation in American history.

Hotel Management Trainee. In this job, you'll work, sometimes in a rotating fashion, in one or more functional areas (such as front desk, housekeeping, catering, event planning, human resources, and operations) of a hotel, learning the detailed functions and procedures of each area, and preparing you for a career managing in one of the areas in which you trained. Besides managing a traditional hotel's operations, you may also find jobs in other lodging establishments, such as camps, inns, boardinghouses, dude ranches, and recreational resorts.

Job Analyst. As a job analyst, you'll work with management of the organization to collect, analyze, and prepare occupational information to assist the personnel, administration, and management functions of an organization. You'll study job functions and interview workers and their supervisors to determine job and worker requirements; analyze occupational data and develop written summaries, such as job descriptions, job specifications, and career advancement paths; and utilize occupational data to evaluate or improve methods and techniques for recruiting, selecting, promoting, evaluating, and training workers.

Labor Relations Specialist. In this job, you'll coordinate and implement industrial labor relations programs, including preparing information for management to use during collective bargaining agreement negotiations, a process that requires the specialist to be familiar with economic and wage data and to have extensive knowledge of labor law and collective bargaining trends. You'll also help interpret and administer the labor contract with respect to grievances, wages and salaries, employee welfare, health care, pensions, union and management practices, and other contractual stipulations. (In nonunion employers, this position may be called an employee relations or personnel management specialist.)

Meeting/Convention Planner. As a meeting/convention planner, you'll coordinate all activities of staff and convention personnel to arrange for group meetings and conventions. You may work as an employee of a hotel or convention center, as an employee for the organization that is running the meeting, or as an independent (event) planner. You'll be involved in the organization of the entire meeting or convention, including the number and type of hotel rooms, meals, meeting rooms, and social events. Before and during events, you'll inspect meeting rooms and resolve any problems or issues. After the event, you'll evaluate events and services so they can be improved for future events.

Training Specialist. In this job, you'll plan, develop, and possibly conduct training and development programs for employees, responding to management and worker service requests. You'll consult with onsite supervisors regarding available performance improvement services and conduct orientation sessions and arrange on-the-job training for new employees, help all employees maintain and improve their job skills, and possibly prepare for jobs requiring greater skill. You'll also help supervisors improve their interpersonal skills to deal effectively with employees. You may set up individualized training plans to strengthen an employee's existing skills or teach new ones, including developing management development programs among employees in lower-level positions.

Other Career Possibilities. Here are some other job and career paths for management, entrepreneurship, and hospitality majors:

Conference Services Manager	Nursing Home Administrator
Country Club Manager	Operations Manager
Food/Beverage Manager	Resorts Manager
Franchise Owner	Restaurant Manager
Guest Services Manager	Retail Manager
Hospital Administrator	Small Business Owner
Hospitality Coordinator	

Skills Needed/Developed

Students who major in management, entrepreneurship, and hospitality develop numerous valuable and transferable skills, but those included here are the most critical to graduates.

Interpersonal (Persuasive) Communications. This skill involves your ability to listen, respond, interact, and communicate successfully, and includes accurately interpreting verbal and nonverbal messages and giving feedback in one-on-one and small-group situations.

The Professor Says

Other transferable skills you gain from these majors include:

◆ Risk-taking

◆ Leadership

◆ Time management

◆ Organizational

Written and Oral Communications. Speaking and writing skills are essential when pursuing a career in management, entrepreneurship, or hospitality. You'll need the ability to clearly express yourself in writing and in speaking.

Creativity. This skill involves your ability to develop, design, and create new applications, ideas, systems, or products to fill a need or solve a problem.

Analytical Skills. This skill deals with your ability to manage large amounts of information and demands through task analysis, time management, and goal-setting.

Teamwork. This skill involves your ability to work with other people—whether they are similar or different—and is one of the most important for any career in business because so much is now done in work teams.

Expected Growth

Graduates with a solid foundation in business will always be in demand, especially in the coming decade, as many retirements will compel businesses to hire even more business grads.

Management Majors

Demand for management professionals and management majors should remain very strong over the next decade because organizations will be facing a talent shortage, especially in management positions.

A source of additional information can be found at the American Management Association (www.amanet.org).

Entrepreneurship Majors

There has never been a better time to be an entrepreneur—or to think of becoming one. During the next few years, the biggest economic growth is expected to come from small businesses. Today's entrepreneurs should find capital available for qualified and imaginative enterprises.

Sources of additional information:

- Entrepreneurs' Organization (www.eonetwork.org)
- National Association for the Self-Employed (www.nase.org)
- Self-Employed Women's Association (www.sewa.org)
- Women Entrepreneurs (www.we-inc.org)

Entrepreneurial Educator Stacey Ellis

Stacey Ellis is the director and founder of Smart Start Tutoring, an educational facility that offers a variety of programs, including one-on-one tutoring, after-school programs, home-schooled student programs, computer tutoring, and career and college planning. Ellis earned her Bachelor's degree in marketing from Stetson University, later pursuing an education certification from Miami (of Ohio) University. She worked as a teacher for a variety of elementary schools, picking up ideas for starting her business as she occasionally tutored students after school. After developing her business plan, she launched her business and has seen it grow over the years. Ellis has received numerous nominations and awards for her teaching, and her company recently received state approval as a No Child Left Behind supplemental education services provider.

Hospitality Majors

Demand for hospitality professionals and hospitality majors with leadership abilities should continue to increase as there is a need to fill managerial and administrative positions in the rapidly expanding hospitality industry. The number of available management positions in the industry continues to exceed the number of hospitality graduates each year.

Additional information can be found at the Hospitality Sales and Marketing Association International (www.hsmai.org).

Benefits Administrators/Specialists

Job growth for benefit administrators and specialists is expected to be faster than the average (18 to 25 percent) for all jobs over the next decade.

Sources of additional information:

◆ International Foundation of Employee Benefit Plans (www.ifebp.org)

◆ International Society of Certified Employee Benefit Specialist (www.iscebs.org)

Wondering what employers look for in a benefits specialist? Here's a sample benefits specialist job description:

Seeking an individual with excellent analytical and communications skills to provide support to employees and field HR contacts on projects and processes related to retirement plans. Responsibilities include planning administration support on retirement plans; delivering superior customer service and communicating consistent message to all stakeholders; serving as liaison with other departments and benefit plan vendors; assisting in annual plan audits and ensuring timely completion; ensuring plan administration complies with plan and regulatory guidelines; documenting benefit administration practices and procedures, focusing on continual improvement; working on problems of diverse scope, exercising judgment, and assisting team in other duties as required; and supporting corporate benefits team with cross-functional support during peak periods. Must be a strong team player, exhibit excellent organizational and time-management skills, display good judgment, and maintain confidentiality. Requires a Bachelor's degree in management, human resources, or related field.

Hotel Management Trainees

Job growth for hotel managers is expected to be about as fast as the average (10 to 15 percent) for all jobs over the next decade.

Additional information can be found at the American Hotel & Lodging Association (www.ahla.com).

Wondering what employers look for in a hotel management trainee? Here's a sample hotel management trainee job description:

> We are seeking a management trainee in the Rooms Division to train in our 200-room, top-rated oceanfront resort in Myrtle Beach. The management trainee will be trained in all aspects of housekeeping, front office, and engineering operations. The candidate will be trained and developed in Myrtle Beach until the candidate can be placed in a department-head position at one of our other hotels. You must have a Bachelor's degree in hotel, hospitality, or business management with some prior experience (internships count) in a full-service hotel or resort. Candidate must be able to travel and relocate.

Job Analysts

Job growth for job analysts is expected to be faster than the average (18 to 25 percent) for all jobs.

Sources of additional information:

- ◆ National Human Resources Association (www.humanresources.org)
- ◆ Society for Human Resource Management (www.shrm.org)

Labor Relations Specialists

Job growth for labor relations specialists is expected to be faster than the average (18 to 25 percent) for all jobs over the next decade.

Wondering what employers look for in a labor relations specialist? Here's a sample labor relations specialist job description:

> This position will assist management and field HR in the identification and resolution of labor relations matters; provide advice on the interpretation and application of the labor contract; develop and interpret labor relations–related policies; assist management in developing and applying the labor relations strategy; advise and assist management in addressing labor relations issues in a manner that promotes a motivated and productive workforce in compliance with labor laws and labor contracts; advise and counsel management and field HR on labor contract interpretation and administration; assist with and participate in labor contract negotiations, including bargaining on existing or new policies and issues; and assist with due diligence and integration-related work in support of merger and acquisition activities. Successful candidates will have knowledge of laws, regulations, and standards related to industrial relations, employment law, human resources policies and procedures, and knowledge of labor contract administration. Need excellent oral and written communications, negotiation, and research skills. Candidates should also have the ability to problem-solve, think analytically, and lead projects to closure.

Meeting/Convention Planners, Specialists

Job growth for media planners is expected to be faster than the average (18 to 25 percent) for all jobs.

Sources of additional information:

◆ Meeting Professionals International (www.mpiweb.org)

◆ Professional Convention Management Association (www.pcma.org)

◆ Society of Corporate Meeting Professionals (www.scmp.org)

Wondering what employers look for in a meeting planner? Here's a sample meeting planner job description:

> As our event planner, you will work in our meeting and convention planning department, handling special events and small meeting planning, including

organization and follow-through of event details. More specifically, the meeting planner will be responsible for various aspects of planning meetings and independently plan small and less-complex meetings. Meeting planning tasks may include site research, site inspection, meeting budgets, ground transportation, amenities, specifications, food and beverage, technology support, security, rooming lists, off-site venues, on-site management, A/V, and meeting evaluations. Must have the ability to work on multiple priorities with a sense of urgency. In addition, the meeting planner may also assist other meeting planners on larger and more-complex programs. Other tasks may include acting as backup for virtual meetings when required, answering the daily Meeting and Event Service hotline and database inquiries, and providing post-meeting summary reports for all meetings. This person must be a team player with excellent interpersonal skills, strong oral and written skills, technology skills, and absolute dedication to detail. The ability to travel a minimum of 35 percent of the time is required.

Training Specialists

Demand for training specialists is expected to be higher than average (18 to 25 percent) over the next decade.

A source of additional information can be found at the American Society for Training & Development (www.astd.org).

The Professor Says _____

Your next step? Pick the couple of careers that most fit your interests with a major in management, entrepreneurship, and hospitality, and dig more deeply into them. Remember that it is always important to learn more about prospective careers by researching online, talking with professors, conducting informational interviews, and job-shadowing.

Earnings Potential $

Management and entrepreneurship graduates typically earn about $39,000, while hospitality graduates earn about $32,000. Thus, management majors make a bit more than average while hospitality majors a bit less than the average annual salary for all college graduates, which is currently around $38,000.

In terms of the specific careers mentioned in this chapter, this section will provide you with some general guidelines of salaries to expect upon graduation. (Remember, salaries vary by employer, industry, and region.)

Benefits Administrator/Specialist. The average starting salary for a benefits specialist is $38,000.

Entrepreneur. Because you set your own salary, and because it partly depends on the success of the business, salaries for entrepreneurs vary greatly.

The Professor Says

Your next step after choosing your major? Gaining work experience. Just about all "entry-level" jobs for college graduates require some work experience outside the classroom. Seek out internships, volunteer, and figure out other ways to gain the experience you need.

Hotel Management Trainee. Beginning salary for a hotel management trainee ranges from $30,000 to $35,000.

Job Analyst. Median annual earnings of an entry-level job analyst is $34,000.

Labor Relations Specialist. The median salary of a labor relations specialist is $49,000.

Meeting/Convention Planner/Specialist. Beginning salary for a meeting planner is about $37,500.

Training Specialist. The median annual salary of a training specialist is $41,000.

The Least You Need to Know

- As a management, entrepreneurship, or hospitality major, you have numerous career paths available that use your passions and creativity.

- Most careers in management and hospitality are expected to have strong gains in the number of openings for new grads.

- If you have a passion for business, some innovative ideas, and a strong desire to control your destiny, a career as an entrepreneur might be right for you.

- Entry-level management and hospitality jobs pay close to the average for jobs in other fields.

Chapter 3

Marketing or Advertising

In This Chapter

- Discover careers that use your passion for marketing
- Use those creativity skills in jobs that demand them
- Learn what classes the marketing and advertising major requires
- Find key job and salary information

Are you the type of person who finds advertisements fascinating? Do you spend hours late at night watching infomercials? See yourself marketing or selling some of your favorite products? Do you watch the Super Bowl purely for the commercials? Love to shop?

If you have a passion for marketing—and all it encompasses (advertising, sales, and branding)—but are unsure of the types of jobs or specific career path you see yourself following, then this chapter is for you!

This chapter reveals rewarding careers for students who major in marketing or advertising.

About the Majors

Students majoring in marketing or advertising typically enjoy working with people and have a flair for creativity, a passion for all things marketing, and a desire to use their powers of persuasion to connect buyers with products.

Marketing

Marketing majors learn both the art and science of undertaking competitive analyses, developing and producing new ideas that will fulfill a market need, researching and cultivating an audience, bringing the product (or service, idea, person) to market, fostering customer satisfaction, and building lasting customer relationships. Marketers use the combination of advertising, business logistics, research, pricing, consumer behavior, brand management, and selling in targeted efforts to satisfy the consumer or the organizational buyer with products and services. The best marketers master marketing processes and situations, think independently (and "out-of-the-box"), communicate effectively, and appreciate their own and other cultures.

Most colleges and universities with a business school offer a major in marketing. In some schools you'll be able to specialize in a particular area of marketing (such as advertising, branding, product development, market research, selling). Typical courses include:

Principles of Marketing	Brand Management
Consumer Behavior	Professional Sales/Selling
Marketing Tools and Skills	Sales Management
Market Research	Services Marketing
Channels of Distribution	Sports Marketing
Global Marketing	New Product Development
Wholesaling	Product Development
Retailing	Strategic Marketing Management
Advertising Management	Marketing E-Commerce

Advertising

Advertising majors acquire the knowledge and skills that will help with a career in advertising or public relations, including topics in marketing, communications, copy writing, advertising creation, and media planning.

While you will find advertising courses in most business schools, the advertising major is typically housed in the college of communications—and typically is only available at larger colleges and universities. Typical courses include:

Principles of Advertising	Advertising and PR Research
Integrated Strategy	Account Planning
Consumer Behavior	Interactive Marketing Design
Advertising and Society	Media Planning
Advertising Campaigns	Promotions and Sponsorships
Advertising Design	Global Advertising
Copywriting and Art Direction	Principles of Public Relations
Advertising Management	

The Professor Says

While marketing and advertising are the big majors for students who are extremely creative and have a passion for marketing and advertising, a few other majors—retailing, sales, and public relations—also cater to creative marketer types. Only a few schools, however, offer these majors.

Background on Careers

The great thing about marketing is that just about everyone needs to do it, so you can find marketing jobs in corporations, government, and nonprofit organizations.

Some top jobs and careers for students earning a Bachelor's degree with a major in marketing or advertising include:

Advertising Account Executive, Junior. As a junior account executive, you'll be part of an account team working in a fast-paced environment and serving as a liaison between current and prospective clients and your marketing or advertising agency,

Major Pitfalls

Some critics of marketing and other business disciplines suggest that the major is too career-focused; thus, while you may find a few grads who decide not to work directly in marketing or sales (such as teaching business at the high school level), most graduates go to work in marketing-related jobs and careers.

always ensuring the client is informed and happy with your agency's efforts. More specifically, you'll work with clients to sell them on the ideas of the agency, explain client goals and expectations to the agency creative and production teams, supervise development of the entire marketing or advertising plan, and follow-up with clients to be certain they are satisfied with the development and implementation of the plan.

Brand Manager, Assistant. In this job, you'll typically start off working with a senior brand manager and plan, direct, and control all marketing efforts related to one or more brands. You'll be involved in marketing research, brand/product research and development, packaging, manufacturing, sales and distribution, advertising and promotion management, and business analysis and forecasting. Entry-level positions usually start managing smaller brands and as you prove yourself, you get promoted to higher-profile and better-known brands. You can specialize in consumer or industrial goods.

E-Commerce Market Analyst. People in these jobs collect and analyze data to evaluate existing and potential online markets to determine potential sales of a product or service. You'll gather information on competitors, prices, sales, and methods of marketing and distribution, and use traffic tracking applications to recognize user patterns and trends to help formulate effective marketing techniques. You may also use survey results to create a marketing campaign based on regional preferences and buying habits.

Marketing Assistant. As a marketing assistant, you'll typically start as a marketing generalist within an organization's marketing department, sometimes rotating among functional areas until the organization places you in a more specific position. You'll assist in the development and distribution of marketing and sales materials and the production and analysis of marketing research projects, as well as in the creation of advertising, marketing brochures, sales kits, or other promotional materials. You may also write articles and design layouts, depending on the size of the organization.

Market Research Analyst. In this job, you'll plan, collect, examine, and report on information relating to issues important to the company, such as customer preferences and satisfaction, brand awareness, product performance, pricing issues, distribution strategies, and marketing competitiveness. You'll often use a variety of market research techniques, such as surveys, observation, and experiments. You'll provide statistical reports and recommendations to management and assist with developing plans for improving the organization's marketing efforts. You'll need to know statistical programs as well as computer-modeling techniques.

Media Planner, Junior. As a junior media planner, you'll work in the (sometimes high-stress) media service department of an advertising agency assisting the account team, applying statistical models to audience, circulation, and media cost to develop a media plan that maximizes a client's advertising goals while minimizing costs—and keeping media buys within the allotted budget. You'll typically evaluate audience claims and negotiate with all media types—print, television, radio, outdoor, and Internet—to get the best media buys for your agency's clients.

The Professor Says

Probably about half of all marketing majors go into sales when they graduate, but that's mainly because those are the jobs that are the most heavily recruited on college campuses. If you love marketing, but don't want a career in sales, there are plenty of other opportunities—you just need to search them out.

Retail Buyer, Assistant. In this typically high-pressure job, you'll manage the buying of merchandise for a specific retailer or department within the retailer. You plan, select, and purchase the range, type, and quantity of products according to several factors, including estimated customer demand, product trends, store policy, and budget. You'll need to have a detailed understanding of customer needs and wants so that you can maximize profits and provide a commercially viable range of merchandise at competitive prices. You'll also need to keep abreast of market trends and react quickly to changes in demand. You typically have a considerable amount of responsibility and autonomy as a buyer.

Sales Representative. As a sales representative, you'll use your marketing talent and your persuasive communication skills to find, evaluate, and sell prospective buyers on the benefits of your organization's products or services. Just about all organizations use salespeople, so you'll find jobs in a wide range of profit and nonprofit organizations, including financial services, insurance, pharmaceutical, office supplies, food, hospitality, and the like. As your career progresses, you can choose to stay in sales or move into sales management, and, in some cases, to the top management of the organization.

Other Career Possibilities. Here are some other job and career paths for marketing and advertising majors:

Advertising Account Coordinator

Business Analyst

Catalog Sales Fulfillment Manager

Club Marketing Manager

Development Officer

Direct Marketing Specialist

Export Manager

Event Planner

Merchandising Manager

Online Marketer/Sales Manager

Packaging Specialist

Public Relations Assistant

Purchasing Agent

Real Estate Agent

Retail Store Management Trainee

Supply Chain Analyst

Skills Needed/Developed

Students majoring in marketing and advertising develop numerous valuable and transferable skills. The following are the most critical to graduates:

Creativity. Perhaps the most essential skill that any marketing or advertising professional possesses—you'll develop, design, and create new applications, ideas, systems, or products to solve a need or problem.

Interpersonal (Persuasive) Communications. This skill involves your ability to listen, respond, interact, and communicate successfully, and includes accurately interpreting verbal and nonverbal messages and giving feedback in one-on-one and small-group situations.

Written and Oral Communications. Speaking and writing skills are essential when pursuing a career in marketing or advertising. You'll need the ability to clearly express yourself in writing and in speaking.

Analytical Skills. This skill deals with your ability to manage large amounts of information and demands through task analysis, time management, and goal-setting.

Teamwork. This skill involves your ability to work with other people—whether they are similar or

The Professor Says

Other transferable skills you gain from these majors include:

◆ Record keeping

◆ Leadership

◆ Time management

◆ Technical/computer

different—and is one of the most important for any career in business because so much work is now completed in work teams.

Expected Growth

Graduates with a solid foundation in business will always be in demand, especially in the coming decade as many retirements will require businesses to hire even more business grads.

Marketing Majors

Demand for marketing professionals and marketing majors should remain very strong (18 to 25 percent) over the next decade because the ever-increasing competitive marketplace demands organizations hire competent and creative marketers to gain an edge over competitors.

Sources of additional information:

◆ American Marketing Association (www.marketingpower.com)

◆ Direct Marketing Association (www.the-dma.org)

◆ Promotion Marketing Association (www.pmalink.org)

Advertising Majors

Demand for advertising professionals and advertising majors should remain solid, though people who specialize in emerging advertising tools and techniques (such as multimedia and online) will have an edge over advertising traditionalists.

◆ American Advertising Federation (www.aaf.org)

◆ American Association of Advertising Agencies (www.aaaa.org)

◆ Association of National Advertisers (www.ana.net)

Advertising Account Executives, Junior

Job growth for advertising account executives is expected to be faster than the average (18 to 25 percent) for all jobs over the next decade.

Wondering what employers look for in a junior advertising account executive? Here's a sample junior advertising account executive job description:

> As one of the area's most dynamic, fun, and creative advertising agencies, we value a motivated, fun, fast-paced working environment; professionalism and integrity; a strong commitment to teamwork; and an outstanding attitude. As a junior account executive, you must be able to hit the ground running as you will assist the team in effectively managing the development and production of all projects. You will be responsible for the continued good administration of the accounts and ensuring a good relationship between the client and agency. You'll also handle the day-to-day smooth running of the accounts in terms of budget, media, and material being ready for publications/electronic media.

Brand Managers, Assistant

Job growth for brand managers is expected to be faster than the average (18 to 25 percent) for all jobs.

Wondering what employers look for in an assistant brand manager? Here's a sample assistant brand manager job description:

> The assistant brand manager is responsible for assisting the brand manager in the development and execution of marketing plans and programs to achieve the brand's short- and long-term business objectives. Specific duties include assisting in the development and execution of annual marketing plan; managing the execution of the brand's promotional programs and materials, including design, development, and production; acting as key liaison with sales; assisting in management of the brand's multi-million-dollar budget, including point-of-sale, consumer promotion, and trade marketing; analyzing scanner, audit, and competitive data and preparing presentations for monthly brand meetings, quarterly reviews, and regular field communications; participating in qualitative and quantitative consumer research and advertising creative meetings; and assisting brand manager on brand-related projects, which may include innovation and/or line extensions. Requires a Bachelor's degree in marketing; excellent verbal, written, and presentation communication skills.

E-Commerce Market Analysts

Job growth for e-commerce and online market analysts is expected to be faster than the average (18 to 25 percent) for all jobs over the next decade.

Wondering what employers look for in an e-commerce market analyst? Here's a sample e-commerce market analyst job description:

> We are seeking an e-commerce marketing analyst to assist in the current and future growth plans of our e-commerce marketing team. This position is responsible for cross-functional teaming with the merchandising team to define web-specific product slotting and promotional strategies. The analyst also owns the day-to-day responsibility for the execution of all product merchandising on the website, including product selection, tracking/reporting, and overall campaign management, as well as responsibility for all website reporting and analytics. Our ideal candidate will possess a Bachelor's degree in marketing and a strong knowledge of web merchandising and retail best practices, an understanding of E-commerce technology applications, including content management, analytics, and site search packages; will be comfortable in a deadline-driven environment with rapidly changing priorities and a high volume of projects; and will be a team player with strong initiative, work ethic, ability to work independently, and an entrepreneurial spirit.

profiles

Marketing Guru Seth Godin

Seth Godin is a best-selling author, entrepreneur, and a self-proclaimed agent of change. Godin is the author of seven books—including *Permission Marketing, Unleashing the Ideavirus, Survival Is Not Enough, Purple Cow, All Marketers Are Liars,* and *Small Is the New Big*—that have changed the way people think about marketing, change, and work. He graduated from Tufts University with a degree in computer science and philosophy. His first job was as a brand manager for Spinnaker Software. He later earned his M.B.A. in marketing from Stanford University and was founder and CEO of Yoyodyne, the industry's leading interactive direct marketing company, which Yahoo! later acquired. He's been called "the ultimate entrepreneur for the Information Age" by *Business Week*.

Marketing Assistants

Job growth for marketing assistants is expected to be faster than the average (18 to 25 percent) for all jobs.

Market Research Analysts

Job growth for market research analysts is expected to be about as fast as the average (10 to 15 percent) for all jobs.

A source of additional information can be found at Marketing Research Association (www.mra-net.org).

Media Planners, Junior

Job growth for media planners is expected to grow faster than the average (18 to 25 percent) for all jobs.

Wondering what employers look for in a junior media planner? Here's a sample junior media planner job description:

> Who said an analytical mindset and creative thinking don't mix? If you have very strong analytical skills and a level of creative thinking that needs more room for expression, the stimulating and varied role that we are now offering at our advertising agency in Manhattan will be a rare opportunity to make the very most of all your talents. As a junior media planner, your prime responsibility will be to produce comprehensive media plans. You'll be comfortable working under minimum supervision and remain calm under pressure when you need to meet urgent deadlines. Our account service team takes care of daily client interaction, but you will maintain contacts with newspaper vendors, trade publications, and online sources to determine rates, sizes, and deadlines, and then work within a budget to plan schedules and have opportunities to come up with creative media ideas. You will sometimes be asked to participate in client meetings, so good communication skills are highly valued. Working under the supervision of the account manager and account executives, you will know the value of close cooperation and teamwork, reliability and, always, great accuracy.

profiles

Marketing Strategist Philip Kotler

Philip Kotler is a great marketing strategist, thinker, and author. He is also the S.C. Johnson & Son Distinguished Professor of International Marketing at the Northwestern University Kellogg Graduate School of Management in Chicago. He earned his Master's degree from the University of Chicago and his Ph.D., from MIT, both in economics. Dr. Kotler has authored or co-authored some of the leading marketing textbooks and trade books, written hundreds of articles in premier business journals (including *Business Horizons, California Management Review, Harvard Business Review, Journal of Marketing,* and *Sloan Management Review*), has received numerous honorary doctoral degrees, and has been presented with several major awards, including the Distinguished Marketing Educator of the Year Award of the American Marketing Association and Marketer of the Year by the Sales and Marketing Executives International (SMEI).

Retail Buyers, Assistant

Demand for retail buyers is expected to be lower than average (under 8 percent) over the next decade as consolidation in retail results in reductions in jobs.

A source of additional information can be found at National Retail Federation (www. nrf.com).

Sales Representatives

Job growth for sales representatives is expected to be as fast as the average (10 to 15 percent) for all jobs, but competition will remain strong for the most attractive sales positions.

Additional information can be found at National Association of Sales Professionals (www.nasp.com).

The Professor Says _____

Variety abounds in sales careers, and one of the fastest-growing—and appealing to many marketing majors—is pharmaceutical sales. However, the number of pharmaceutical sales positions for new college graduates is limited, and the ones that are available are extremely competitive. Thus, if you want an edge, work as many sales jobs during college as you can, and take some basic life science courses.

Earnings Potential $

Marketing graduates earn about $37,000, compared to advertising grads, who earn about $31,000, with the difference partly explained by the business skills the marketing graduates obtain. Still, both majors earn less than the average annual salary for all college graduates, which is currently around $38,000.

The following section provides some general guidelines of salaries to expect upon graduation. Remember, salaries vary by employer, industry, and region.

Advertising Account Executive, Junior. The average salary for a junior account executive is $34,000.

Brand Manager, Assistant. The average salary for an assistant brand manager is $48,000 a year.

The Professor Says _____

Not sure about these career choices? These are just some of the career possibilities for a major in marketing and advertising. Remember that it is always important to learn more about prospective careers by researching online, talking with professors, conducting informational interviews, and job-shadowing.

E-Commerce Market Analyst. Beginning salary for an e-commerce market analyst ranges from $40,000 to $50,000.

Marketing Assistant. Median annual earnings of a marketing assistant are $35,400.

Market Research Analyst. The median salary of a market research analyst is $43,000.

Media Planner, Junior. Beginning salary for a junior media planner is about $30,000.

Retail Buyer, Assistant. The median starting salary of an assistant buyer is $40,000.

Sales Representative. Salaries for sales representatives vary widely because most are paid on a commission basis, but most earn a salary of $44,000+.

The Professor Says _____

Remember that you're not done once you pick your college major—in fact, it's just begun, because the next thing you need to do is gain work experience. Just about all "entry-level" jobs for college graduates require some work experience outside the classroom. Seek out internships, volunteer, and figure out other ways to gain the experience you need.

The Least You Need to Know

◆ If you have a flair for creativity and enjoy working with people, majoring in marketing or advertising is a good fit.

◆ Most careers in marketing and advertising are expected to have strong gains in the number of openings for new grads.

◆ You should be able to find plenty of jobs in marketing, advertising, and sales with just an undergraduate degree.

◆ Entry-level marketing and advertising jobs don't pay as well as jobs in other fields.

Chapter 14

Real Estate

In This Chapter

◆ Discover careers that use your passion for real estate

◆ Use your sales skills in jobs that demand them

◆ Learn the classes a typical real estate major requires

◆ Find out what kinds of jobs and salaries to expect

What do you do for a career if you love looking at properties and picturing how you could improve them and sell them? If you can't get enough of the real estate section in your local paper? Do you see yourself as the next Donald Trump?

This chapter reveals rewarding careers for students majoring in real estate.

About the Major

When most people think real estate, they immediately think of real estate agents. But real estate majors learn much more and prepare for a variety of career paths.

Real Estate

Real estate majors learn all the business basics (accounting, marketing, management, finance) while also learning how to develop, appraise, buy, sell, and manage properties and buildings—preparing students for entry-level positions in private, public, and not-for-profit real estate organizations. Some majors also include courses on real estate law and taxation.

Real estate is a fairly specialized major, but you'll typically find it at larger universities that have a school of business (typically housed in the finance department). Typical courses include:

Real Estate Principles	Real Estate Capital Markets
Real Estate Valuation	Asset Management
Real Estate Investment	Real Estate Construction Process
Real Estate Finance	Nonprofit Housing Development
Real Estate Development	Real Estate Market Analysis
Real Estate Law	

Background on Careers

Real estate graduates are prepared for a variety of careers in real estate, including real estate appraisal, real estate brokerage, corporate real estate, mortgage lending, property management, and real estate investment. You may work within the real estate asset management department of a large corporation (such as a restaurant chain, searching out potential new sites for future restaurants); as part of a team of a development company (that acquires land and then plans shopping centers, residential developments, and the like); or as a property manager overseeing the operations of apartment complexes or office buildings.

Some top jobs and careers for students earning a Bachelor's degree with a major in real estate include:

Development Specialist/Assistant Project Manager. As a development specialist or assistant project manager, you'll work with a developer or development company to turn land into profitable and marketable residential, commercial, or industrial developments. You'll be involved with determining market potential, locating and acquiring potential sites, planning and designing the layout of the project, analyzing costs and arranging financing, contracting and supervising construction of buildings, promoting the finished development, and working with a sales team to sell to the prospects for whom the development was planned.

Mortgage Loan Officer. In this job, you'll work in a bank or other financial institution and assist people who want to buy houses or other real estate or get new real estate loans for property they already own. You'll gather personal information from prospective clients to ensure that an informed decision is made regarding the creditworthiness of the borrower and the probability of repayment. Loan officers may provide guidance about alternative borrowing methods to prospective loan applicants who have problems qualifying for traditional loans. Loan officers who specialize in evaluating a client's creditworthiness—conduct financial analyses or other risk assessments—are often called loan underwriters.

Property Management Specialist/Leasing Agent. As a property management specialist or leasing agent, you manage all aspects of one or more rental properties, with the goal of protecting and increasing the value of the owner's investment. Your job consists of developing informational packets about the property (and specific units) and surrounding amenities (such as schools, shops, libraries); producing marketing and promotional materials to attract prospective tenants; showing properties or rental units to prospective tenants; collecting and verifying applications from prospective tenants; entering data and compiling information for property management database and producing monthly management reports; and performing inspections, drive-bys, and walk-throughs of units.

Real Estate Agent. Working with a real estate broker, you'll seek out both commercial or residential buyers and sellers, listing and showing homes or other properties, and making an income from the commissions of real estate sales. In working with the buyers, you'll need to know what they can afford and be knowledgeable about the homes you show them. In working with the sellers, you'll help them set the asking price, make recommendations for ways to increase the sale value, and market the property. You'll need to apply for and pass a test to get licensed by your state to be a real estate agent. Many real estate agents are also Realtors, which means they belong to the National Association of Realtors (and must adhere to the association's strict code of ethics).

The Professor Says _____

Here are just a few of the 17 articles of ethical practice that Realtors must adhere to:

◆ Pledge to put the interests of buyers and sellers ahead of their own and to treat all parties honestly and fairly.

◆ Shall refrain from exaggerating, misrepresenting, or concealing material facts; and is obligated to investigate and disclose when situations reasonably warrant.

◆ Shall cooperate with other brokers and agents when it is in the best interests of the client to do so.

◆ Shall not provide professional services in a transaction where the agent has a present or contemplated interest without disclosing that interest.

◆ Shall not collect any commissions without the seller's knowledge nor accept fees from a third-party without the seller's expressed consent.

◆ Must engage in truth in advertising.

Source: National Association of Realtors

Real Estate Appraiser/Trainee. As an appraiser, you'll provide an unbiased estimate of the value of properties, including vacant or developed land, single or multiple-family dwellings, and commercial businesses or sites, typically so that buyers and sellers can move forward with their deals. Real estate is appraised to determine many types of values, including assessment for tax purposes, investment value or present value for potential investors, "book" value for accounting purposes, rental value for income projections, and insurable value. Working for a bank or an appraisal firm—often as an independent contractor—and typically specializing in residential or commercial property, you'll locate comparable sales and make a final value judgment on the value of the real estate in relation to selling prices of nearby properties.

Real Estate Broker. In this job, you'll work with one or more salespersons (commonly called real estate agents; see above) to assist sellers in marketing their commercial or residential property and selling it for the highest possible price under the best terms. A real estate broker is an independent businessperson with a license to run a real estate office. As a broker, you hire employees and salespeople, determine their compensation, and supervise their activities. You may also actively pursue new business, service existing clients, review and assess the current market value of properties, and market your firm's listings and services.

Other Career Possibilities. Here are some other job and career paths for real estate majors:

Building Inspector

Building Superintendent

Community Development Representative

Construction Manager

Credit Counselor

Direct Marketing Specialist

Housing Project Manager

Insurance Agent/Broker

Market Analyst

Personal Financial Adviser

Real Estate Attorney

Real Estate Consultant

Retail Buyer

Sales/Marketing Analyst

Sales Representative

Title Examiner/Searcher

The Professor Says

Wondering about the difference between a career in commercial versus residential real estate? Typically, commercial real estate—which involves the buying/selling/leasing of office buildings, retail space, hotels, and other commercial properties—pays better but is much harder to break into than residential real estate—which deals mainly with the buying and selling of· houses and vacant lots.

Skills Needed/Developed

Students majoring in real estate develop numerous valuable and transferable skills. The following are the most critical to graduates.

Persuasion/Negotiating Skills. Probably one of the most important skills that you'll learn or perfect as a real estate major is the ability to negotiate deals and use persuasion to close them.

Interpersonal Communications. You'll need to possess the ability to talk and listen in one-on-one and small-group situations, one of the core elements of business decision-making.

Written and Oral Communications. Speaking and writing skills are essential when pursuing a career in real estate. You'll need the ability to clearly express yourself.

Analytical Skills. This skill deals with your ability to manage large amounts of information and demands thorough task analysis, time management, and goal-setting.

Math and Statistics. As with many business majors, you'll need to have strong math and statistics skills and abilities.

> **The Professor Says** _____
>
> Other transferable skills you gain from these majors include:
> - Decision-making
> - Problem-solving
> - Goal-oriented
> - Technical/computer

Expected Growth

Graduates with a solid foundation in business will always be in demand, especially in the coming decade as many retirements will require businesses to hire even more business grads.

Real Estate Majors

Demand for real estate majors should remain strong over the next decade because of population growth and ongoing demand in residential and commercial developments.

Additional information can be found at National Association of Realtors (www.realtor. org).

Development Specialists/Assistant Project Managers

Employment is expected to grow about as fast as the average (10 to 15 percent) for all jobs over the next decade.

Wondering what employers look for in a development specialist? Here's a sample development specialist job description:

> The assistant development project manager is engaged in all aspects of real estate development from inception to completion, and assists the project manager in tasks related to site selection and identification of market demand, pre-development project planning and due diligence; environmental and historic research and compliance, financial analysis, design, permitting, and construction. Duties include assisting in development and monitoring of project schedules and

budgets; project reporting; researching and compiling data; assisting in the preparation of reports; monitoring activities of consultants hired to perform project-related tasks; preparing and/or monitoring project contracts; coordinating meetings for assigned projects; maintaining project files and drafting correspondence and reports related to duties; assisting in preparation of lease provisions and exhibits and assisting in negotiating leases and development agreements; monitoring the design, permitting, and construction process and ensuring delivery of projects; preparing purchase requests; assisting in developing marketing tools; and coordinating the production of graphic presentation materials. Requires any combination of training, education, and experience equivalent to a Bachelor's degree in public or business administration, architecture, real estate development, real estate or land use law, or a related field.

profiles

Pioneering Developer James Rouse

James Rouse had an amazing career as a developer, pioneering urban renewal in decaying cities, creating the concept of shopping malls, constructing one of the earliest planned developments, and revitalizing rundown historic structures. He attended college and law school at the University of Maryland, and after earning his degrees, he worked for the Federal Housing Administration before becoming a partner at a mortgage banking firm. He joined the National Housing Task Force and coined (or at least helped popularize) the term "urban renewal" to describe the recommendations made by that task force to revitalize city slums. He then went on to build the Harundale Mall, the first enclosed shopping center east of the Mississippi River, coining the term "mall" to describe it. He later turned his attention to planned communities, developing the city of Columbia, Maryland, one of the largest and most successful of American planned cities. Finally, his company was also involved in major historic preservation projects, including Faneuil Hall, South Street Seaport, and Harborplace. In 1981, *Time* magazine labeled Rouse "the man who made cities fun again." President Bill Clinton presented Rouse with the Presidential Medal of Freedom Award, the highest civilian honor, in recognition of humanitarian service through his Enterprise Foundation.

Mortgage Loan Officers

Employment is expected to grow more slowly than the average (under 8 percent) for all jobs over the next decade.

Additional information can be found at National Association of Responsible Loan Officers (www.narlo.com).

Wondering what employers look for in a residential mortgage loan officer? Here's a sample loan officer job description:

> As a Mortgage Loan Officer, this individual will originate mortgage loans; solicit new business; analyze credit and approve applications of new customers and perform loan pre-qualifications by processing applications, analyzing credit reports, registering loan with investor and receiving underwriter's approval. Responsibilities include answering customers' questions and requesting supporting documents; coordinating time-sensitive activities among insurance and title companies, Realtors, appraisers, investors, and the customer; sending disclosures and ordering various appraisals; sending in applicable verifications; and confirming closing fees and rate as well as setting up closing time. Prefer someone with some sales experience, strong analytical and communications skills, and great work ethic.

Property Management Specialists/Leasing Agents

Job growth is expected to be about as fast as the average (10 to 15 percent) for all careers over the next decade.

Sources of additional information:

- Institute of Real Estate Management (www.irem.org)
- National Association of Residential Property Managers (narpm.org)
- Property Management Association (www.pma-dc.org)

Wondering what employers look for in a property management specialist? Here's a sample leasing agent job description:

> As a leasing consultant, you'll work with the property manager in achieving the long-term financial and operational goals established for the property by having budget awareness, marketing diligence, and maintaining high occupancy, as well as assisting with the day-to-day operations of the community, including leasing, collections, resident services, maintenance, administration, and policy and procedures compliance. More information for you: leasing agents are the main point of contact with customers—whether they call our office or visit online or in person. The leasing agent is the property's sales representative whose primary duties are to greet prospects, present the features and benefits of apartment community, secure lease agreements from qualified persons, and address the needs of current residents. A leasing agent is very service-oriented and your focus is to strive to make everyone feel welcome and comfortable in his or her apartment and successfully highlight the advantages of our communities.

Real Estate Agents

Job growth is expected to be about as fast as the average (10 to 15 percent) over the next decade.

	A Day in the Life ... of a Real Estate Agent
7:00 A.M.	Up early and already at my home computer responding to e-mails from current and prospective clients and printing out some new listings that I'll use later today.
9:00 A.M.	A quick stop at the office to check voicemail and confirm my appointments for the day.
9:30 A.M.	My first appointment of the day is meeting with a former client who is selling her house. I need to inspect it and the surrounding neighborhood so I can assist her with setting an asking price.
11:00 A.M.	Back to the office to finalize all the paperwork to make the listing official and to get the ball rolling on having the house added to some of our marketing materials. Check mortgage rates online.
12:00 P.M.	Showing a young couple a few houses over their lunch hour. I have carefully selected these properties, so I am hopeful. I see my job as a matchmaker, putting people and houses together.
1:00 P.M.	Taking a client buying a second rental home through a more detailed inspection of a property.
3:00 P.M.	A visit with the local building permit office to check on some questionable work found at one of the houses from earlier in the day. I need to protect my clients, so I feel as though I really need to be an expert in all things real estate.
4:30 P.M.	Arrive back at the office to check e-mails and voicemails. You have to be a people-person.
5:00 P.M.	Grab a bite to eat because I have an open house tonight.
6:00 P.M.	Work the open house. I hope some of the people who looked tonight come back and make an offer.
8:00 P.M.	Time to go home for one last e-mail check.

Real Estate Appraisers/Trainees

Job growth is expected to be about as fast as the average (10 to 15 percent) for all careers over the next decade.

Sources of additional information:

◆ American Society of Appraisers (www.appraisers.org)

◆ Appraisal Institute (www.appraisalinstitute.org)

Wondering what employers look for in a commercial real estate appraiser trainee? Here's a sample appraiser trainee job description:

> We are known in the industry for delivering quality, timely reports to our clients, using the most sophisticated appraisal technology available. You'll be responsible for assisting staff appraisers in the appraisal of real estate properties. This position is a trainee position under the guidance of a certified staff appraiser while completing the educational courses toward state certification. Responsibilities will include daily updating of our web-based notification system. Diligence in receiving orders and setting inspection appointments as well as quick reaction time to inquiries made by office manager or clients is required. Requirements include a Bachelor's degree in real estate, business, or a relevant field or three to five years work experience in a closely related job; strong verbal and written communications; strong PC skills including Microsoft Word, Access, and Excel; and must be willing to obtain state certification for a Real Estate General Appraiser license, which includes completing required educational courses. If you are a team player who is looking for a great career in appraising and enjoys the advantages of working with a professional organization, then apply for this position.

Real Estate Brokers

Job growth is expected to be as fast as the average (10 to 15 percent) for all occupations over the next decade.

Additional source information can be found at National Association of Real Estate Brokers (www.nareb.com).

profiles

Mega-Developer Donald Trump

Donald Trump is a billionaire real estate speculator and developer—and larger-than-life personality—who is chairman, president, and chief executive officer of the Trump Organization, which owns several pieces of high-profile New York City real estate; 25 percent of Trump Entertainment Resorts (formerly Trump Hotels & Casino Resorts); Trump Restaurants, Trump Mortgage; Trump University; and other holdings, including a Florida resort and 50 percent of the Miss USA, Miss Teen USA, and Miss Universe beauty pageants. Trump attended the University of Pennsylvania's Wharton School of Finance, and after earning his degree in economics, started out immediately tackling big building projects in Manhattan. In the 1990s, Trump experienced what many developers fear (though not on the scale of Trump) when he went from highly successful developer to nearly bankrupt and losing many of his holdings, to successful developer again. In 2004 he began a hit reality series *The Apprentice* (coining the ever-popular "You're fired," when dismissing contestants). Some of his books include *Trump: The Art of the Deal, Trump: Surviving at the Top, Trump: The Art of the Comeback, Trump 101: The Way to Success, Trump University Real Estate 101: Building Wealth With Good Investments,* and *Why We Want You to be Rich: Two Men—One Message* (co-written with Robert T. Kiyosaki).

Earnings Potential $

Real estate majors have a starting salary around $45,000, more than the average for all college graduates, which is currently around $38,000.

The following section provides some general guidelines of salaries to expect upon graduation. Remember, salaries vary by employer, industry, and region.

Development Specialist/Assistant Project Manager. Median annual salary of an assistant project manager is $44,000.

Mortgage Loan Officer. Beginning salary for a mortgage loan officer is $31,000.

Property Management Specialist/ Leasing Agent. Median annual earnings of a property management specialist are $35,000.

The Professor Says

There are many career possibilities for a major in real estate beyond the ones featured here. Remember that it is always important to learn more about prospective careers by going online, talking with professors, conducting informational interviews, and job-shadowing.

Real Estate Agent. The average salary for an entry-level real estate agent varies because salary is based on commissions, but tends to be about $36,000+.

Real Estate Appraiser/Trainee. The median annual base salary of a real estate appraiser is $37,000.

Real Estate Broker. The average salary for an entry-level real estate broker varies because salary is based on commissions, but tends to be about $45,000+.

The Professor Says _____

Your next step after choosing your major? Gaining work experience. Just about all "entry-level" jobs for college graduates require some work experience outside the classroom. Seek out internships, volunteer, and figure out other ways to gain the experience you need.

The Least You Need to Know

- ◆ Students who have a passion for real estate and a gift for selling should find jobs upon graduation as job growth is expected in most fields.

- ◆ Just about all the careers in real estate involve working with people, and networking is essential.

- ◆ As is the case with many fields, you can get a good entry-level job with just an undergraduate degree in real estate, though some jobs require an additional license.

- ◆ Several careers in real estate pay purely on commission from sales, and thus have more risks and rewards than salaried jobs.

Part 4

Careers in the Sciences Using a Major in ...

This part highlights the wide variety of careers available to you if you choose to major in one of the "hard" sciences—also referred to as the "natural sciences"—such as chemistry or biology, as well as engineering or physics. Whether you want to help farmers grow better crops, solve the climate-change crisis, find a cure for cancer, discover untold universes, design rocket propulsion systems, or save polar bears from extinction, there's a science major that fits your vision for your future career—and multiple career paths to fit your choice of science major.

You'll find information on the life sciences, earth sciences, chemistry and biochemistry, engineering, the geosciences, physics and astronomy, and zoology.

"That's it! I'll be a physics major."

Chapter 15

The Life Sciences

In This Chapter

◆ Find careers that use your research skills and your love of living organisms

◆ Learn about careers focusing on your natural curiosity

◆ Learn the courses that typical life sciences majors require

◆ Discover what kind of jobs and salaries to expect

Do you spend a lot of your time outside or in the lab studying all types of living organisms? Do the life cycles of various plants and animals fascinate you? Are you curious about how living things work and interact together? Are you interested in a career working with an agriculture-related business?

This chapter reveals rewarding careers for students who major in one of the life sciences—including biology, botany, and agriculture.

About the Majors

The life sciences deal with a very broad category of sciences concerned with the study of living organisms (including plants, animals, and humans). This chapter focuses on biology (the biggest of the life sciences), botany, and agriculture. We cover earth sciences in Chapter 16.

As you begin to look at majors, you'll find that many schools offer a mix of life science majors. We'll separate them in this chapter so you have a complete understanding of each discipline.

Biology

Biology is the study of living organisms—how they live, interact with other living things, and how they evolve. Most biology majors receive a broad introduction into the many facets of the field, touching on a wide range of topics, including molecular and cellular biology, biotechnology, microbiology, entomology, genetics, physiology, evolution, and ecology.

Biology is a very common major at most colleges and universities. Typical courses include:

Principles of Biology	Molecular Biology
Microbiology	Cell Biology
Molecular and Cellular Biology	Plant Physiology
Evolutionary Biology	Animal Physiology
Scientific Theory and Practice	Biotechnology
Marine Biology	Neurobiology
Plant Biology	Entomology
Ecology	Epidemiology
Genetics	Virology
Evolution	Genomics

Botany

Botany is the study of plants—how they function, what they look like, how they are related to each other, where they grow, and how they evolve. It's the study of plants from algae to giant redwoods. Plants are at the core of all environmental communities—from providing shelter to animals to filtering the air and supplying remedies to common ailments.

Botany is a fairly specialized major (often combined with another of the life sciences), so you will need to seek out universities with this major.

Typical courses include:

Environment Appreciation	Natural Resource Management
Plant Form and Function	Algology
Evolutionary Survey of Plants	Taxonomy of Vascular Plants
Ethnobotany	Hydrology
Plant Anatomy and Morphology	Intermountain Flora
Plant Physiology	Plant Evolution
Plant Genetics	Cell Culture
Plant Geography	Soils
Biology of the Plant Cell	Plant Reproduction
Mycology	Global Botanical Change

Agriculture/Horticulture

Agriculture and horticulture majors grow, market, and use fruits, vegetables, flowers, landscape plants, and turfgrass. The courses focus on a broad number of topics, including plant science, soil science, horticulture, agricultural engineering, agricultural education, and agribusiness. The major prepares students for applied careers in the education, design, or management of farms, nurseries, orchards, vineyards, garden centers, botanical gardens, and fields and parks.

Both agriculture and horticulture are fairly specialized majors, so you will need to seek out universities with this major.

Typical courses include:

Turfgrass Management	Nursery Management
Plant Pathology	Herbaceous Ornamental Plants
Integrated Pest Management	Plant Propagation
Vegetable Production	Garden Center Management
Plant Physiology	Landscape Design
Greenhouse Operations	Soil Fertility
Greenhouse Crop Production	Insect Pest Management

Pesticide Safety and Management

Plant Micropropagation

Plant Biotechnology

Horticulture Technology

Seed Production and Technology

Soil and Water Engineering

Seed, Crop, and Grain Analysis

Arboriculture

Agricultural Economics

Farm Management

Agricultural Irrigation and Water Systems

Computer Applications in Agriculture

Agriculture Education, Extension, and Leadership

Background on Careers

There are myriad specialized fields in the life sciences, and the list continues to grow. You may specialize in a particular kind of organism, such as snakes, fish, or roses. Or you may specialize in a specific system within all living organisms, such as cells, tissues, or organs.

Major Pitfalls

Biology graduates are most frequently employed as technicians in biology laboratories; however, many other careers are possible outside the lab for those students who see their future elsewhere, but still in the field.

Biology graduates have the most career options because of the breadth of the major, including becoming a research technician (at hospitals, biotech firms, pharmaceutical companies, academic institutions, or government agencies), a naturalist (at state or national parks or with a school system), a biostatistician (in industry or government), a technical/science writer, or a science teacher, or pursuing a career in health care (see also Chapter 25).

Botany graduates may work in the field, conducting plant research as a field botanist, or working as an ecologist, park ranger, or environmental inspector. You could also work in a laboratory as a research technician, in industry or with a governmental agency, as a teacher, or as a technical/science writer.

Agriculture/horticulture graduates tend to go into very applied careers, trying to improve plant culture methods for increasing crop quality and yields in management or marketing positions for an agriculture-related business, landscape design and maintenance firm, or plant and food inspection or education with a governmental agency. Some graduates do go into the science side, becoming plant scientists or researchers.

Some top jobs and careers for students earning a Bachelor's degree with a major in one of these life sciences include:

Agriculture Extension Educator. As an extension agent/educator, you'll serve as an expert in one of a network of local and regional agricultural extension offices affiliated with a state office located at its land-grant state university, providing useful, practical, and research-based information to agricultural producers, small-business owners, youth (working with local 4-H clubs—Head, Heart, Hands, and Health), consumers, and others in rural areas and communities of all sizes. Agricultural extension agencies also offer opportunities to serve in developing nations through international agencies.

Agronomist/Plant Scientist. In this job, you'll study plants at the cellular and whole-plant levels and work to improve the quality and production of crops for the producers of food, feed, and fiber crops. You'll evaluate multiple growing methods, field management and rotation, and pest and disease prevention practices, and work to improve the nutritional value of crops. You'll also evaluate soil samples and conduct topographic analyses and take an active role in environmental issues related to all phases of seed production, as well as plan, conduct, and supervise experiments related to the planting, cultivating, and harvesting of crops.

Biologist. Few fields are as broad as biology, where the study can span the characteristics of a single cell all the way to an entire ecosystem. Biologists study the basic principles of plant and animal life, collecting and analyzing biological field data to further the science. Many biologists specialize in a particular aspect of biology or plants, animals, or region. Some biologists work for universities while others work for industry and governmental agencies, often examining environmental impacts of the pollution, development, or use of present and potential land and water areas.

Biostatistician. In this job, you'll contribute to an assessment team in a health-related field (including medical therapies and pharmaceutical trials, epidemiology, and public health) in the design and preparing of clinic studies, from forming hypotheses to sample selection; evaluating, interpreting, and reporting study findings; and preparing regulatory submissions to governmental agencies. You may also develop statistical programs to perform detailed analyses and prepare data results. The job requires strong expertise in both biological sciences and theoretical and applied statistics.

Biology Lab Research Technician. As a research technician, you'll typically perform many types of work, testing, examining, and analyzing research materials. In some larger labs, you may specialize. This job is typically a critical first job for many biology graduates, one in which you'll hone your research skills while providing key laboratory support, such as inspecting, cleaning, testing, calibrating, adjusting, and maintaining lab equipment. Advancement is usually to higher level positions within the laboratory, academic institution, or hospital. You may work in research, quality control, or in a manufacturing environment.

Field Botanist. As a field botanist, you'll study plants and the environment in the field, observing conditions in the actual natural environment, identifying and classifying plants, often conducting research or surveys, and keeping botanical inventories that examine the effects of rainfall, temperature, climate, and soil on plant growth. Some botanists study all kinds of plant life, including algae, fungi, lichens, mosses, ferns, conifers, and flowering plants; others specialize in such areas as identification and classification of plants, the structure of plants, or the causes and cures of plant diseases.

Naturalist. In this job, you'll inspire and educate others on the importance and fragility of the environment. Naturalists need to have a passion for the environment, a concern for living things, and a desire to share their knowledge with others. You may work for an educational institution or park system. Working as a naturalist is the perfect combination for someone who loves nature but also has a passion to be an educator. You'll often spend days visiting schools, leading field trips and trail hikes, or conducting educational programs. You'll also often take pictures, write copy, and develop educational materials, such as brochures, posters, and displays.

Major Pitfalls

While you can get a job in any of these careers with just a Bachelor's degree, the more lucrative and rewarding jobs in the life sciences require at least a Master's degree.

Other Career Possibilities. Some other job and career paths for biology, botany, and agriculture/horticulture majors include:

Biomedical Engineer	Marine Lab Technician
Community Ecologist	Medical Library Specialist
Conservation Biologist	Microbiologist
Criminologist	Molecular Biologist
Environmental Specialist	Mycologist
EPA Inspector	Nursery Management
Horticulturalist	Pharmaceutical Sales Representative
Hospital Administrator	Plant Taxonomist
Immunologist	

Range Manager   Technical Writer

Soil Scientist   Wildlife Biologist

Skills Needed/Developed

Students majoring in some area of the life sciences develop numerous valuable and transferable skills. The following are the most critical to graduates:

Problem-Solving. One of the most important skills for life scientists, this skill involves your ability to identify complex problems, review existing conditions and restrictions, and develop and evaluate alternative solutions to the problem.

Scientific Method. Like all science majors, you'll possess an understanding of the scientific method, which involves the formulation of a hypothesis concerning some phenomena, experimentation to demonstrate the truth or fallacy of the hypothesis, and a conclusion that validates or modifies the hypothesis.

Synthesizing Information. All of the life sciences involve working with multiple sources of information and data, and your ability to bring all this information together in a logical manner is an essential skill.

The Professor Says _____

Other transferable skills you gain from these majors include:

- ◆ Research and planning
- ◆ Recordkeeping/ handling details
- ◆ Gathering information
- ◆ Communications
- ◆ Observation

Technical/Computer Skills. Because many of the jobs in the life sciences require using computers and specific software applications, key technical and computer skills are indispensable.

Teamwork. Many of the jobs in this field involve working with others, whether in a laboratory or in the field, so your ability to work well with teams is critical.

Expected Growth

The demand for life scientists in general is expected to continue to be strong over the next decade, as the number of students studying biological sciences has declined over the past decade, while at the same time there are already shortages of skilled technical personnel and a growing demand for biotechnological and molecular biological researchers.

Sources of additional information:

- EnviroLink Network (www.envirolink.org)
- NatureServe (www.natureserve.org)

Agricultural Extension Agents/Educators

Job growth for agricultural extension agents is expected to increase about as fast as the average (10 to 15 percent) for all careers over the next decade.

Sources of additional information:

- National Association of Agricultural Educators (www.naae.org)
- National Association of Extension 4-H Agents (www.nae4ha.org)

Agronomists/Plant Scientists

Job growth for agronomists and agricultural scientists is expected to be about as fast as the average (10 to 15 percent) for all careers over the next decade.

Sources of additional information:

- American Society of Agronomy (www.agronomy.org)
- Crop Science Society of America (www.crops.org)
- Soil Science Society of America (www.soils.org)

Wondering what employers look for in a plant scientist? Here's a sample plant scientist job description:

> We're seeking a highly motivated, team-oriented individual to provide support in the development, optimization, and implementation of high-quality laboratory and greenhouse disease bioassays and field experiments in our Soybean Group. The primary role is to support the proper maintenance and production of inoculums of a number of soybean disease pathogens for lab, greenhouse, and field bioassays. This position will require the initiative and foresight to execute and assist in the daily routine operations associated with a comprehensive soybean

disease-screening program. Other responsibilities include planting, inoculation, generation, and collection of high quality disease data, laboratory support, and greenhouse germplasm resistance screening and pathogen diagnostic techniques. Supervise and ensure safety of contract workers and seasonal employees. Field responsibilities include the establishment of disease nurseries to evaluate tolerance of soybean germplasm to various soybean diseases.

Biologists

Demand for biologists should remain strong over the next decade, with job growth expected to be about as fast as the average (10 to 15 percent) for all careers over the next decade.

Sources of additional information:

◆ American Institute of Biological Sciences (www.aibs.org)

◆ American Society for Cell Biology (www.ascb.org)

◆ American Society for Microbiology (www.asm.org)

◆ Federation of American Societies for Experimental Biology (www.faseb.org)

Wondering what employers look for in an entry-level biologist? Here's a sample biologist job description:

Responsibilities of this biologist job include assisting staff in GIS-based analyses of bird and habitat data; manipulating data and conducting statistical analyses as requested; preparing maps and other summary products from the GIS information; and providing technical assistance to federal agency personnel as requested. Knowledge of bird biology, basic computer skills, and basic statistics are required. You will develop biological information for modeling studies and presentations over the Internet; conduct a variety of data manipulations and analyses and conduct statistical and spatial analyses requiring a critical analysis and evaluation of project objectives, past practices, and source materials; and assist with preparation of reports, manuscripts, and Internet communications. Qualifications: Bachelor's degree in biology or zoology, ecology, botany, and/or wildlife biology. Knowledge of GIS and SAS.

Biologist Nettie Stevens

Nettie Stevens, an early American geneticist, was one of the first female scientists to make a name for herself in the biological sciences when her work with Edmund Beecher Wilson was published describing the chromosomal basis for sex in meal worms and other species of insects. She completed her undergraduate studies in just two years at what is now Westfield State College, graduating at the top of her class. She earned a Master's degree in biology at Stanford University, where she studied marine life. She then attended Bryn Mawr College, where she earned a Ph.D., in biology. She is credited with expanding the fields of embryology and cytogenetics.

Biostatisticians

Job growth for biostatisticians is expected to be faster than the average (18 to 25 percent) for all careers over the next decade, partly because of a current shortage of biostatisticians.

Sources of additional information:

◆ American Statistical Association (www.amstat.org)

◆ International Society for Clinical Biostatistics (www.iscb.info)

Wondering what employers look for in an entry-level biostatistician? Here's a sample biostatistician job description:

> Our company helps improve health care worldwide by providing a broad range of professional services, information, and partnering solutions to the pharmaceutical, biotechnology, and health-care industries. We are currently seeking a qualified candidate for the position of biostatistician. The person in this position will participate on one or more project teams as biostatistician, which involves preparing analysis plans and writing detailed specifications for analysis files, consistency checks, tables, and figures; communicating with clients regarding statistical analysis issues as they arise; and interpreting analyses and writing statistical sections of study reports. The biostatistician may also serve the role of statistical programmer, in addition to biostatistician, on projects. B.S. degree in statistics or biostatistics and some statistical experience in the clinical trials environment is a minimum. Excellent written and oral communication skills, the ability to work as part of a team, and excellent attention and accuracy to details required. Must have strong working knowledge of SAS.

Biology Lab Research Technicians

Employment for laboratory research technicians is expected to grow faster than average (18 to 25 percent) for all jobs over the next decade.

Wondering what employers look for in a laboratory technician? Here's a sample lab tech job description:

> This is an exciting opportunity for an entry-level biologist to get on board with one of the area's premier biotech companies. The ideal candidate will be familiar with the techniques used in viral purification and cell culture. This position provides the successful candidate with the opportunity to hone your molecular and cell biology skills by working side-by-side with senior-level scientists. The company is looking for a candidate with a Bachelor's degree in a life science. Previous experience with purification and cell culture preferred. Some previous experience in industry is preferred, although candidates completing internships and special projects while in school will be given consideration.

Field Botanists

Job growth for botanists is expected to be about as fast as the average (10 to 15 percent) over the next decade.

Sources of additional information:

◆ American Society of Plant Biologists (www.aspb.org)

◆ American Society for Horticulture Science (www.ashs.org)

◆ Botanical Society of America (www.botany.org)

Naturalists

Employment of naturalists projects to increase slower than the average (under 8 percent) for all occupations over the next decade.

Sources of additional information:

◆ The American Society of Naturalists (www.amnat.org)

◆ Association for Environmental & Outdoor Education (www.aeoe.org)

◆ National Recreation & Park Association (www.nrpa.org)

◆ North American Association of Environmental Education (www.naaee.org)

Botanist Liberty Hyde Bailey Jr.

Liberty Hyde Bailey Jr. so transformed the field of botany, revolutionized methods in the field of agricultural education, and founded the discipline of landscape architecture that some people label him as the father of horticulture in America. He was instrumental in getting botanists, plant physiologists, and geneticists to work together in the field of horticulture. He also established the American Society for Horticulture Science and the Botanical Society of America, authored hundreds of books and articles on botany, and is perhaps best known for his encyclopedia of plants, *Hortus*. He earned his Bachelor's and Master's degrees from what is now Michigan State University. He worked at Harvard University (in the gardens and greenhouses), and taught at both Michigan State and Cornell Universities. He was also considered both a naturalist and rural sociologist.

Wondering what employers look for in a naturalist? Here's a sample naturalist job description:

The Professor Says

Your next step? Pick the couple of careers that most fit your interests with a major in biology, botany, or agriculture and dig more deeply into them. Remember that it is always important to learn more about prospective careers by going online, talking with professors, conducting informational interviews, and job-shadowing.

We're a residential outdoor science school, with a primary focus in science education, not recreation. We seek an educator to instruct fifth- and sixth-grade students in the principles of ecosystem science, with topics such as geology and soils, plant adaptations, wildlife habitat, comparative ecosystems, and human ecology. You will also lead some evening programs, provide occasional student supervision, and train volunteer cabin leaders. To qualify, you need a Bachelor's degree in life science (biology, botany, etc.), with coursework including general ecology, botany, earth science, and field natural-history experience, as well as a willingness to work irregular hours and lead teaching hikes in a semi-wilderness setting.

Earnings Potential $

Graduates with a Bachelor's degree in one of these life science majors earn a starting salary of about $33,000—less than the average annual salary for all college graduates, which is currently around $38,000—however, salaries vary widely.

The following section provides some general guidelines of salaries to expect upon graduation. Remember, salaries vary by employer, industry, and region.

Agricultural Extension Educator. Beginning annual salary for a new graduate is about $28,000.

Agronomist/Plant Scientist. Median annual earnings of an agronomist is about $30,500.

Biologist. Median annual salary for an entry-level biologist is about $42,300.

Biostatistician. The median annual salary of an entry-level biostatistician is about $55,000.

Biology Lab Research Technician. The median annual salary of an entry-level lab technician is about $35,000.

Field Botanist. The median annual salary of an entry-level botanist is $55,000.

Naturalist. The median starting salary for a naturalist varies by type of employer. Annual entry-level salaries for park naturalists are about $44,000, while those working in schools are much lower.

The Professor Says

Remember that you're not done once you pick your college major—in fact, it's just begun, because the next thing you need to do is gain work experience. Just about all "entry-level" jobs for college graduates require some work experience outside the classroom. Seek out internships, volunteer, and figure out other ways to gain the experience you need.

The Least You Need to Know

- A major in one of the life sciences is the perfect fit for someone who has a passion about all living creatures and an interest in plants, agriculture, or the outdoors.

- If you have a strong interest in math and biology, consider a career as a biostatistician, the career path most in demand in the life sciences, and also one of the highest paying.

- If you are interested in working in nature rather than being stuck in an office somewhere, a career in the life sciences should be one you consider.

Chapter 16

The Earth Sciences

In This Chapter

- Discover careers that use your love of the outdoors
- Learn the typical classes that Earth science majors require
- Find out what kind of jobs and salaries to expect

Do you spend a lot of your time outside hiking, fishing, and camping? Do you enjoy the serenity of nature? Are you a tree-hugger? Do you desire to make a positive impact on the future of our environment in conserving our forests and other natural resources?

This chapter reveals rewarding careers for students majoring in one of the earth sciences—including environmental science, forestry, and wildlife ecology.

About the Majors

The earth sciences deal with a very broad category of sciences that focus on the study of the problems and solutions related to the environment, ecology, and ecosystems. This chapter focuses on environmental science, forestry, and wildlife ecology.

As you begin to look at majors, you'll find that many schools have a mix of earth science majors. We'll separate them in this chapter so you have a complete understanding of each discipline.

Environmental Science

Environmental science is the study of interactions among the physical, chemical, and biological components of the environment. Typically, this major focuses on pollution and degradation of the environment related to human activities and strategies for sustainability, solving and managing environmental problems for the future.

Environmental science is often an interdisciplinary major that draws resources not only from the sciences, but also from economics, law and policy, international studies, and the social sciences, and can be found at some colleges and universities.

Typical courses include:

Earth, Environment, and Society

Conservation Biology and Applied Ecology

Technology and the Environment

Energy and the Environment

Organic Pollutants in the Environment

Ecosystems, Patterns and Processes

Atmospheric Processes and Climate

Introduction to Environmental History

Environmental Ethics, Policies, and Law

Environmental Assessment

Environmental Economics and Planning

Ecology and Environmental Problem-Solving

Atmosphere, Ocean, and Environmental Change

Structure, Function, and Development of Trees

Forestry

The major in forestry provides students with the knowledge and understanding of forest ecosystems—and the concepts needed for the sustainable management of those forests. Students learn about forest biology, forest health, wildlife management, forest inventory, and resource economics and policy. Graduates of forestry programs learn to manage forests to meet the many societal needs, including water and soil quality protection, forest products, wildlife protection, and recreation through a variety of additional courses in conservation, economics, quantitative methods, and communications.

Forestry is a fairly specialized major, so you will need to seek out universities with this major.

Typical courses include:

Dendrology and Forest Plants	Forest Health Management
Forest Water Resources	Forest Economics
Natural Resource Sampling	Forest Resource Information Systems
Forests and the Future	
Forest Ecology	Forests, Conservation, and People
Silviculture	Environmental Education Program Development
Tree Biology	
Agroforestry	Integrated Natural Resource Management
Urban Forestry	
International Forestry	Forest Operations and Wood Utilization

Wildlife Ecology

Wildlife ecology and wildlife management majors are typically interdisciplinary and prepare students for professional positions in planning, developing, and managing private and public lands for recreational purposes. Students learn the basic principles associated with using leisure time and the relationship of natural resources to the constructive use of leisure time.

Wildlife is a fairly specialized major (often combined with forestry or environmental science), so you will need to seek out universities with this major.

Typical courses include:

Forestry and Natural Resources	Wildlife Damage Management
Wildlife Ecology	Wetlands
Ecology of Natural Resources	Water Resource Management
Forest Protection	Water Science

Forests, Fisheries, and Wildlife

Fisheries Science

Bio-Atmospheric Resources

Limnology

Natural Resource Policy

Wildlife Techniques

Biology of Wildlife Populations

Background on Careers

Environmental science graduates are the leaders that help the public understand and solve environmental problems and issues caused by overpopulation, residential and commercial development, and waste and other pollutants. They often find employment in government-funded organizations and other conservation and environmental planning and action groups.

The Professor Says

Here are a few of the biggest environmental action groups:

- ◆ Clean Water Network (www.cwn.org)
- ◆ Conservation International (www.conservation.org)
- ◆ EarthWatch (www.earthwatch.org)
- ◆ Environmental Working Group (www.ewg.org)
- ◆ Friends of the Earth (www.foe.org)
- ◆ Greenpeace (www.greenpeace.org)
- ◆ National Wildlife Federation (www.nwf.org)
- ◆ The Nature Conservatory (www.nature.org)
- ◆ Union of Concerned Scientists (www.ucsusa.org)
- ◆ The Wilderness Society (www.wilderness.org)

Forestry graduates perfect the science, art, and practice of creating, managing, using, and conserving forests in a sustainable manner. These graduates find careers in industry, academic institutions, or the government as forest managers or consultants, urban foresters, forest scientists, and forest educators.

Wildlife ecology and wildlife management graduates typically work in a natural-resources–based recreation setting on private or public lands, including local, state, and national parks, and with other state and federal agencies and nonprofit organizations providing outdoor recreational opportunities.

Some top jobs and careers for students earning a Bachelor's degree with a major in one of these earth sciences include:

Environmental Analyst. As an environmental analyst, you'll work closely with construction contractors and engineers, GIS technicians, and industry, environmental, and community groups to conduct research studies to develop theories or methods of abating or controlling sources of environmental pollutants. You'll also determine data collection methods to be employed in research projects and surveys, plan and develop environmental research models, identify and analyze sources of pollution to determine their effects, and collect and synthesize data from atmospheric monitoring, meteorological and mineralogical information, and soil or water samples. Analysts are also responsible for preparing graphs, charts, and statistical models from synthesized data, and analyzing data to assess pollution problems, establish standards, and to develop approaches to pollution control.

Major Pitfalls

As in many of the sciences, some graduates continue their studies in graduate school rather than working after earning their Bachelor's degree, as more (and more lucrative) jobs tend to be available for those with a graduate degree.

Environmental Specialist. In this job, you'll conduct research or perform investigations to identify, abate, or eliminate sources of pollutants or hazards that affect the environment. You'll collect, synthesize, study, model, report, and take action on how to clean the environment based on data derived from measurements or field observations of air, soil, water, and other sources. As an environmental specialist, you may specialize in a relatively narrow field, for example: agricultural runoff, air pollution, drinking and ground water, hazardous waste, or solid and infectious waste. You'll also mediate conflict resolutions, meet with attorneys, hold hearings, or even appear in court as an expert witness.

Forest Biologist. As a forest biologist, you will provide the technical expertise to conserve the biological diversity of forests and grasslands and work to protect and recover endangered species. You'll research the origins, behavior, diseases, genetics, and life processes of trees and wildlife, and may specialize in forest research and management, including collecting and analyzing biological data to determine the environmental effects of present and potential use of land and water areas. Work also includes educating and supervising the public and forest users who hunt, fish, birdwatch, and vacation in the forest acreage. Forest biologists often work as partners with state and national wildlife agencies, conservation organizations, and special interest groups to manage the forests and wildlife habitat and populations.

Forester. As a forester, you may work at sites that vary from glaciers to laboratories, tropical rain forests to grasslands, and offices to mountainsides. Your responsibilities may span the full spectrum of natural resources—water, soil, air, range, fish, wildlife, wood, minerals, recreation, and wilderness. The job includes a wide range of activities—developing, implementing, or administering plans for recreation activities and site development, trail construction maintenance, and interpretive/educational services; wilderness protection; timberland improvements; forest habitat analyses and enhancements; land exchanges or purchases; timber sales; special permits for mineral exploration and other land uses; and prescribed fire management and wildlife suppression.

Hydrographic Survey Technician. As a hydrographic survey technician, you'll employ a variety of tools, instruments, and equipment, ranging from sonar systems to computers and peripherals, GPS, surveying instruments, sampling equipment, and deck equipment to chart ocean waters, landforms, and underwater features. More specifically, you'll conduct surveys to ascertain the locations of natural features and human-made structures on the earth's surface, underground, and underwater; prepare topographic and contour maps; and maintain equipment.

Urban Forester. In this job, you'll work with city leaders to develop, manage, and/or monitor activities related to the conservation, preservation, and proliferation of trees in an urban setting. You'll likely oversee the application of pesticides, insecticides, and fertilizers; inspect and treat trees for diseases and parasites; confer with architects, developers, and contractors to discuss tree preservation techniques; draft/write and enforce ordinances and policies relating to arboricultural and urban forestry practices; manage and/or coordinate specific tree programs; review construction plans, specifications, and contracts for compliance with codes, ordinances, and zoning related to trees; and develop and implement plans, strategies, and programs to conserve, preserve, and proliferate trees and urban forests within the city's limits.

Wildlife Refuge Manager. As a wildlife refuge manager, you'll perform a variety of duties related to wildlife habitat management, including planning, organizing, and conducting field inventories for wildlife habitats; setting objectives and goals, developing monitoring plans, and analyzing data for input into refuge-planning documents. You'll also develop long-range plans for developing or expanding the wildlife refuge, as well as manage other land-use plans, work with various organizations and governmental agencies related to any endangered species living in the refuge, and collaborate with local groups and organizations to promote and sustain wildlife conservation interest.

Other Career Possibilities. Some other job and career paths for environmental science, forestry, and wildlife ecology majors include:

Agroforester	Forest Economist
Air Pollution Analyst	GIS Specialist
Arborist	Hydrologist
Conservation Lands Manager	Land Acquisition Specialist
Conservation Specialist	Naturalist
Ecotour Guide	Reforestation Specialist
Environmental Lobbyist	Silvicultural Researcher
Extension Agent	Timber Dealer

Skills Needed/Developed

Students majoring in some area of earth science develop numerous valuable and transferable skills. The following represent the most critical to graduates.

Problem-Solving. One of the most important skills for earth scientists, this is the ability to identify complex problems, review existing conditions and restrictions, and develop and evaluate alternative solutions to the problem.

Creativity. This skill involves brainstorming innovative solutions to ongoing environmental issues, developing specific plans to implement the solutions, and modifying the plans as needed.

Scientific Method. All science majors must understand the scientific method, which involves the formulation of a hypothesis concerning some phenomena, experimentation to demonstrate the truth or fallacy of the hypothesis, and a conclusion that validates or modifies the hypothesis.

Communications (in writing and verbally). All majors must perfect the following critical skills: the ability to report and present the results of your

The Professor Says

Other transferable skills gained from these majors include:

- Research and planning
- Recordkeeping/handling details
- Gathering information
- Compute
- Observation

scientific research, to develop educational and informative literature, and to be persuasive when speaking with a group.

Teamwork. Since many environmental jobs require working as part of at least one team, the ability to work, communicate, and lead groups of peers is an essential skill.

Expected Growth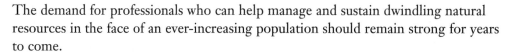

The demand for professionals who can help manage and sustain dwindling natural resources in the face of an ever-increasing population should remain strong for years to come.

Sources of additional information:

◆ Ecological Society of America (www.esa.org)

◆ National Association of Environmental Professionals (www.naep.org)

---

profiles

Environmentalist Dr. David Suzuki

Dr. David Suzuki is an award-winning environmentalist, scientist, and broadcaster. He also serves as chair of the David Suzuki Foundation, which has worked to use science and education to find ways for society to live in balance with the natural world by focusing on three areas—oceans and sustainable fishing, climate change and clean energy, and sustainability. He graduated with honors from Amherst College with a Bachelor's degree in biology and has a Doctorate in zoology from the University of Chicago, as well as 18 honorary Doctorates. He is Professor Emeritus at the University of British Columbia, host of a popular Canadian science television series, *The Nature of Things*, author of 43 books, including *Introduction to Genetic Analysis*, and is a world leader in sustainable ecology. He has received numerous awards, including the Kalinga Prize for Science, the United Nations Environment Program Medal, and the Roger Tory Peterson Award from Harvard University.

Environmental Analysts

Job growth for environmental analysts is expected to be much faster than the average (18 to 25 percent) for all careers over the next decade as new environmental regulations, awareness, and policy drive jobs.

Wondering what employers look for in an environmental analyst? Here's a sample environmental analyst job description:

> We're seeking an environmental analyst/engineer. Candidates with a Bachelor's degree in environmental engineering, geology, or environmental science preferred. Ability to conduct environmental assessments and write technical reports required. You'll also need the ability to communicate complex technology issues to wide-ranging audiences; strong analytic, problem-solving, organizational, planning, and communication (both verbal and written) skills; and familiarity with standard office software applications. Field and remediation experience a plus.

Environmental Specialists

Job growth for environmental specialists is expected to be about as fast as the average (10 to 15 percent) over the next decade.

Wondering what employers look for in an environmental specialist? Here's a sample environmental specialist job description:

> This position is responsible for providing technical expertise in support of environmental compliance and regulatory approvals associated with management of solid waste at coal, nuclear, and gas/oil-fired electric generating plants. This position requires excellent written and verbal communication skills. You'll provide daily support to power plant personnel regarding waste classification/disposal and other solid-waste–related issues; ensure timely and accurate submission of environmental reports to achieve compliance with regulatory standards; and provide technical expertise and recommendations to management regarding due diligence investigations and remediation projects. Bachelor of Science in environmental science, geology, or similar degree with an understanding of groundwater and associated environmental regulations required.

Forest Biologists

Demand for forest biologists is expected to grow slower than the average (under 8 percent) for all careers over the next decade.

Foresters

Job growth for foresters is expected to be slower than the average (under 8 percent) for all careers over the next decade.

A source of additional information is the Society of American Foresters (www.safenet.org).

Wondering what employers look for in a forester? Here's a sample forester job description:

> Performs duties related to the management of vegetation such as silviculture, timber management, reforestation, timber stand improvement, and fuels management; develops new or proposed plans, policies, procedures, and guidelines and makes recommendations on the need for new or modified policies regarding forestland management programs and policies; implements forestry land management plans and performs work involving the review and analysis of forestry resource issues in order to implement forestry resource plans and/or management programs; plans, initiates, and/or conducts surveys, studies, or evaluations of forest resource management projects and programs and provides complete documentation of information accumulated from the review and the resulting procedures established or changed; gathers, analyzes, and interprets scientific data through development and use of computer software and automated systems. Must have knowledge of forestry land-management principles and practices, reforestation methods, and harvesting systems used to perform plant management work and must complete a full four-year course of study in an accredited college or university leading to a Bachelor's or higher degree in forestry.

profiles

Forester Bruce Zobel

Bruce Zobel is a legend in forestry, forest improvement, and forest genetics. He was a professor of forestry, ran a forestry cooperative, and had his own forestry consulting business, picking up numerous awards over the years, including the Governor's Award for Conservation, Barrington Moore Memorial Award (Biological Research), and the North Carolina Forestry Association's Man of the Year. After earning a Bachelor's degree in forestry from the University of California at Berkeley, he worked as an assistant logging engineer, forestry officer, and senior lab assistant. He then went on to complete both his Master's degree and Ph.D., in forestry, also from the University of California at Berkeley. Before getting into teaching, he worked several years as a silviculturist (forest manager).

Hydrographic Survey Technicians

Employment is expected to grow about as fast as average (10 to 15 percent) for all jobs over the next decade.

Wondering what employers look for in a hydrographic survey technician? Here's a sample hydrographic survey technician job description:

> We are seeking a professional to assist our engineering staff in carrying out studies and designs typically pertaining to surface water resources, watershed characteristics, and/or system flow characteristics. You'll determine basic stage-discharge-storage relationships through the compilation, manipulation, and interpretation of hydraulic, hydrologic, and basic survey data; use CAD and GIS software to develop maps and designs; and participates in field data collection activities pertaining to land or hydrographic surveys. Field duties may include, but not be limited to, river transect surveys, discharge measurements, and topographic surveys. Bachelor's degree required. Some experience in engineering, earth, physical or natural science, soil conservation, or survey a plus.

Urban Foresters

Job growth for urban foresters is expected to be about as fast as the average (10 to 15 percent) as more communities implement plans for protecting and managing trees along their streets and parks.

Sources of additional information:

◆ International Society of Arboriculture (www.isa-arbor.com)

◆ Society of Municipal Arborists (www.urban-forestry.com)

Wondering what employers look for in an urban forester? Here's a sample urban forester job description:

> We have an opening for an entry-level urban forester, which requires you to have a Bachelor of Science degree in urban forestry, forest management, arboriculture, or a related field from an accredited four-year institution, with proven competency in urban forestry, plant identification, and wildlife ecology—qualifications you'll need to secure status of Certified Arborist within one year of hiring. Your responsibilities will include performing protected tree inventories for private landowners, performing urban tree inventories for public entities, reviewing trees for health defects, and making management recommendations.

You'll assist with environmental permitting activities, including wetland delineation, performing threatened/endangered wildlife species surveys, and drafting permit applications. You'll also assist with general forest management activities, including prescribed burning, preparing management plans, and assessing timber resources.

A Day in the Life ... of a Forester

8:00 A.M.	I like to arrive early and take a quick ride through the main forest trails. I love the fact that while others are going to their offices in some stuffy building, the forest is my office.
9:00 A.M.	We have a quick staff meeting to go over plans for the day. Our plans vary by season, and in the winter months, we do a lot of maintenance.
9:30 A.M.	Most of the morning will be spent clearing trails and footpaths and pruning trees while they're dormant.
12:00 P.M.	Lunch always seems to taste better after a morning of hard work. While eating, I'm looking over the plans for a new covered walkway in an area of the forest we are just beginning to develop for public use.
1:00 P.M.	Time to take one of the trucks to where we were working this morning and dispose of the debris.
2:00 P.M.	Off to the construction site to make sure the work is being completed properly and with as little harm to surrounding ecosystems as possible.
3:00 P.M.	Arrive at our greenhouse to check on the plantings and seedlings we have growing for when spring arrives, so we can spruce up the park.
4:00 P.M.	The end of the day, as the forest gets dark quickly with these shorter days, is always a good time to catch up on paperwork and handle some of the administrative duties that come with the job. My main task today is putting the finishing touches on the wording of some new educational signs we plan to have in place in time for spring.

Wildlife Refuge Managers

Employment of wildlife refuge managers projects to increase about as fast as average (10 to 15 percent) for all occupations over the next decade.

Wondering what employers look for in a wildlife refuge manager? Here's a sample wildlife refuge manager job description:

> The person we hire will be responsible for the protection, management, and improvement of wildlife. You'll monitor wildlife activity program activities for selected wildlife species; conduct annual surveys to determine the status of endangered, threatened, and sensitive wildlife species; and prepare reports with recommendations as required. You'll also conduct and monitor special studies on the habitat of unique, rare, threatened, and endangered species, and make recommendations for habitat protections. You'll also provide assistance in preparing and reviewing environmental assessments and environmental impact statements affecting wildlife resources. Finally, either individually or through participation on interdisciplinary teams, you'll study and plan proposed management activities, and coordinate and/or implement approved resource management plans.

The Professor Says

Not sure about these career choices? These are just some of the career possibilities for a major in one of the earth sciences. Remember that it is always important to learn more about prospective careers by going online, talking with professors, conducting informational interviews, and job-shadowing.

Earnings Potential $

Graduates with a Bachelor's degree in one of these earth science majors earn a starting salary of about $36,000—less than the average annual salary for all college graduates, which is currently around $38,000—however, salaries vary widely.

The following provides some general guidelines of salaries to expect upon graduation. Remember, salaries vary by employer, industry, and region.

Environmental Analyst. Beginning annual salaries for new graduates range from $30,000 to $35,000.

Environmental Specialist. Median annual earnings of an environmental specialist are about $35,500.

Forest Biologist. Beginning annual salary for an entry-level forest biologist ranges from $30,000 to $40,000.

The Professor Says

Your next step after choosing your major? Gaining work experience. Just about all "entry-level" jobs for college graduates require some work experience outside the classroom. Seek out internships, volunteer, and figure out other ways to gain the experience you need.

Forester. Beginning salary for an entry-level forester ranges from $20,000 to $32,000.

Hydrographic Survey Technician. The median annual salary of an entry-level hydrographic survey technician is $24,000.

Urban Forester. Beginning salaries for urban foresters range from $25,000 to $37,000.

Wildlife Refuge Manager. Beginning annual salaries for a wildlife refuge manager range from $20,000 to $30,000.

The Least You Need to Know

◆ Careers for students majoring in one of the earth sciences require a passion for the environment and strong math and science skills.

◆ If you love the environment and have a desire to find solutions to ongoing environmental problems, then one of these earth science careers ought to be perfect for you.

◆ Environmental jobs are not the most lucrative—especially at the Bachelor's degree level—but the impact you can make for future generations is enormous.

◆ If working indoors in an office setting is the opposite of what you want and desire in your career, then one of these majors (along with the life and geosciences) might be right for you.

Chapter 17

Chemistry and Biochemistry

In This Chapter

- ◆ Discover careers that use your love of working in the lab
- ◆ Learn the typical classes that chemistry and biochemistry majors require
- ◆ Find out what kind of jobs and salaries to expect

Do you spend a lot of your time in your high school science laboratory? Do you enjoy combining chemicals and monitoring the reactions? Are you interested in understanding the physical universe in which we live? Do you own a set of beakers and test tubes?

This chapter reveals rewarding careers for students majoring in chemistry and biochemistry.

About the Majors

Chemistry examines the composition, structure, properties, and reactions of matter. It is often referred to as the central science because it joins together physics and mathematics, biology and medicine, and the earth and environmental sciences. Simply, chemistry looks at the way two or more chemicals react with each other.

Biochemistry majors study the chemistry of living things—the molecular compounds, substances, and physiology that make them tick—to develop an understanding of every aspect of the structure and function of living things at the molecular level. Studying the nature of chemicals and chemical processes provides insights into a variety of physical and biological phenomena—because everything boils down to a collection of chemicals.

As you begin to look at majors, you'll find that almost all schools offer a chemistry major, sometimes with a biochemistry option and sometimes with a full biochemistry major. We'll separate the two in this chapter so you have a complete understanding of each discipline.

Chemistry

Chemistry majors gain a greater understanding as to how the physical world operates by studying the atomic and molecular structure of matter. The major typically includes studies in physical chemistry, analytical chemistry, organic chemistry, and inorganic chemistry. Chemists examine the most basic qualities of matter, master strategies of chemical synthesis, solve chemical mysteries in the laboratory, and learn to communicate facts and theories about chemistry to others.

Just about all colleges and universities offer a major in chemistry. Typical courses include:

General Chemistry I	Polymer Chemistry
General Chemistry II	Environmental Chemistry
Organic Chemistry I	Spectroscopy
Organic Chemistry II	Modern Physical Spectroscopy
Physical Chemistry I	Radiochemistry
Physical Chemistry II	Chemical Quantitative Analysis
Nuclear Chemistry	Introduction to the Chemical Literature

Biochemistry

This major is ideal for the student wishing to pursue an interdisciplinary degree with extensive study in both chemistry and biology. With training in biochemistry, analytical chemistry, molecular biology, and genetics, this major also serves as an excellent preparation for medical school or graduate work in the health sciences. It also prepares students for graduate study or employment in forensic science or pharmaceutical chemistry.

Biochemistry is a fairly specialized major, so you will need to seek out universities with this major. Typical courses include:

General Chemistry I	Immunology
General Chemistry II	Introductory Virology
Organic Chemistry I	Anatomy and Physiology
Organic Chemistry II	Bioinformatics
Introductory Biochemistry	Biostatistics
Advanced Biochemistry	Metabolic Biochemistry
Biophysical Chemistry	Molecular Mechanism of Drugs and Disease
Molecular Biology	

Background on Careers

Chemistry graduates, with their broad knowledge of science, go into any number of fields, ranging from pharmaceuticals to biotechnology to environmentalism. Chemistry majors work in a variety of organizations, including industry, health care, education, and public service.

Biochemistry graduates study the minute, discrete characteristics of every organism and biological process. They prepare for careers in industry, hospitals, agriculture, research institutes, education, and associated areas.

Some top jobs and careers for students earning a Bachelor's degree with a major in chemistry or biochemistry include:

Pharmaceutical Chemist. As a pharmaceutical chemist, you'll develop and evaluate new medications that prevent, cure, and relieve symptoms of disease, and improve analytical techniques for monitoring the levels of drugs in the body. Pharmaceutical chemists use both sophisticated instruments and simple experimental procedures

Major Pitfalls

As in many of the sciences, some chemistry and biochemistry graduates continue their studies in graduate school—with further education in medicinal chemistry, biochemistry, pharmacology, analytical chemistry, inorganic chemistry, and polymer chemistry.

to study the safety and reliability of existing and experimental drugs and chemicals present in drug samples or blood or tissue samples taken from humans or animals that have been treated with a drug. You'll typically work in teams of professionals during the development and testing of new drugs. For more regarding health-related careers, see Chapters 23 and 25.

Bench Chemist. In this job, a very typical one for new chemistry graduates, you'll work as a member of a project team, conducting and interpreting chemical experiments to help achieve the project team's goals by examining the composition, structure, chemical reactivity, and properties of unfamiliar substances and chemical compounds. You'll analyze the results of your experiments and write detailed reports with recommendations for further research. You'll typically work closely with other experts, including chemical engineers, who convert chemical discoveries into products; sales representatives, who need to understand the products to sell them; and academic chemists, who share information at cutting-edge levels. From this job, you can be promoted to a senior bench chemist position or move into a broader area of laboratory work.

Forensic Chemist. As a forensic chemist, you will analyze evidence—applying knowledge from diverse disciplines such as chemistry, biology, materials science, and genetics—that is brought in from crime scenes or from the body of a criminal suspect and reach a conclusion based on tests run on the evidence. A forensic chemist's job is to identify the evidence as part of the larger process of solving a crime, with the results of your work used in police investigations and court trials. You may be called upon to provide expert testimony and explain your findings to a jury. The career path for most forensic chemists is through federal, state, or county labs associated with the medical examiner's office.

Food Scientist/Technologist. As a food scientist you'll apply your knowledge of chemistry, engineering, biology, and nutrition to study the chemical composition of food and food ingredients, develop new food products, improve existing food products, and ensure that the food is healthy, desirable, safe to consume, and easy to use. You'll also evaluate the physical, biological and biochemical properties of foods; the microbiology of foods; and the interaction of food constituents with each other and their environment. Food scientists work in food quality management, processing, research and development, and marketing and distribution. You'll work for companies that manufacture retail food products as well as companies supporting food manufacturers.

Patent Examiner. As a patent examiner, you'll employ a variety of research methods to assess patent applications which are granted to inventors, giving them the right to stop others from using, selling, or making their inventions. You'll conduct a substantive investigation, including a detailed examination of the description and claims; review the invention from a technical standpoint; scrutinize each application to ascertain that the invention is described clearly and in a manner sufficient to allow a skilled person to use it; and search online databases of previous patents to ascertain that the application is novel.

Scientific Equipment Sales Representative. In this job, you'll combine a love of science with a passion for selling by working for a scientific manufacturing company and making sales calls to prospective customers to pitch scientific equipment. Specifically, you should expect to call prospective customers and introduce products and services with the goal of developing prospects into customers; to increase sales-level volume from existing customers; to provide the technical expertise to explain products and answer technical questions; to maintain accurate records of all sales activity; and to coordinate negotiations with customers.

The Professor Says

Some students major in chemistry and biochemistry to get the science foundation required for advanced studies in their pursuit of professional degrees and careers. These careers include:

◆ College Professor
◆ Dentist
◆ Doctor
◆ Patent Attorney
◆ Veterinarian

Other Career Possibilities. Some other job and career paths for chemistry and biochemistry majors include:

Analytical Chemist

Associate Chemist

Clinical Technician/Specialist

Environmental Inspector

EPA Inspector

FDA Inspector

Geochemist

Laboratory Research Assistant

Molecular Biologist

Pharmaceutical Sales Representative

Pollution Control Technician

Polymer Chemist

Quality Control Technician

Science Writer

Toxicologist

Water Purification Chemist

Skills Needed/Developed

Students majoring in chemistry and biochemistry develop numerous valuable and transferable skills. The following are the most critical to graduates:

Observation and Attention to Detail. Perhaps the most important skill for chemists is that of keen observation of even seemingly unimportant details. Laboratory experiments often take long hours of observation and meticulous attention to detail.

Intellectual Curiosity and Reasoning. These majors require an endless desire to find answers and solutions, combining pieces of sometimes unrelated information to form general rules or conclusions.

Scientific Method. All science majors understand the scientific method, which involves the formulation of a hypothesis concerning some phenomena, experimentation to demonstrate the truth or fallacy of the hypothesis, and a conclusion that validates or modifies the hypothesis.

The Professor Says

Other transferable skills you gain from these majors include:

◆ Research and planning
◆ Organization
◆ Active listening
◆ Gathering information
◆ Computer and math

Communications (in writing and verbally). You must perfect the ability to report and present the results of your scientific research, to translate the technical into information the layperson can understand, and to be persuasive when speaking with a group.

Teamwork. Since many chemistry and biochemistry jobs require working as part of at least one team, the ability to work, communicate, and lead groups of peers is an essential skill.

Expected Growth

The demand for chemistry and biochemistry professionals should remain strong for years to come; however, overall job creation for chemists is expected to be slower than the average (under 8 percent) over the next decade.

Sources of additional information:

◆ American Chemical Society (www.chemistry.org)
◆ American Institute of Chemists (www.theaic.org)

◆ American Society for Biochemistry & Molecular Biology (www.asbmb.org)

◆ Association of Analytical Chemists (www.aoac.org)

◆ Society of the Chemical Industry (www.aoac.org)

---

profiles

Polymer Chemist Dr. Ralph Hansen

Dr. Ralph Hansen (1923–1997) was a pioneering chemist and polymer researcher (and father of the author) who specialized in troubleshooting plastics additives and processing. He earned his Bachelor's degree in chemistry from Cornell University, later adding a Master's degree and a Ph.D., in organic chemistry from New York University. In a long career in the telecommunications industry, Dr. Hansen made contributions in the stabilization of polymers and polymer additives and pioneered in the field of plasma treatment of polymers. He was awarded 18 patents, authored chapters in 7 books, and published countless articles in technical journals. He was recognized numerous times in his career, receiving the Union Carbide Award from the American Chemical Society, the Mobay Award from the Society of Plastics Industry, and the Polyolefins Award from the Society of Plastics Engineers. While Dr. Hansen spent most of his career in industry, he later served as a research professor and director of the Polymer Durability Center at Polytechnic University.

Bench Chemists

Job growth for bench chemists is expected to be about as fast as the average (10 to 15 percent) for all careers over the next decade.

Wondering what employers look for in a bench chemist? Here's a sample bench chemist job description:

> With a focus on lighting solutions, precision materials, and components, we are seeking a bench chemist who will be responsible for problem solving through chemical analysis for materials, products, and processes throughout the company. You'll perform chemical analyses on assigned samples; apply existing analytical methodologies to production/research problems; develop analytical methodologies as necessary; and provide expert consultation to research/production staff. This position requires the demonstrated knowledge of quantitative chemical analysis including classical wet chemical analysis and instrumental analysis, including a broad knowledge in the various fields of chemistry; detailed knowledge in analytical chemistry, especially inorganic chemical analysis; familiarity

with analytical instrumentation; and possession of the technical skills to function as a bench chemist. Bachelor of Science in chemistry required, with some advanced laboratory work (including university-level and internships) preferred.

Food Scientists/Technologists

Job growth for food scientists is expected to be about as fast as the average (10 to 15 percent) for all careers over the next decade.

Sources of additional information:

◆ Institute of Food Science & Technology (www.ifst.org)

◆ Institute of Food Technologists (www.ift.org)

Wondering what employers look for in a food scientist? Here's a sample food scientist job description:

> Leading food supply company seeks food scientist. Under direct supervision, researches, conducts experiments, gathers data, develops preliminary findings, and prepares written reports for the development of new products from conception through successful commercialization. Follows established protocols and work plans. Drafts for review technical proposals and reports. You must be a proactive self-starter, willing to accept responsibility for business tasks; able to plan, prioritize, and complete tasks effectively and efficiently; be a clear, concise written and verbal communicator; able to complete project objectives under the direction of supervisor; able to maintain accurate and complete records; work with pilot plant equipment under supervision; learn and utilize online specification system; execute experiments and prepare results for review; develop prototypes that deliver project objectives. Requires Bachelor's degree in science or chemistry.

Forensic Chemists

Demand for forensic chemists is expected to grow at least as fast as the average (10 to 15 percent) for all careers over the next decade, as continued interest in the use of DNA analysis is expected to create more jobs.

A source of additional information is the American Academy of Forensic Sciences (www.aafs.org).

Patent Examiners

Employment is expected to grow about as fast as average (10 to 15 percent) for all jobs over the next decade.

Wondering what employers look for in a patent examiner? Here's a sample patent examiner job description:

> Major duties of the patent examiner (biotechnology/organic chemistry) include reviewing patent applications to assess if they comply with the basic format, rules, and legal requirements; determining the scope of the protection claimed by the inventor; researching relevant technologies to compare similar prior inventions with the invention claimed in the patent applications; and communicating the examiner's findings to patent practitioners/inventors with reasons on the patentability of applicant's inventions. Patent examiners are responsible for the quality, productivity, and timely processing of patent applications, which is the basis of their performance evaluation. Biotechnology/organic/chemistry positions require a four-year course of study leading to a Bachelor's degree from an accredited college or university in chemistry or biochemistry.

Pharmaceutical Chemists

Job growth for pharmaceutical chemists is expected to be faster than the average (18 to 25 percent) for all careers over the next decade as the pharmaceutical industry continues to increase spending on new drug development and clinical trials.

A source of additional information is the American Association of Pharmaceutical Scientists (www.aapspharmaceutica.com).

Wondering what employers look for in a pharmaceutical chemist? Here's a sample pharmaceutical chemist job description:

> We are in need of qualified pharmaceutical chemists to work at a global pharmaceutical company. Chemist will coordinate analytical development and chemistry-related activities for new over-the-counter (OTC) products under direction of the associate director of analytical development or an analytical development team leader. The pharmaceutical chemist will contribute to the preparation of the analytical portions of regulatory submissions. Has close interaction with other functions and departments, including all other departments in OTC research and development. Primary responsibilities of this position include performing chemistry-related testing of R&D batches, validation batches, and

stability testing of products or characterization of drug substances. Qualified pharmaceutical chemist must have a Bachelor of Science degree in chemistry or biochemistry and a GPA of 3.5 or higher. Undergraduate research experience (outside of required lab courses) is a plus.

---

profiles

Nobel Prize Biochemist Dr. Kary Mullis

Dr. Kary Mullis invented the polymerase chain reaction (PCR), with which scientists can determine the order of nucleotides in a gene. The process has multiple applications in medicine, genetics, biotechnology, and forensics, and has been called one of the monumental scientific techniques of the twentieth century. He earned a Bachelor of Science degree in chemistry from the Georgia Institute of Technology and later earned his Doctorate in biochemistry from the University of California at Berkeley. Dr. Mullis received a Nobel Prize in chemistry for his invention of the PCR. His many other awards include California Scientist of the Year Award, the National Biotechnology Award, and the William Allan Memorial Award of the American Society of Human Genetics. Dr. Mullis has an honorary Doctorate from the University of South Carolina and was inducted into the National Inventors Hall of Fame. Dr. Mullis holds numerous patents and has published a large number of articles in scholarly journals, and has even written his autobiography, *Dancing Naked in the Mind Field* (Pantheon Books). He is currently a distinguished researcher at Children's Hospital and Research Institute.

Scientific Equipment Sales Representative

Job growth for scientific sales representatives is expected to be about as fast as the average (10 to 15 percent) for all occupations over the next decade.

Wondering what employers look for in a scientific equipment sales representative? Here's a sample scientific sales representative description:

> We are a dynamic and industry-recognized laboratory equipment distributor for the life science industry that is currently seeking an outgoing self-starter for our Metro NYC sales territory. If you have the science background and love the sales environment, then this truly is an opportunity that you cannot pass up. Candidates must possess a BA/BS in biology, chemistry, or related field; a passion for winning; excellent written, oral, and presentation communication skills; ability to set a personal schedule with minimal input from management; and ability to travel extensively throughout the designated region.

A Day in the Life ... of a Scientific Equipment Sales Rep

6:00 A.M.	Early starts are critical in this business, so I am up at 6:00 and on the road by 7:00.
7:00 A.M.	Hit the road to make my first morning appointments. I like to catch doctors and administrators as early in the day as possible.
9:30 A.M.	After completing my morning appointments, this time is best spent updating my notes and placing orders on my laptop, as well as returning phone calls. Did I mention that my car is my office?
11:00 A.M.	Time to squeeze in a few unscheduled calls before lunch—sometimes I get lucky and walk right in, other times I can schedule a future appointment.
12:00 P.M.	Food and meals are important in this business, and today I am doing a lunch meeting and presentation with the executive board of a local physician group. Feed them and sell them ... that's my mantra.
2:30 P.M.	Back on the road to conduct some scheduled sales calls, but I have mapped my route to also make a few quick stops along the way to drop off some (food) goodies and win over the staff while trying to get some future appointments.
5:00 P.M.	With my sales calls done for the day, it's now time for more updating of notes, placing orders, and responding to e-mails. I also need to download some product specifications of new equipment we are rolling out later in the year. In this job, you need to be an expert on the equipment you sell as well as a great salesperson. You also need to be an expert on the competition.
6:00 P.M.	Sometimes I have dinner meetings and presentations—you have to adjust to your clients' schedules, but on this day, I am done with my work, so I begin the journey home.

The Professor Says

There are many career possibilities for chemistry and biochemistry majors beyond the ones featured here. Remember that it is always important to learn more about prospective careers by going online, talking with professors, conducting informational interviews, and job-shadowing.

Earnings Potential $

Graduates with a Bachelor's degree in chemistry or biochemistry earn a starting salary of about $40,000—more than the average annual salary for all college graduates, which is currently around $38,000—however, salaries vary widely.

The following provides some general guidelines of salaries to expect upon graduation. Remember, salaries vary by employer, industry, and region.

Bench Chemist. Beginning annual salaries for new graduates range from $33,000 to $37,000.

> **The Professor Says**
>
> Remember that you're not done once you pick your college major—in fact, it's just begun, because the next thing you need to do is gain work experience. Just about all "entry-level" jobs for college graduates require some work experience outside the classroom. Seek out internships, volunteer, and figure out other ways to gain the experience you need.

Food Scientist/Technologist. Median salary for an entry-level food scientist is $48,000.

Forensic Chemist. Beginning annual salaries for entry-level forensic chemists are in the range of $35,000 to $40,000.

Patent Examiner. Median salary for an entry-level patent examiner is $40,000.

Pharmaceutical Chemist. The median annual salary of an entry-level pharmaceutical chemist is $40,000.

Scientific Equipment Sales Representative. Beginning salaries for scientific sales representatives vary widely since total compensation is based on commission and salary, though most first-year sales-people make between $70,000 and $100,000.

The Least You Need to Know

◆ If you have a general passion for science, a chemistry career ought to be perfect for you.

◆ If you have an interest in pharmaceutical research or forensics, a biochemistry major is the right one for you.

◆ The outlook for careers for chemistry and biochemistry majors is good, with certain career paths expected to grow faster than others.

◆ The salaries for newly graduated chemistry and biochemistry majors are generally better than the average for all college grads.

18

Engineering

In This Chapter

- ◆ Discover careers that use your problem-solving skills
- ◆ Find careers within engineering that are right for you
- ◆ Learn about the many different types of engineering majors
- ◆ Find out what kind of jobs and salaries to expect

Do you spend your time thinking about how things work? About how to improve planes, buildings, spaceships, motors, or other machines and devices? As a child, did you enjoy building stuff? Are you fascinated by how bridges, skyscrapers, airplanes, and the like are designed and built?

This chapter reveals rewarding careers for students majoring in some aspect of engineering.

About the Major

Engineering is a combination of applied math and science, where you develop solutions to technical problems. Engineers invent, design, create, construct, test, and improve things from cars to buildings to airplanes to medical equipment. It's one of the most difficult majors, but also one of the few that are always in high demand by employers.

As you begin to look at majors, you'll find that in many schools, they offer majors in only a few of the many fields of engineering. The most common majors you'll find are likely to be civil, electrical, and mechanical. Also included in this chapter are aerospace, biomedical, chemical, environmental, and industrial.

Aerospace Engineering

Aerospace engineering majors learn to use math and engineering to design and develop better and stronger high-speed transportation vehicles, such as aircraft, missiles, and space-related vehicles.

Typical courses you might find in an aerospace engineering major include:

Air and Space Vehicles

Introduction to System Engineering

Compressible Aerodynamics

Incompressible Aerodynamics

Orbital and Space Flight Mechanics

Atmospheric Flight Mechanics

Aerospace Instrumentation

Propulsion

Gas Dynamics

Fluid Mechanics

Introduction to Aerospace Plasmas

Computer Tools for Aerospace

Aircraft Design—Basics

Aircraft Design—Advanced

Aerospace Heat Transfer

Spacecraft and Space Systems Design I

Spacecraft and Space System Design II

Finite Element Structural Analysis

Composite Materials for Aerospace Structures

Flight Test Engineering

The Professor Says _____

If you're still in high school, one of the best ways to prepare for an engineering major in college is to take as many math courses, especially IB and AP courses, as you possibly can.

Biomedical Engineering

Biomedical engineering majors integrate engineering with fundamentals of biology, chemistry, and medicine to prepare graduates to work with physicians to monitor, restore, and improve the functions of the human body.

Typical courses you might find in a biomedical engineering major include:

Biomedical Engineering Principles

Electrical Circuits in Biomedical Engineering

Biomedical Fluid Mechanics and Energy Transport

Biomedical Control Systems

Biomedical Instrumentation Systems

Introduction to Clinical Engineering

Biomedical Instrumentation and Biosensors

Biomedical Engineering Design

Biomedical Signal Analysis

Bioheat and Mass Transfer

Biostatistics

Biomaterials

Biomechanics

Advanced Biomedical Instrumentation Systems

Biomedical Imaging

Biological Systems

Cell and Tissue Mechanics

Biofluids

Tissue Engineering

Neural Engineering

The Professor Says

If you're a woman interested in engineering, many colleges are clamoring for your application. Women received only 18 percent of the 78,200 engineering degrees given out in 2003–2004, per the latest data available from the U.S. Department of Education. That's the same percentage as in 1998. A study by the University of Michigan's Institute for Research on Women and Gender found that females choose other careers because they don't see engineering as a way to help others, yet engineering is all about solving problems and finding solutions.

Chemical Engineering

Chemical engineering majors learn both chemistry and engineering so they can solve problems and find more efficient methods for accomplishing chemical processing and manufacturing processes.

Typical courses you might find in a chemical engineering major include:

Molecular Modeling in Engineering and Science

Introduction to Fuel Cells

Introduction to Chemical Engineering

Chemical Engineering Fundamentals

Elementary Chemical Processes

Applied Chemical Engineering Thermodynamics

Advanced Chemical Processes

Kinetics and Reactor Design

Introduction to Biological Engineering

Applied Mathematics in Chemical Engineering

Chemical Materials Engineering

Chemical and Environmental Technology

Air Quality Management

Chemical Engineering Design

Chemical Process Dynamics and Control Laboratory

Chemical Plant Design Project

Mathematics Analysis in Chemical Engineering

Kinetics and Catalysis

Chemical Reactor Design

Catalysis and Surface Science of Materials

Fluid Mechanics

Civil Engineering

Civil engineering majors combine math, physics, and geology with engineering to design and supervise the construction of infrastructure, such as roads, buildings, tunnels, airports, dams, bridges, and water supply and sewage systems.

Typical courses you might find in a civil engineering major include:

Probabilistic and Statistical Methods in Civil Engineering

Methods of Civil Engineering

Engineering Geology

Civil Engineering Materials

Introduction to Structural Engineering

Computational Methods in Civil Engineering

Geotechnical Engineering

Structural Analysis

Air Pollution Engineering

Environmental Engineering

Transportation Engineering

Wastewater System Design

Groundwater Hydrology

Legal, Ethical, and Business Relations in Engineering

Introduction to Water Chemistry and Treatment

Advanced Mechanics of Solids

Finite Elements in Structural Mechanics

Structural Systems

Structural Steel Design

Construction Management

Reinforced Concrete Design

Electrical Engineering

Electrical engineering majors combine courses in technology with engineering to design and develop everything related to electrical devices and systems and the use of electricity, including power plants, computer and Internet equipment and systems, and electrical networks for buildings.

Typical courses you might find in an electrical engineering major include:

Programming Concepts for Engineers

Semiconductor Devices and Analog Electronics

Fundamental Electric and Digital Circuit Laboratory

Numerical Techniques in Engineering

Electromagnetic Wave Propagation

Microelectronics Design Laboratory

Basic Circuit Theory

Digital Logic Design

Digital Electronics

Electronic Circuits Design

Signal and System Theory

Engineering Probability

Computer Organization

Power Electronics

Environmental Engineering

Environmental engineering majors combine studies in biology and chemistry with engineering to develop solutions to environmental problems.

Typical courses you might find in an environmental engineering major include:

Principles of Environmental Engineering

Introduction to Mechanics of Materials

Construction Engineering

Surveying Engineering

Transportation Engineering

Fluid Mechanics

Hydraulic Engineering

Environmental Engineering— Water and Air Quality

Constructional Materials

Basic Soil Mechanics

Elementary Structures

Environmental Engineering Systems

Graphics Communication and Computer-Aided Design

Basic Environmental Engineering Computing

Infrastructure Construction

Construction Planning and Scheduling

Traffic Engineering Fundamentals

Foundation Design

Industrial Engineering

Industrial engineering majors combine studies in business and psychology with engineering to examine and evaluate methods of production and recommend ways to improve them.

Typical courses you might find in an industrial engineering major include:

Introduction to Industrial Engineering

Introduction to Production Systems

Economic Analysis of Engineering Projects

Statistical Control of Quality

Production Systems Planning

Production Systems Operations

Project Management for Engineers

Engineering Management Techniques

Total Quality Engineering

Facilities Location, Layout, and Material Handling

Design and Analysis of Industrial Systems with Simulation

Human Factors and Ergonomics

Principles of Programmable Automation

Manufacturing Systems Design

 Major Pitfalls

If you are considering a major in engineering, you must have a strong aptitude for math and science; otherwise, you will not succeed in this major.

Mechanical Engineering

Mechanical engineering majors learn the techniques to both study the behavior of materials when under distress and design elements to survive the distress, as well as develop and produce the tools used by other engineers.

Typical courses you might find in a mechanical engineering major include:

Foundations of Mechanical Systems

Foundations of Thermal and Fluid Sciences

Computer Analysis in Engineering

Materials for Mechanical Engineering Applications

Thermodynamics and Heat Transfer

Modeling and Analysis of Dynamic Systems

Fundamentals of Machine Design

Mechanical Engineering Design

Manufacturing Processes and Their Application

Kinematics and Dynamics of Machinery

Control of Mechanical Systems

Mechatronics System Design

Finite Element Analysis in Mechanical Engineering Design

Energy Sources and Their Utilization

Mechanics of Composite Materials

Design for Manufacturing

Fundamentals of Robotics

Computer-Aided Engineering Analysis and Design

Principles of Structural Stability

Fracture Mechanics

Advanced Engineering Design

Materials Selection in
Engineering Design

Background on Careers

Most engineers specialize in a certain field of engineering, usually combining their passion for engineering with some other field(s). While at least 25 engineering specialties exist (and are listed in the detailed career section), this chapter focuses on the eight most common engineering career fields.

Aerospace Engineer. As an aerospace engineer, you'll design and develop machines that fly in the earth's atmosphere and beyond, and tend to work in the aviation, defense systems, and space-exploration industries. Some aerospace engineers specialize in certain elements (such as aerodynamics, thermodynamics, or propulsion) while other specialize by project (jets, missiles, helicopters). You may work in an office or lab, but also may work in the field testing and exploring system failures.

Biomedical Engineer. In this job, you'll often work with a team of health-care professionals to design, develop, and test new materials, devices, and equipment that solve medical and health-related problems, including artificial organs, prostheses, instrumentation, medical information systems, and medical imaging systems. You may also design or modify equipment for clients with special needs in a rehabilitation setting or manage the use of clinical equipment in hospitals and the community.

Chemical Engineer. As a chemical engineer, you'll solve problems and find more efficient ways of doing things, taking ideas from chemists and putting them into practice—converting scientific discoveries into marketable products. You may develop and design processes for manufacturing new chemicals and chemical solutions, from fertilizers to new drugs. Frequently, engineers specialize in one area, such as food, pharmaceuticals, heat transfer and energy conversion, petrochemicals (chemicals made from petroleum or natural gas), or consumer products.

Civil Engineer. As a civil engineer, you'll design and supervise the creation of structures—buildings, tunnels, airports, pipelines, subdivisions, water systems, and more—to meet the needs of a growing population. Many civil engineers work in a specific field, such as construction, land development, structural or hydraulic design, soil mechanics, waste water treatment, or solid waste management. Some civil engineers also work with specialists on general problems such as soil or ground water contamination or energy development and conservation.

Electrical Engineer. As an electrical engineer, you'll design and develop all kinds of electronic equipment—power generators, motors, lighting systems, and more. Typically electrical engineers specialize in power systems engineering—managing issues associated with large-scale electrical systems such as power transmission and motor control—or in electrical equipment manufacturing by dealing with developing small-scale electronic systems, including computers and integrated circuits.

Environmental Engineer. As an environmental engineer, you'll analyze water and air pollution control, recycling, waste disposal, and public health issues. You'll study the impact of proposed construction projects, advise on the treatment and containment of hazardous waste, design wastewater treatment systems, and work to minimize the effects of acid rain, global warming, auto emissions, and ozone depletion on both local and global levels.

Industrial Engineer. In this job, you'll analyze and evaluate production methods and suggest strategies to improve the process and increase productivity by determining the most effective and efficient ways to use the basic factors of production—people, machines, materials, information, and energy. Some industrial engineers specialize in such areas as assembly, raw-materials processing, and administrative practices. Often working closely with management to make improvements, some industrial engineers actually move out of engineering into management.

Mechanical Engineer. As a mechanical engineer, you'll research, design, and create a wide variety of mechanical devices that meet the specific requirements for a particular job or process—including tools, engines, and machines. Mechanical engineering is one of the broadest engineering disciplines, and thus many mechanical engineers also design tools for use by other engineers. Mechanical engineers search for new engineering solutions, look to develop new or existing products and processes, and work to develop more efficient production processes.

Other Career Possibilities. Some other job and career paths for engineering majors include:

Architectural Engineer	Petroleum Engineer
Automotive Engineer	Production Engineer
Health and Safety Engineer	Structural Engineer
Marine Engineer	Systems Analyst
Materials Engineer	Urban Planning Engineer
Nuclear Engineer	

Skills Needed/Developed

Students majoring in engineering develop numerous valuable and transferable skills, but those included here are the most critical to graduates.

Active Listening. Because engineers are the problem-solvers, before they can find a solution to the problem, they need to get full and detailed information describing the problem.

The Professor Says

Other transferable skills gained from these majors include:

◆ Communications (verbal and written)

◆ Gathering information

◆ Spatial relations

◆ Teamwork

◆ Technical/computer

Complex Problem-Solving. Perhaps one of the most important skills for engineers, problem-solving involves your ability to identify complex problems, review existing conditions and restrictions, and develop and evaluate alternative solutions to the problem.

Critical Thinking. This skill involves your ability to use logic and reasoning and apply them to complex situations to better understand the situation and underlying issues.

Quantitative Analysis. Because all the fields of engineering use mathematical formulas and equations, you must have strong quantitative skills and abilities.

Expected Growth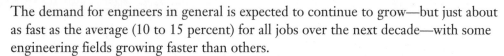

The demand for engineers in general is expected to continue to grow—but just about as fast as the average (10 to 15 percent) for all jobs over the next decade—with some engineering fields growing faster than others.

Sources of additional information:

◆ American Association of Engineering Societies (www.aaes.org)

◆ American Engineering Association (www.aea.org)

◆ American Institute of Engineers (www.members-aie.org)

◆ National Society of Black Engineers (national.nsbe.org)

◆ National Society of Professional Engineers (www.nspe.org)

◆ Society of Women Engineers (www.swe.org)

Aerospace Engineers

Job growth for aerospace engineers, while favorable, is expected to be slower than the average (under 8 percent) for all careers over the next decade.

A source of additional information is the American Institute of Aeronautics & Astronauts (www.aiaa.org).

Wondering what employers look for in an aeronautics engineer? Here's a sample aeronautics engineer job description:

> We are searching for an entry-level thermal engineer to work on a number of innovative spaceflight missions and projects. The successful candidate will work under the direction of the technical project manager to provide engineering expertise, skills, and technical knowledge for the design and development activities supporting thermal control system design, thermal analysis, analytical thermal model development, fabrication, assembly, integration, and test verification. You will perform thermal design, analysis, and verification tests to evaluate alternative thermal designs and to predict/verify the detailed temperature distributions; and support the development, fabrication, and test of various thermal designs. Qualifications include a Bachelor of Science degree in aeronautical engineering or a related field. A minimum of 1–4 years of experience in the thermal design and analysis of spaceflight subsystems is preferred.

Biomedical Engineers

Job growth for biomedical engineers is expected to be much faster than average (18 to 25 percent) over the next decade.

Sources of additional information:

◆ American Society for Healthcare Engineering (www.ashe.org)

◆ Biomedical Engineering Society (www.bmes.org)

Wondering what employers look for in a biomedical engineer? Here's a sample biomedical engineer job description:

> Develop and administer Biomedical Engineering Technology Management Systems (BETMS) and related systems applying knowledge of engineering biology and biomechanical principles. Develop database access methods, organization, security, documentation, and statistical methods. Integrate and enhance coordination of systems and processes. Plan for support of new technology and

accounts, manage assigned projects, provide technical support, and oversee quality assurance. Requires a Bachelor's degree in biomedical or clinical engineering. You must also possess basic statistical knowledge and the ability to interact and effectively communicate both written and orally with a wide variety of people. Computer literacy and working knowledge of statistical software preferred. Some previous experience, including experience in a hospital environment, is preferred.

Chemical Engineers

Demand for chemical engineers should remain strong over the next decade, with job growth expected to be about as fast as the average (10 to 15 percent) for all careers over the next decade. A source of additional information is the American Institute of Chemical Engineers (www.aiche.org).

Civil Engineers

Job growth for civil engineers is expected to be about as fast as the average (10 to 15 percent) for all careers over the next decade.

Sources of additional information:

◆ American Society of Civil Engineers (www.asce.org)

◆ Chartered Institution of Building Services Engineers (www.cibse.org)

Wondering what employers look for in a civil engineer? Here's a sample civil engineer job description:

National engineering consulting firm is looking for an entry-level civil engineer. Working under supervision of senior engineers, you will prepare construction documents and drawings for a wide variety of civil engineering projects in our Airports Group. Successful candidates will have 0–5 years experience working on civil design projects. *Ideal* candidates will have design experience in transportation, airports, and/or survey/site development. Engineer-In-Training certification is required (or are currently signed up for the next exam). Must have strong verbal and written communication skills and proficiency with AutoCAD. Must be able to work well both individually and as part of a team. We are a progressive engineering firm that hires on skills and looks for the right personality fit.

Electrical Engineers

Employment for electrical engineers is growing about as fast as the average (10 to 15 percent) for all jobs over the next decade. A source of additional information is the Institute of Electrical and Electronics Engineers (www.ieee.org).

Supercomputer Creator Seymour Cray

Seymour Cray created the CRAY-1 in 1976, considered the first supercomputer. His father was a civil engineer who spurred Cray's interest in science. When he was a child, his parents let him use the basement of their house as a laboratory for his studies and research, where among other things, he designed a device that would generate Morse code signals based on punched tape that was passed through it. He earned a Bachelor of Science degree in electrical engineering at the University of Minnesota and found a job at Engineering Research Associates. In his spare time he earned a Master's degree in applied mathematics. He later joined Control Data Corp. He left CDC to start his own company, CRAY Research, and shortly before his death, yet another company, SRC Computers.

Environmental Engineers

Job growth for environmental engineers is expected to be faster than the average (18 to 25 percent) for all jobs over the next decade. A source of additional information is the American Academy of Environmental Engineers (www.aaee.net).

Wondering what employers look for in an entry-level environmental engineer? Here's a sample environmental engineer job description:

> An environmental and engineering consulting firm is looking to add an environmental engineer to its staff. This is a worldwide firm and this is an excellent opportunity to get your foot in the door. We are looking for a lightly experienced environmental engineer with 0–2 years experience. This employee will study and perform remediation services, which involve working in the office and in the field. The field work will involve studies and remediation work. The office time will be spent doing data analysis validation and evaluation report preparation and design work. The design work will be basic engineering calculations following standard methods and principles using engineering analysis. Other work will include maintaining engineering records and preparing basic sketches for drafting and incorporation in final design plans. Candidate will also perform

studies and analysis on specific portions of a project that includes research, investigation, and coordination. Bachelor of Science degree in civil or environmental engineering is required.

Industrial Engineers

Employment of industrial engineers projects is expected to increase about as fast as average (10 to 15 percent) for all careers over the next decade. A source of additional information is the Institute of Industrial Engineers (www.iienet2.org).

Wondering what employers look for in an entry-level industrial engineer? Here's a sample industrial engineer job description:

> We are a global food industry manufacturing company that is actively searching for an entry-level industrial engineer to assist our facilities transition to Lean Manufacturing. This person will design lean layouts for new facilities and be responsible for in-depth studies and business analysis for existing processes and new processes and products. Will work with various factory locations and corporate functions to implement cost-saving plans. Candidates need teamwork, project management, and good interpersonal skills. Any AutoCAD experience is a plus. Minimum required is a Bachelor of Science degree in industrial engineering or equivalent. Understanding and comprehension of the core principles of industrial engineering and their applications for Lean Manufacturing and fluency in a second language is a plus. Travel will be about 25 percent of job. Entry position offers a fast progression in the Engineering Technology Department.

Mechanical Engineers

Job growth for mechanical engineers is expected to be about the same as the average (10 to 15 percent) for all jobs over the next decade.

Sources of additional information:

◆ American Society of Mechanical Engineers (www.asme.org)

◆ International Association of Mechanical Engineers (www.iasme.org)

Engineer and Astronaut Dr. Bonnie Dunbar

Dr. Bonnie Dunbar, a veteran of five Space Shuttle flights, is president and CEO of the Museum of Flight, Seattle, Washington, one of the largest air and space museums in the world. She earned a Bachelor of Science degree in ceramic engineering from the University of Washington and went on to work as a systems analyst for Boeing Computer Services. She then went back to college to earn her Master's in ceramic engineering, also from the University of Washington. She then accepted a senior research engineer position with Rockwell International Space Division, where she was involved in research that included developing equipment and processes for the manufacture of Space Shuttle's thermal protection system—a system that would later protect her (and her crewmates) on her Shuttle missions. She later earned a Doctorate in mechanical/biomedical engineering from the University of Houston and worked at NASA for more than 25 years, serving as a mission specialist astronaut for a majority of that time. Dr. Dunbar has been honored by numerous professional societies and universities, as well as by NASA, and has been inducted in the Women in Technology International Hall of Fame.

Earnings Potential $

Graduates with a Bachelor's degree in one of these engineering majors earn a starting salary of about $51,000—much more than the average annual salary for all college graduates, which is currently around $38,000—however, salaries vary widely.

The following provides some general guidelines of salaries to expect upon graduation. Remember, salaries vary by employer, industry, and region.

Aerospace Engineer. Beginning annual salaries for new graduates average about $51,400.

Biomedical Engineer. Median annual earnings of an entry-level biomedical engineer are about $49,500.

Chemical Engineer. Beginning annual salary for an entry-level chemical engineer is about $56,300.

The Professor Says

Your next step? Pick the couple of careers that most fit your interests with a major in engineering and dig more deeply into them. Remember that it is always important to learn more about prospective careers by going online, talking with professors, conducting informational interviews, and job-shadowing.

The Professor Says _____

Your next step after choosing your major? Gaining work experience. Just about all "entry-level" jobs for college graduates require some work experience outside the classroom. Seek out internships, volunteer, and figure out other ways to gain the experience you need.

Civil Engineer. The median annual salary of an entry-level civil engineer is about $46,000.

Electrical Engineer. Beginning annual salaries for electrical engineers are about $53,300.

Environmental Engineer. The median annual salary of an entry-level environmental engineer is $47,400.

Industrial Engineer. The median starting salary for an industrial engineer is $51,500.

Mechanical Engineer. Beginning annual salaries for mechanical engineers are $51,800.

The Least You Need to Know

◆ Numerous (and mostly growing) career options are available for people with a passion for engineering.

◆ So many different fields of engineering exist that no matter what your other interests are, you can likely combine them with your interest in engineering to create a rewarding career.

◆ If you enjoy solving complex technical problems and developing innovative solutions to those problems, an engineering major may be perfect for you.

◆ Engineering grads are traditionally some of the highest-paid of all undergraduate majors.

Chapter 19

Geosciences: Geography, Geology, and Geophysics

In This Chapter

- ◆ Discover careers that use your passion for the planets

- ◆ Use your interest in the forces of nature in a career

- ◆ Learn the classes a major in one of the geosciences requires

- ◆ Find out what kinds of jobs and salaries to expect

Do you spend your time thinking about our planet, its historical development, and the people who inhabit it? Are you in awe of the power of natural forces in our lives? Do you spend way too much time watching weather patterns? Do you dream of discovering the next big oil reserve?

This chapter reveals rewarding careers for students who major in some aspect of geoscience—including geography, geology, and geophysics.

About the Majors

The geosciences deal with the investigation and development of scientific understanding about this and other planets. The major embraces an enormous range of topics, including the evolution of life, the nature of planetary interiors, the causes of earthquakes and volcanic eruptions, environmental impacts, earth-surface processes, effects and patterns of weather, and the origin and behavior of oceans and atmosphere.

As you begin to look at majors, you'll find that in many schools, they have combined two or more of these studies together, such as geology and geophysics, or geography and geology. We'll separate them in this chapter so you have a complete understanding of each discipline.

Geography

Geography is all about the study of the relationships between the earth's landscapes, people, places, and environments. The study of geography helps with understanding the world we live in, dealing with issues from climate change to world trade. In human geography, you study the dynamics of cultures, societies, and economies, while in physical geography, you seek a deeper understanding of physical landscapes and environmental processes.

Geography is a fairly common major at larger universities. Typical courses include:

Introduction to Geography

Resources and People

Global Physical Environments

World Regions

Map Reading and Interpretation

Climatology

Soil: Ecosystem and Resource

Soils of the World

History of Cartography

Biogeography

Elementary Photogrammetry

Geomorphology

Modern Urban America

Population, Migration, and Diffusion

Geography of Social Organization

Geography, Politics, and Territoriality

Settlement Patterns and Processes

Physical Systems of the Environment

Atmospheric Environment and Society

Spatial Organization of Human Activity

Economic Geography: Locational Behavior

Analysis of the Physical Environment

Landforms and Landscapes of North America

The Human Role in Changing the Face of the Earth

Geology

Geology is the study of the earth, its history, and how the earth's materials, structures, processes, and organisms have changed over time—thus increasing our knowledge about natural resources, allowing us to better understand Earth's history and help foresee how events and processes of the past might influence the future.

Geology is a fairly specialized major (often combined with another of the earth sciences), so you will need to seek out universities with this major. Typical courses include:

Introductory Geology

Lithology

Air Photo Interpretation

Geochemistry

Forensic Geology

Geomorphology

Structural Geology

Tectonics

Stratigraphy and Sedimentation

Field Geology

Sedimentary Petrology

Subsurface Geology

Lunar and Planetary Geology

Hydrology

Crystal and Optical Mineralogy

Introduction to Environmental Geology

Dinosaurs, Earthquakes, and Volcanoes

Geophysics

Geophysics provides students with a solid background in the essentials of math, physics, and geology. The major brings together the traditional sciences of physics and geology to prepare students for various geoscience careers.

Geophysics is a fairly specialized major (often combined with geology), so you will need to seek out universities with this major. Typical courses include:

GIS in Science

Principles of Geophysics

Computational Geosciences

Petroleum Geophysics

Advanced Field Geophysics

Seismic Exploration

Geoscience Technology

Paleomagnetism

Solid Earth Geophysics

Tectonophysics

Seismic Modeling

Geomechanics

Environmental and Geotechnical Geophysics

Rock Physics for Seismic Applications

Introduction to Seismic Processing

Introduction to Seismic Stratigraphy

Background on Careers

Geoscientists are the historians and researchers of the earth—both its surface and its deeper elements. As a geoscientist, you'll play an essential role in gathering information for understanding the earth and the impact societies have on its future. You'll help in establishing governmental policies for resource management, environmental protection, and public welfare.

Geography graduates have the most career options, after having learned the practical use of computers for such tasks as the interpretation of images of the earth from space, drawing of maps and diagrams (including global positioning systems—GPS), and analysis of economic data. Other job-related skills you'll learn include environmental planning and conducting studies of the impact of major construction works, such as power stations, on surrounding communities.

Geology graduates may work in the field, explore the earth for new mineral or oil reserves, study the history of the earth, work on solving critical environmental issues and problems, conduct research on a variety of topics related to the earth, or teach secondary school science.

Geophysics graduates tend to go into resources exploration or global analysis. In resources exploration, you'll apply geophysical theories and data to the search for resources such as oil, gas, minerals, and water. In global analysis, you may find yourself studying earthquakes (seismology), thermal dynamics of the planet's inner layers, magnetic fields, or other phenomena.

Some top jobs and careers for students earning a Bachelor's degree with a major in one of the geosciences include:

Aerial Photo Interpreter/ Photogrammetric Technician. In this job, you'll apply photogrammetric principles and procedures to the production of large-scale topographical maps for use in highway or similar engineering and design projects. In order to develop these maps, you'll select mapping control point locations, obtain geodetic field data, record field data, and operate computer-aided plotting instruments and CADD work stations.

Major Pitfalls

As in many of the sciences, some graduates continue their studies in graduate school rather than working after earning their Bachelor's degree, as there tend to be more lucrative jobs available for those with a graduate degree.

Assayer. In this job, you'll typically work in a laboratory analyzing geologic materials, milling products, and waste by-products, testing these materials using spectrographic analysis, chemical solutions, and various laboratory equipment. You'll evaluate the results to determine the nature, value, quality, and quantity of the ore and its component metals and minerals. Assayers may specialize in the testing and analyzing of specific minerals or metals.

Geologist. As a geologist, you'll study the materials, processes, products, physical nature, and history of the earth. You may study rock cores, cuttings, and samples; examine fossilized life forms and date rock strata; explore specific areas of the earth; undertake ground magnetic and gravity surveys; prepare geological models to describe processes and predict future situations; and create geological reports and maps.

Geophysical Technician. In this job, you'll apply the principles of physics to studies of the earth's interior and investigate such things as the earth's magnetic, electric, and gravitational fields. As a geophysical technician, you may develop mathematical models as an aid to interpreting geophysical survey results; design instrumentation for taking physical measurements; study earthquakes and earthquake risk, time variations, and the distribution of the earth's magnetic and gravity fields; and design, develop, and operate computer systems and software for processing and interpreting geophysical data sets.

Hydrologist. As a hydrologist, you'll study the occurrence, movement, abundance, distribution, and quality of underground and surface waters (including oceans, seas, rivers, lakes, estuaries, and the water in channels and pipes) and related geological aspects of subsurface waters. In this job, you may select, install, maintain, and repair instruments that monitor water levels, rainfall, and sediments; design, construct, install, and maintain civil works associated with water-related projects and activities; and compile navigational charts and other data for the safe navigation of waters.

Mineralogist. In this job, you'll study mineral formation, composition, and properties—everywhere from the surface of the earth to its core—by isolating specimens from ore, rocks, or matrices and making microscopic examinations to determine shape, surface markings, and other physical characteristics. You'll also perform physical and chemical tests and make x-ray examinations to determine the composition of specimen and the type of crystalline structure, identify and classify all samples, and develop theories on mode of origin, occurrence, and possible uses of minerals.

Meteorologist/Climatologist. In this job, you'll study the atmosphere and atmospheric phenomena, including the weather, to improve the understanding of climate. As a meteorologist, you may use and develop scientific techniques to forecast and interpret climatic conditions; prepare weather forecasts for the public and for specific users; work with physicists and engineers to develop observation equipment and distribute information on climate-related issues and conditions; and study climate and identify climatic change.

Other Career Possibilities. Some other job and career paths for geography, geology, and geophysics majors include:

Air/Water Quality Control Specialist

Computer Mapper

Ecologist

Environmental Impact Analyst

Geomagnetist

Hazardous Waste Planner

Heavy Oil Geologist

Land-Use Analyst

Map Librarian/Curator

Marine Geologist

Petroleum Technician

Seismologist

Soil Analyst

Volcanologist

Skills Needed/Developed

Students majoring in some area of the geosciences develop numerous valuable and transferable skills. The following are the most critical to graduates:

Problem-Solving. One of the most important skills for geoscientists, problem-solving is your ability to identify complex problems, review existing conditions and restrictions, and develop and evaluate alternative solutions to the problem.

Scientific Method. All science majors must possess an understanding of the scientific method, which involves the formulation of a hypothesis concerning some phenomena, experimentation to demonstrate the truth or fallacy of the hypothesis, and a conclusion that validates or modifies the hypothesis.

Quantitative Analysis. All of the geosciences involve working with numbers and math, so you'll develop key math and computational skills.

Communications (in writing and verbally). You'll perfect the ability to summarize, report, and present the results of your scientific research in a clear and understandable manner.

Technical/Computer Skills. Many jobs in the earth sciences require the use of computers and specific software applications, so you'll acquire key technical and computer skills.

The Professor Says

Other transferable skills you gain from these majors include:

◆ Research and planning

◆ Recordkeeping/ handling details

◆ Gathering information

◆ Operations analysis

◆ Teamwork

◆ Observation

Expected Growth

The demand for geoscientists in general is expected to continue to grow—but just about as fast as the average (10 to 15 percent) for all jobs over the next decade—as dwindling energy, mineral, and water resources, along with increasing concerns about the environment and stricter public policy, present new challenges and increase the number of people in these occupations.

Sources of additional information:

◆ American Geophysical Union (www.agu.org)

◆ Association for Women Geoscientists (www.awg.org)

◆ Earth Science World—Gateway to the Geosciences (www.earthscienceworld.org)

Aerial Photo Interpreters/Photogrammetric Technicians

Job growth for photogrammetric professionals is expected to be about as fast as the average (10 to 15 percent) for all careers over the next decade as new mapping technology drives the industry.

Sources of additional information:

◆ American Society for Photogrammetry & Remote Sensing (www.asprs.org)

◆ Management Association for Private Photogrammetric Surveyors (www.mapps. org)

Wondering what employers look for in a photogrammetric technician? Here's a sample photogrammetric technician job description:

> We're a national, geospatial services industry leader seeking photogrammetric technicians to be part of our highly successful photogrammetry team. The chosen candidates will have the chance to work for one of the top mapping companies in the United States and work with the latest remote-sensing technology. Positions require a Bachelor's degree in geography, GIS, engineering, or related field. Previous GIS and photogrammetry experience a plus. Successful candidates will have the opportunity to train in a variety of skill set areas, including photogrammetric tasks utilizing aerial film, digital imaging, and LiDAR sensors.

Assayers

Job growth for assayers is expected to be slower than average (under 8 percent) as declines in mining employment reduce the number of jobs.

Additional information can be found at The Society of Mineral Analysts (www.sma-online.org).

Geologists

Demand for geologists should remain strong over the next decade, with job growth expected to be about as fast as the average (10 to 15 percent) for all careers over the next decade.

Sources of additional information:

◆ American Association of Petroleum Geologists (www.aapg.org)

◆ American Geological Institute (www.agiweb.org)

- American Institute of Professional Geologists (www.aipg.org)

- Association of Environmental & Engineering Geologists (www.aegweb.org)

- Geological Society of America (www.geosociety.org)

- Society for Sedimentary Geology (www.sepm.org)

profiles

Geologist Michel Halbouty

Michel Halbouty is a legend in the geology, geophysics, and petroleum engineering professions and serves as chairman of the board and chief executive officer of the Michel T. Halbouty Energy Company. He has been instrumental in the discovery of many oil and gas fields throughout the world and was the first independent "wildcatter" to make an oil discovery in Alaska. He is the author of more than 300 articles on geology and petroleum engineering, several books on petroleum, and numerous contributions in encyclopedias and is unique among his peers in having been awarded the highest honors of both the American Association of Petroleum Geologists and the American Institute of Mining, Metallurgical and Petroleum Engineers (AIME). Halbouty graduated with a Bachelor of Science degree in geology. He also has a Master's degree in both geology and petroleum engineering, as well as earning a Professional Geological Engineering degree. He is also the recipient of two honorary degrees, a Doctor of Engineering and a Doctor of Geoscience.

Geophysical Technicians

Job growth for geophysical technicians is expected to be about as fast as the average (10 to 15 percent) for all careers over the next decade.

Additional information can be found at the Society of Exploration Geophysicists (www.seg.org).

Hydrologists

Employment is expected to grow much faster than average (18 to 25 percent) for all jobs over the next decade, spurred by increased demand and potential shortages and the need for organizations to comply with complex environmental laws and regulations.

Sources of additional information:

- The American Institute of Hydrology (www.aihydro.org)

- American Water Resources Association (www.awra.org)

- International Association of Hydrologists (www.iah.org)

- International Association for Environmental Hydrology (www.hydroweb.com)

- National Groundwater Association (www.ngwa.org)

Mineralogists

Job growth for mineralogists is expected to increase slower than the average (under 8 percent) for all jobs over the next decade.

Sources of additional information:

- Mineralogical Society of America (www.minsocam.org)

- International Mineralogical Association (www.ima-mineralogy.org)

Meteorologists/Climatologists

Employment of atmospheric scientists (meteorologists and climatologists) projects to increase about as fast as average (10 to 15 percent) for all occupations over the next decade.

Sources of additional information:

- American Meteorological Society (www.ametsoc.org)

- International Association of Meteorology and Atmospheric Sciences (www.iamas. org)

- International Association for Urban Climate (www.urban-climate.org)

- National Council of Industrial Meteorologists (www.ncim.org)

- National Weather Association (www.nwas.org)

profiles

Meteorologist Susan Zevin

Dr. Susan Zevin manages the daily operations of the National Weather Service in her role as the deputy assistant administrator for operations. Prior to her current position, she served as Eastern Regional Director. She has also served as a senior hydrologist for the department of program plans and analysis at the National Weather Service headquarters. Dr. Zevin earned her Bachelor's degree in geography from the University of Pittsburgh, a Master's in geography from the University of Tel Aviv, and her Ph.D. in hydrology and water resources from the University of Arizona. She is a Fellow with the American Meteorological Society, and is a member of both the World Meteorological Organization's Commission on Hydrology and Commission for Basic Services.

Earnings Potential $

Graduates with a Bachelor's degree in one of these geoscience majors earn a starting salary of about $36,000—less than the average annual salary for all college graduates, which is currently around $38,000—however, salaries vary widely.

The following provides some general guidelines of salaries to expect upon graduation. Remember, salaries vary by employer, industry, and region.

Aerial Photo Interpreter/Photogrammetric Technician. Beginning annual salary for a new graduate ranges from $30,000 to $40,000.

Assayer. Median annual earnings of an entry-level assayer are about $32,000.

Geologist. Beginning annual salary for a geologist ranges from $50,000 to $60,000.

The Professor Says

Not sure about these career choices? These are just some of the career possibilities for a major in one of the geosciences. Remember that it is always important to learn more about prospective careers by going online, talking with professors, conducting informational interviews, and job-shadowing.

Geophysical Technician. The median annual salary of a geophysical technician is about $35,000.

Hydrologist. The median annual salary of an entry-level hydrologist is $36,000.

Mineralogist. The median annual salary of an entry-level mineralogist is $36,000.

Meteorologist/Climatologist. Median annual earnings of meteorologists and climatologists range from about $25,000 to $35,000, depending on the employer, with government jobs paying on the higher side.

The Professor Says

Remember that you're not done once you pick your college major—in fact, it's just begun, because the next thing you need to do is gain work experience. Just about all "entry-level" jobs for college graduates require some work experience outside the classroom. Seek out internships, volunteer, and figure out other ways to gain the experience you need.

The Least You Need to Know

◆ Numerous career options exist for people with a passion for gaining a deeper understanding of the physical nature and characteristics of our planet.

◆ Some geoscience careers lead to a better understanding of the earth's development, while others lead to the discovery of valuable resources.

◆ If you enjoy dirt, rocks, and being one with the earth, a geoscience major may be perfect for you.

◆ Some careers in the geosciences are growing faster than others over the next decade, but overall, jobs should be available when you graduate.

20

Physics and Astronomy

In This Chapter

◆ Find jobs using your understanding of time and space

◆ Use your analytical skills in careers that demand them

◆ Learn the classes that typical physics and astronomy majors require

◆ Find out what kinds of jobs and salaries to expect

What do you do if you love understanding how and why things work? If you enjoy discovering the fundamental laws that govern matter, energy, space, and time? Do you stare at the stars at night and think deep thoughts about faraway celestial bodies? Are you a weather geek?

This chapter reveals rewarding careers for students who major in physics or astronomy.

About the Majors

Physics studies the properties and laws of matter, motion, heat, light, and electricity to develop a quantitative understanding of the inorganic, physical world. As the basic science, the results of research in physics have also had an impact on a wide variety of other fields, such as medicine, engineering, chemistry, ecology, archaeology, and, of course, astronomy.

Physics

Physics majors study the fundamental laws of nature governing the inner workings of everything, from a bullet's speed to black holes, and learn to express these natural laws in mathematical language.

Physics is a reasonably common major at most colleges and universities. Typical courses include:

Introduction to Physics	Ethical Issues in Physics
Electricity and Magnetism	Vibration and Sound
Laboratory Techniques	Electrical Measurements
Optics	General Astronomy
Mechanics	Atomic and Nuclear Physics
Electronics	Fluid Dynamics
Mathematical Modeling	Atmospheric Thermodynamics
Modern Physics	Atmospheric Science
Heat and Thermodynamics	Physical Meteorology
Quantum Mechanics	Cloud Physics
Electromagnetic Theory	Kinetic Theory and Statistical Mechanics
Advanced Topics	

Astronomy

Astronomy majors study the planets, stars, galaxies, and the universe as a whole, including their origins and how they have evolved over time. The astronomy major is an observational, not an experimental science, in which celestial events are viewed and data collected, analyzed, and interpreted using the tools of theoretical physics.

Many colleges offer a course or two on astronomy, but as a major, astronomy is fairly specialized, so you will need to seek out universities with this major. Typical courses include:

Exploring the Universe	Stars and the Galaxies
The Solar System	History of Astronomy

Weather and Our Atmosphere

Planetary Science

Modern Astrophysics

Cosmology

Astronomical Techniques

The Milky Way Galaxy

Galactic and Extragalactic Astronomy

Techniques of Optical and Infrared Astronomy

Techniques of Radio Astronomy

Background on Careers

Physics and astronomy graduates are in demand because of the basic scientific skills these majors develop. And because these majors have a solid foundation of physics, they serve as grounding for becoming a teacher of the physical sciences at the primary or secondary levels.

All fields of engineering employ physics graduates for basic and applied research in physics, materials science, astronomy, optics, chemical physics, geophysics, biophysics, and meteorology. (If you have an interest in engineering, see Chapter 18.)

Astronomy graduates are often employed at observatories, planetariums, science museums, and in industry, where they contribute to research or education programs.

Some top jobs and careers for students earning a Bachelor's degree with a major in physics or astronomy include:

Astrophysical Research Specialist. In this job, you'll work as part of a team—most likely in an observatory or other scientific institution—that studies some aspect of the physical properties of celestial bodies. You'll apply physical laws and theories to astronomical objects and phenomena, especially stars and galaxies, with the aim of deriving theoretical models and simulations to explain their behavior.

Geophysics Operations Technician. As a geophysics operations technician, you'll apply physics and mathematics in practical ways and use sophisticated instruments to measure the physical properties beneath the surface of the earth. You may contribute to the understanding of the internal structure

Major Pitfalls

Many physics graduates continue study in graduate school rather than working after earning their Bachelor's degree. Later, after earning at least one graduate degree, they find work as professional physicists in industry, universities, or government laboratories.

and evolution of the earth, earthquakes, the ocean, and many other physical phenomena; seek out new reserves of resources, such as oil, natural gas, gold, diamonds, coal, iron, copper, and other minerals; or conduct geophysical surveys prior to the construction of major engineering structures, such as dams, bridges, or roadwork.

Meteorologist/Climatologist. In this job, you'll study the atmosphere and atmospheric phenomena, including the weather, to improve the understanding of climate. As a meteorologist, you may use and develop scientific techniques to forecast and interpret climatic conditions; prepare weather forecasts for the public and for specific users; work with physicists and engineers to develop observation equipment and distribute information on climate-related issues and conditions; and study climate and identify climatic change.

Physics Engineer. As a physics engineer, you'll work individually as well as collaboratively in an engineering or research laboratory on various projects, combining the elements of physics and engineering in developing, researching, testing, measuring, documenting, modeling, and reporting results suitable for publication and presentation. You may also assist with diagnostic maintenance and design enhancements to improve measurement capabilities, reliability, and accuracy, as well as developing calibration sources and instrumentation to support experimental activities.

Physics Laboratory Technician. As a physics laboratory technician, you'll help physicists conduct tests, experiments, and analyses. Laboratory technicians are employed in a wide variety of industries, educational institutions, and research organizations. Specific duties vary according to the industry, the purpose of the laboratory, and the type of tests completed, but can include setting up laboratory and field equipment, preparing samples for testing and analysis, and recording and compiling test results.

Science Writer. In this job, you'll work either as a journalist—for a journal, magazine, newspaper, radio, television, or the Internet—or as a science public information officer—or in a university, private research foundation, governmental agency or laboratory, science museum, corporation, or nonprofit science organization. You'll write about new developments in all aspects of science, from advances in biotechnology to discoveries in astrophysics, as well as feature articles on some broader aspects of science or scientific discovery.

Other Career Possibilities. Some other job and career paths for physics and astronomy majors include:

Acoustics Physicist   Automotive Engineer

Air Traffic Control Specialist   Fluids Physicist

Forensic Scientist

Geodesist

Geophysics Operations
Technician

Metallurgical Engineer

Molecular Physicist

Nuclear Power Plant Specialist

Physics Engineer

Plasma Physicist

Research and Development
Engineer

Satellite Missions Analyst

Science Museum Administrator

Skills Needed/Developed

Students majoring in physics or astronomy develop numerous valuable and transferable skills. The following are the most critical to graduates.

Observation. Keen observation skills are essential for any physicist or astronomer. After all, these sciences rely on the observation of phenomena instead of data manipulation.

Problem-Solving. Another important skill for physics and astronomy majors, problem-solving involves your ability to identify complex problems, review existing conditions and restrictions, and develop and evaluate alternative solutions to the problem.

Scientific Method. All science majors must possess an understanding of the scientific method, which involves the formulation of a hypothesis concerning some phenomena, experimentation to demonstrate the truth or fallacy of the hypothesis, and a conclusion that validates or modifies the hypothesis.

Quantitative Analysis. Because physics is grounded in mathematics, you'll possess and develop key math and computational skills.

Communications (in writing and verbally). All majors must perfect the ability to summarize, report, and present the results of scientific research in a clear and understandable manner.

The Professor Says

Other transferable skills gained from these majors include:

◆ Teamwork

◆ Analytical

◆ Recordkeeping/ handling details

◆ Technical/computer

Expected Growth

Job growth for physics and astronomy graduates is expected to be slower than the average (under 8 percent) of all jobs over the next decade, as government cutbacks in funding will reduce demand for these jobs.

Astrophysical Research Specialists

Job growth for astrophysical research specialists is expected to be slower than the average (under 8 percent) for all careers over the next decade.

Sources of additional information:

◆ American Astronomical Society (www.aas.org)

◆ International Planetarium Society (www.ips-planetarium.org)

---

profiles

Cosmologist Stephen Hawking

Stephen Hawking—professor, researcher, author—is a leading figure in cosmology and astrophysics. He graduated from Oxford's University College with a degree in physics and later earned his Ph.D., in cosmology from Cambridge University, where he later worked as a professor of theoretical and gravitational physics. His work has included developing a quantum theory of gravity that links quantum mechanics and relativity—the two major theories of modern physics. His ongoing work with quantum theory lends support to a model of the universe known as inflationary theory, and his current work focuses on better understanding black holes in the universe. He has published many articles and books, including *A Brief History of Time* and *Black Holes and Baby Universes and Other Essays*. He has been awarded 12 honorary degrees and been the recipient of numerous awards, medals, and prizes, and is a Fellow of The Royal Society and a member of the National Academy of Sciences.

Wondering what employers look for in an astrophysical research specialist? Here's a sample research specialist job description:

> We have an entry-level data specialist position in our Astrophysical Observatory, providing support for astrophysical research. Duties may include specifying, testing, writing, modifying, debugging, and/or documenting software for data analysis, proposal planning, mission planning, simulations, and modeling; running software and analyzing data output; developing and analyzing algorithms;

developing and maintaining databases; drafting and maintaining materials for websites; and providing support to users via personal interaction and e-mail. To qualify, candidates should possess, at a minimum, a Bachelor's degree in astronomy, physics, or a related field, which must include some computer-related coursework. Experience in computer operations and/or software development, ideally in a UNIX environment, is required.

Geophysics Operations Technicians

Job growth for geophysical technicians is expected to be about as fast as the average (10 to 15 percent) for all careers over the next decade. A source of additional information can be found at the Society of Exploration Geophysicists (www.seg.org).

Wondering what employers look for in a geophysics operations trainee? Here's a sample geophysics operations trainee job description:

As a result of our continued expansion, we have created a new position for an operations trainee. The successful applicant will be trained to assist the operations team with all stages of oil exploration projects, from preparation of tenders and contracts, to project start-up, monitoring, and billing. Once the initial training period has been successfully completed, the intention is that the trainee will be promoted to operations technician, as a first stage in career development within the company. Specific duties will include assisting with preparation of tenders and contracts related to oil exploration; managing jobs in progress; reconciling daily reports; and ensuring that all required administration is undertaken to enable surveys to start on time.

Meteorologists/Climatologists

Employment of atmospheric scientists projects to increase about as fast or slightly faster as average (15 to 20 percent) for all occupations over the next decade.

Sources of additional information:

- ◆ American Meteorological Society (www.ametsoc.org)
- ◆ International Association of Meteorology and Atmospheric Sciences (www.iamas.org)
- ◆ International Association for Urban Climate (www.urban-climate.org)

- National Council of Industrial Meteorologists (www.ncim.org)
- National Weather Association (www.nwas.org)

Physics Engineers

Job growth is expected to increase slower than average (under 8 percent) over the next decade.

Sources of additional information:

- American Institute of Physics (www.aip.org)
- American Physics Society (www.aps.org)
- National Society of Black Physicists (www.nsbp.org)

Physics Laboratory Technicians

Job growth is expected to increase slower than the average (under 8 percent) for all occupations over the next decade.

---

profiles

Physics Pioneer Marie Curie

Marie Curie (1867–1934), along with her husband, Pierre Curie, was a pioneer in the study of radioactivity, which led to the discovery of the elements radium and polonium in 1898. She spent many years in poverty working as a teacher and a governess before moving to Paris to study physics and mathematics at the Sorbonne, earning degrees in both. In 1903, she obtained her Ph.D., for a thesis on radioactive substances, and along with her husband and Henri Becquerel, she won the Nobel Prize for physics for the joint discovery of radioactivity. Later, she became the first female lecturer at the Sorbonne, and, in continuing her research, she was awarded a second Nobel Prize, this time for chemistry, for her work in radioactivity and the isolation of pure radium. She was appointed director of the Curie Laboratory in the Radium Institute of the University of Paris. She dedicated the rest of her career to the study of the chemistry of radioactive materials for medical purposes, including the development of the use of X-rays. She received many honorary science, medicine, and law degrees over the course of her life.

Science Writers

Job growth for science writers is expected to be about as fast as the average (10 to 15 percent) for all careers, though Internet-based jobs may grow faster than traditional media.

Sources of additional information:

◆ International Science Writers Association (internationalsciencewriters.org)

◆ National Association of Science Writers (www.nasw.org)

Wondering what employers look for in a science writer? Here's a sample science writer job description:

> We are an employee-owned company of over 600 professionals who support the diverse technical, scientific, and administrative needs of the Federal government. We are currently searching for a science writer to support the National Institutes of Health (NIH). The science writer will be responsible for performing a variety of writing and editing assignments for administrative and scientific reports, presentations, and publications, including understanding and analyzing complex biomedical information and research findings. More specifically, duties include preparing required scientific or technical documents; assisting in creating scientific summaries and updates for internal and external use; maintaining and developing sources of information to gather data; transmitting findings in areas of biomedical science; working with graphic artists to ensure manuscript accuracy; and designing and creating documents, using desktop publishing software and office tools.

The Professor Says

There are many career possibilities for physics and astronomy majors beyond the ones featured here. Remember that it is always important to learn more about prospective careers by going online, talking with professors, conducting informational interviews, and job-shadowing.

Earnings Potential $

Physics and astronomy graduates earn $45,000, more than the average annual salary for all college graduates, which is currently around $38,000.

The following provides some general guidelines of salaries to expect upon graduation. Remember, salaries vary by employer, industry, and region.

Astrophysical Research Specialist. Median annual salary of an astrophysical research specialist is approximately $48,000.

Geophysics Operations Technician. Salaries for geophysics operations technicians start at about $40,000.

The Professor Says

Your next step after choosing your major? Gaining work experience. Just about all "entry-level" jobs for college graduates require some work experience outside the classroom. Seek out internships, volunteer, and figure out other ways to gain the experience you need.

Meteorologist/Climatologist. Median annual earnings of meteorologists and climatologists range from about $25,000 to $35,000, depending on the employer, with government jobs paying on the higher side.

Physics Engineer. The median annual salary of a physics engineer is about $48,000.

Physics Laboratory Technician. The median annual salary of a physics laboratory technician ranges from $35,000 to $40,000.

Science Writer. The average starting salary for a magazine staff science writer is $30,000. Some science writers work as freelancers, and their salaries vary.

The Least You Need to Know

◆ Students with a passion for understanding the universe should be able to find jobs upon graduation as some job growth is expected.

◆ As one of the basic sciences, a major in physics provides you with an excellent foundation in science.

◆ As is the case with many fields, you can get a good-paying entry-level job with just an undergraduate degree.

◆ Jobs that utilize physics and astronomy are some of the highest-paying of all the sciences (not counting engineering).

Chapter 21

Zoology

In This Chapter

◆ Discover careers that use your love of animals

◆ Learn the classes that a typical zoology major requires

◆ Find out what kind of jobs and salaries to expect

Do you love animals? Do you worry about the polar bears and other animals that are being adversely affected by environmental conditions and development? Spend too much time at your local zoo or aquarium—or observing wildlife?

This chapter reveals rewarding careers for students majoring in zoology.

About the Major

Zoology is the scientific study of animals and their ecosystems and involves the broad topics of animal behavior, structure, development, function, evolution, genetics, and ecology. Some people call it the study of animal biology.

Zoology majors learn about all animals, ranging from single-celled animals (protozoans) to birds and mammals (vertebrates), gaining knowledge through fieldwork, direct laboratory experimentation, and independent research projects. Besides zoology courses, the major is usually supplemented with coursework in other areas, such as chemistry, physics, and mathematics.

Zoology is a fairly specialized major (though you might be able to find a few zoology courses in most biology majors), so you will need to seek out universities with this major. Typical courses include:

General Zoology

Animal Physiology

Field Zoology

Wildlife Diseases

Wildlife Ecology and
Management

Endocrinology

Fisheries Biology

Fisheries Management

Conservation Biology

Ichthyology

Vertebrate Histology

Entomology

Aquatic Invertebrate Taxonomy

Animal Behavior

Herpetology

Ornithology

Issues in Aquatic Ecology

Avian Biology

Fundamental Genetics

Neurobiology

Zoo and Aquarium Science

Evolution

Environmental System Science

Writing in the Biological
Sciences

Background on Careers

Zoology prepares students for careers in human and animal health, medical and biological research, teaching, animal care, conservation, and environmental biology. Zoologists regard an animal as any living thing that is not a plant, fungus, virus, or bacterium. Graduates typically specialize in a particular group of animals (such as mammals, insects, or mollusks) or focus on the interactions of organisms with one another and their environment (such as fishery, conservation, or wildlife).

Some top jobs and careers for students earning a Bachelor's degree with a major in zoology include:

Conservation Officer. As a conservation officer (sometimes referred to as an environmental conservation officer), you'll be a sworn police officer who enforces conservation laws and protects a state's natural resources and environment. These officers investigate complaints to detect and document state and federal environmental conservation law felonies, misdemeanors, and violations. You'll also conduct community educational programs—meeting with school groups, service groups, and hunter's and angler's clubs—to promote compliance with environmental conservation law, which includes fish and wildlife law.

 Major Pitfalls

Zoology graduates, like many other science graduates, can get a job in any of these careers with just a Bachelor's degree; however, the more lucrative and rewarding jobs often require at least a Master's degree.

Environmental Research Technician. In this job, you'll collaborate with one or more environmental scientists, either in the lab or in the field, and oversee anything from animal care to habitat management to data collection. You'll use the principles and theories of zoology to solve problems in research and development and to help invent and improve products and processes. Technicians set up, operate, and maintain laboratory instruments, monitor experiments, make observations, calculate and record results, and often develop conclusions. You might assist in the documentation and preparation of reports to show compliance with governmental regulations.

Fishery Biologist. As a fishery biologist, you'll study the biology of fish, including habitats, population, life histories, diseases, and forage bases, to develop programs to help protect, manage, and improve the lives of fish. You may work for industry, helping manage the raising of fish in fish hatcheries, or work for state or federal agencies. You may also meet with the general public and develop education programs; undertake special studies on rare, threatened, or endangered fish; conduct studies on stream productivity and how streams are being used as fish habitats; and monitor the biological characteristics of the fish population.

Naturalist. In this job, you'll serve an important role by inspiring and educating others on the importance and fragility of the environment. You'll need a passion for the environment, a concern for living things, and a desire to share your knowledge with others. You may work for an educational institution or park system. Working as a naturalist is the perfect occupation for someone who loves nature but also has a passion to be an educator. Days are often spent visiting schools, leading field trips and trail hikes, or conducting educational programs. You'll also take pictures, write copy, and develop educational materials, such as brochures, posters, and displays.

Veterinary Technician. In this job, you'll work in veterinary offices or hospitals assisting the veterinarian staff in a number of ways, including general assistance with animals and their owners (including admittance, discharge, and filling prescriptions), supporting surgical procedures (including surgery prep work, assisting during the actual surgery, and post-operative care), providing limited medical treatments and therapies (as directed by the veterinarian), and offering training and guidance to non-technical staff members.

Wildlife Biologist. As a wildlife biologist, you'll study animals and wildlife—their origin, behavior, diseases, and life processes—typically in the animals' natural habitats. You'll plan research studies and implement management practices pertaining to habitat, production, distribution, and natural balance to ensure sound management and conservation of the wildlife. You may also collect and analyze biological data to determine the environmental effects of current and potential use of land and water areas and disseminate your findings by writing reports, scientific papers, or journal articles, and by delivering presentations and giving talks for schools, clubs, interest groups, and park interpretive programs.

The Professor Says

Some students major in zoology to get the science foundation required for advanced studies in their pursuit of professional degrees and careers. These careers include:

- ◆ College Professor
- ◆ Dentist
- ◆ Doctor
- ◆ Environmental Lawyer
- ◆ Veterinarian

Zookeeper. As a zookeeper, you'll assist in the care and management of wild animals in zoos, animal and safari parks, bird collections, and aquariums. You'll help create and modify animal living spaces, maintain clean and safe living conditions, supervise dietary and food needs, record information about individual animals, and monitor overall health and well-being. You'll also contribute to the development of educational materials and programs for zoo/park visitors, and respond to general questions and inquiries of guests. Some zookeepers may also play an important role in protecting rare and endangered animal species.

Other Career Possibilities. Some other job and career paths for zoology majors include:

Animal Trainer	Environmental Planner
Aquarist	Fish and Wildlife Technician
Cell Culture Operator	Genetic Researcher
Conservation Biologist	Hatchery Technician
Environmental Educator	Herpetologist

Marine Mammal Scientist/ Biologist

Museum Zoologist

Park Ranger

Range Conservationist

Wildlife Refuge Manager, Assistant

Wildlife Rehabilitation Officer

Skills Needed/Developed

Students majoring in zoology develop numerous valuable and transferable skills. The following are the most critical to graduates.

Analyzing and Synthesizing Information. You'll develop the ability to bring information together in a logical manner while analyzing a situation, and sometimes work with multiple sources of information and data.

Scientific Method. All science majors must possess an understanding of the scientific method, which involves the formulation of a hypothesis concerning some phenomena, experimentation to demonstrate the truth or fallacy of the hypothesis, and a conclusion that validates or modifies the hypothesis.

Communications (in writing and verbally). Because many of the jobs in zoology require reporting and presenting research findings or developing educational materials, you must develop strong writing and speaking skills.

Teamwork. Many of these jobs involve working with others, whether in a laboratory, office, park, or in the field, so your ability to work well with teams is a critical skill to master.

The Professor Says _____

Other transferable skills gained from these majors include:

- ◆ Planning
- ◆ Recordkeeping/ handling details
- ◆ Gathering information
- ◆ Interpersonal communications
- ◆ Observation

Expected Growth

The demand for graduates with the skills developed from a zoology major should continue to be strong over the next decade, with expected overall job growth to be at least as fast as all other career paths (10 to 15 percent), and with some zoology careers growing faster than the average (18 to 25 percent).

Sources of additional information:

◆ American Society of Animal Science (www.asas.org/)

◆ Zoological Association of America (www.zaoa.org/)

profiles

Zoologist and Author Richard Dawkins

Richard Dawkins was born in Nairobi, Kenya, and is the author of a number of best-selling books about evolutionary biology including *The Selfish Gene, The Extended Phenotype, The Blind Watchmaker, River Out of Eden, Climbing Mount Improbable,* and *Unweaving the Rainbow.* He earned a degree in zoology at Balliol College, Oxford, where he was so inspired by the Dutch biologist Niko Tinbergen that he went on to earn his Doctorate under the tutelage of Tinbergen (a Nobel Prize winner for his pioneering work on animal behavior). Dr. Dawkins taught zoology at the University of California at Berkeley and Oxford. He is the Charles Simonyi Professor of the Public Understanding of Science at Oxford University. He was awarded the Silver Medal of the Zoological Society of London and the Royal Society Michael Faraday Award for the advancement of the public understanding of science. He also won the Nakayama Prize for Human Science and was awarded an honorary Doctorate in literature from the University of St. Andrews. He won both the Royal Society of Literature Award and the Los Angeles Times Literary Prize for *The Blind Watchmaker.*

Conservation Officers

Job growth for conservation officers is expected to be about as fast as the average (10 to 15 percent) for all careers over the next decade.

A source of additional information can be found at the North American Wildlife Enforcement Officers Association (www.naweoa.org).

Wondering what employers look for in a conservation officer? Here's a sample conservation officer job description:

> Our conservation officers work in one of five primary areas: wildlife and wildlife damage management, fisheries management, land and habitat management, conservation law enforcement, and public relations. Once hired, you will enter the Law Enforcement Training Academy and complete 12 weeks of training in general law enforcement curriculum to become certified as a law enforcement officer. Following certification, you will begin a 15-week field assignment designed to train you in various functions of conservation law enforcement,

community policing, and problem-solving, plus an additional 2 weeks of classroom training in wildlife damage and habitat management. You must have knowledge of the principles of biology associated with zoology, mammalogy, ornithology, ecology, ichthyology, and fish and wildlife management.

Environmental Research Technicians

Job growth for environmental research technicians is expected to be much faster than the average (18 to 25 percent) for all careers over the next decade.

Sources of additional information:

◆ National Association of Environmental Professionals (www.naep.org)

◆ Union of Concerned Scientists (www.ucsusa.org)

Wondering what employers look for in an environmental research technician? Here's a sample environmental research technician job description:

> Initially, the successful candidate will work with a senior research scientist in analyzing environmental issues associated with wetlands, wildlife, and natural resource development. The work will entail exploring ways of moving beyond compliance associated with environmental management systems to new approaches for maximizing environmental performance. The position could lead to leadership opportunities and could involve extensive collaborative work with public and private sector institutions, grant writing, and future program development. The successful candidate must be capable of working on multiple project teams and supporting a range of research projects. A team-oriented approach and effective communication skills are required. A Bachelor's degree in zoology, ecology, environmental science, or wildlife management is the minimum to be considered for this position.

Fishery Biologists

Demand for fishery biologists should remain strong over the next decade, but because supply exceeds demand, job growth is expected to be somewhat slower than the average (under 8 percent) for all careers.

Additional information can be found at the American Fisheries Society (www.fisheries. org).

Wondering what employers look for in an entry-level fishery biologist? Here's a sample fish biologist job description:

> This position provides expertise and support in cold-water fisheries, water quality, and riparian habitat management to the field office manager and staff, as well as other agencies. Provides advice and develops plans related to the protection and management of aquatic resources, including fish passage, stream inventory, stream productivity, stream utilization, physical and biological characteristics, endangered and sensitive species, and habitat improvements or rehabilitation programs. Works as a member of a team to resolve resource issues within the field office. Develops watershed assessments and drainage activity plans in coordination with other agencies and private landowners. Conducts inventories. Collects information on fish, water quality, and physical factors relating to fisheries resources within the district, including the collection and recording of data on fish, water quality parameters, and physical habitat factors affecting both fisheries and water quality. Must have a degree with coursework in general zoology, vertebrate zoology, comparative anatomy, physiology, entomology, parasitology, ecology, cellular biology, and genetics.

Naturalists

Employment of naturalists is projected to increase slower than the average (under 8 percent) for all occupations over the next decade.

Sources of additional information:

- The American Society of Naturalists (www.amnat.org)
- Association for Environmental & Outdoor Education (www.aeoe.org)
- National Recreation & Park Association (www.nrpa.org)
- North American Association of Environmental Education (www.naaee.org)

Veterinary Technicians

Job growth for veterinary technicians is expected to be much faster than the average (18 to 25 percent) for all careers over the next decade.

Sources of additional information:

- ◆ American Veterinary Medical Association (www.avma.org)

- ◆ National Association of Veterinary Technicians (www.navta.net)

Wondering what employers look for in an entry-level veterinary technician? Here's a sample veterinary technician job description:

> The ideal candidate will be working with the department of animal services, assisting in the spay and neutering program for small animals. You will perform many pre-surgery preparatory activities, assist during actual sterilization surgeries, and provide post-surgery care of animals. Instruction, guidance, and supervision are received from a veterinary surgeon. You will also assist in the physical examinations of animals, both pre- and post-surgery, prepare instruments and supplies for veterinarian's use, assist the veterinarian in the treatment of all other shelter animals, and observe the general shelter population for illness and/or injury. Must have a degree in animal health, animal science, or zoology. Some experience in a veterinary clinic or small animal hospital preferred. Must possess valid certificate as an animal health technician.

Wildlife Biologists

Employment for wildlife biologists is expected to grow faster than the average (18 to 25 percent) for all jobs over the next decade.

Additional information can be found at Association of Fish and Wildlife Agencies (www.iafwa.org).

Wondering what employers look for in a wildlife biologist? Here's a sample wildlife biologist job description:

> Major duties of this position include developing biological study proposals and survey designs; conducting complex biological field investigations involving wildlife species and habitats, including population and harvest studies, biological sampling, population health studies, animal collecting, food habitat studies, and population modeling; preparing issue papers, briefing documents; and providing verbal briefings to supervisors, regional directors, and others regarding issues that could affect the ecological integrity of resources within our jurisdiction. You will also be expected to maintain a working knowledge of emerging and current international, national, and regional resource conservation and natural resource management issues, activities, policies, and research.

Wildlife Biologist Jane Goodall

Jane Goodall is most well-known for her work with chimpanzees, in which she changed and enriched the field of primatology through her innovative research techniques. She is considered the world's foremost authority on chimpanzees and has observed their behavior for the past 45 years in the jungles of the Gombe Game Reserve in Tanzania, Africa. She earned her Doctorate in ethology from Cambridge University. Dr. Goodall has received 28 honorary Doctorates and is a member of countless environmental organizations. She has received numerous awards and honors for her work, including the French Legion of Honor, the UNESCO Gold Medal Award, the National Organization of Women's Intrepid Award, the Nierenberg Prize for Science in the Public Interest, the Gold Medal of the Society of Women Geographers, and The National Geographic Society Hubbard Medal for Distinction in Exploration, Discovery, and Research. Dr. Goodall's list of publications is extensive, including two overviews of her work at Gombe—*In the Shadow of Man* and *Through a Window*. She founded the Jane Goodall Institute for Wildlife Research, Education and Conservation to provide ongoing support for field research on wild chimpanzees, and continues to serve as a trustee.

Zookeepers

Job growth for zookeepers is expected to be slower than the average (under 8 percent) for all careers over the next decade.

Sources of additional information:

◆ American Association of Zookeepers (www.aazk.org)

◆ Association of Zoos and Aquariums (www.aza.org)

Wondering what employers look for in an entry-level zookeeper? Here's a sample zookeeper job description:

> Under general supervision, performs a variety of semi-technical tasks involving the care, feeding, training, doctoring, and custody of the animal collection within the large-mammal department of the zoo, working with large carnivores and hoof-stock. You'll observe animals for behavioral changes, maintain and repair cages, exhibits, and general zoo facilities and grounds; provide quality customer service to zoo visitors by giving tours, answering questions, and conducting demonstrations, working with the animals during public shows and presentations;

maintain and operate a variety of equipment; and keep accurate reports and records. Requires a college degree in zoology, biology, or related field, as well as some experience in a zoo-related setting.

The Professor Says

Your next step? Pick a couple of careers that most fit your interests with a zoology major and dig more deeply into them. Remember that it is always important to learn more about prospective careers by going online, talking with professors, conducting informational interviews, and job-shadowing.

Earnings Potential $

Graduates with a Bachelor's degree in zoology earn a starting salary of about $35,000—less than the average annual salary for all college graduates, which is currently around $38,000—however, salaries vary widely.

The following provides some general guidelines of salaries to expect upon graduation. Remember, salaries vary by employer, industry, and region.

Conservation Officer. Beginning annual salaries for new graduates are about $28,000.

Environmental Research Technician. Median annual earnings of an environmental research technician are about $27,000.

Fishery Biologist. Median annual salary for an entry-level fishery biologist is about $32,000.

Naturalist. The median starting salary for a naturalist varies by type of employer. Annual entry-level salaries for park naturalists are about $44,000, while those working in schools are much lower.

Veterinary Technician. Median annual salary for an entry-level veterinary technician is about $27,000.

The Professor Says

Remember that you're not done once you pick your college major—in fact, it's just begun, because the next thing you need to do is gain work experience. Just about all "entry-level" jobs for college graduates require some work experience outside the classroom. Seek out internships, volunteer, and figure out other ways to gain the experience you need.

Wildlife Biologist. New graduates can expect to make a starting salary of around $27,000.

Zookeeper. Median annual salary for an entry-level zookeeper is about $29,000.

The Least You Need to Know

- Having a passion for animals and nature can lead you to rewarding careers in zoology.

- A major in zoology is the perfect fit for someone who has an interest in working with animals, along with an aptitude for science.

- While the salaries with this major are decent, the fulfillment you will get from making a difference in working with these animals is indescribable.

- If you have an interest working outside and with animals, you should find enough job growth for employment in one of these careers.

Part 5

Careers in Service to People Using a Major in ...

This part invites you to learn more about careers that have a direct impact on helping people—with majors in education, health care, exercise science, and pre-med and pre-pharmacy. If you have a driving passion to make an impact on people's lives, then the chapters that follow should be of special interest to you. Does your vision of your future career involve empowering students, providing quality care to people who are ill, or saving lives through medical procedures? If so, then you'll want to pay special attention to the various career paths for majors related to the service to people.

In the following pages, you'll find information on a multitude of careers related to education, health services, exercise science and recreation and leisure services, and health science.

"I want to go back to school. Be a doctor."

22

Education

In This Chapter

- ◆ Discover careers that use your passion for teaching
- ◆ Use those empowerment skills in jobs that demand them
- ◆ Learn what classes the typical education major requires
- ◆ Find key job and salary information

What do you do if you've always enjoyed helping others learn? Been the teacher's pet at school? What if you have a strong desire to teach? Love working with kids? Want to make a difference in the lives of children?

This chapter reveals rewarding careers for students majoring in education.

About the Major

A major in education, sometimes referred to as teacher education, typically offers several tracks for students to choose from. These tracks include early childhood education (for students seeking certification to teach pre-K through grade 3), elementary education (for students seeking certification to teach grades 1–6 and middle school), special needs education (for students seeking certification to teach students with disabilities), subject-specific secondary education (for students seeking certification to teach

English, math, science, social studies, foreign language, music, or art in grades 7–12), and English for speakers of other languages (ESOL).

Education

Education majors learn to be ethical, competent, effective, and knowledgeable facilitators of learning; build learning communities within a diverse student body; and empower students to take charge of their education and future. Besides classes, education majors must perform at least one field experience in student teaching.

Education is a fairly specialized major, though you should find it at larger universities. Typical courses include:

Educational Psychology

Technology in the Classroom

Assessment and Evaluation

Educational Psychology

Applied Linguistics

Student Teaching Experience

Developmental Theory and Practice

Issues in Teacher Education

Foundations of Education: The School Curriculum

Instructional Strategies and Classroom Management

Establishing the Learning Environment

Creating Successful Classrooms

Integrating Teaching and Learning

Urban and Multicultural Education

Adolescent Development and Cognition

Principles and Methods of Instruction for Diverse Learners

Introduction to Exceptional Student Education

Methods of Integrating Arts in the Elementary School

The Early Childhood Educator

Foundations of Reading Instruction

Language Arts and Literature for Children

Introduction to Learning Disabilities

Instructional Strategies for Students with Mild Handicaps

Nature and Needs of Mildly Handicapped Students

Curriculum and Methods for Students with Severe Disabilities

Teaching Reading and Writing in the Elementary Schools

Teaching Mathematics in the Elementary Schools

Improving Reading and Writing Skills in the Middle Schools

Nature and Needs of the Gifted

Educational Procedures and Curriculum for the Gifted

Teaching Methods for the High School Classroom

Methods of Teaching English to Speakers of Other Languages

ESOL Instruction and Assessment

Legal, Ethical, and Professional Issues in Teaching

The Professor Says _____

One of the most important things you need to know is that you'll need a teaching certificate from the state in which you seek to teach if you want to teach in the public school system. The best teacher education programs have designed their curriculum, of course, to meet all the certification requirements for their particular state.

Background on Careers

Deciding to become a teacher is one of the most unselfish things you can do in your life, and the impact you can make on the students who attend your classes is immense. That said, the skills you develop in this major can also be used in a variety of other teaching-related and educational careers.

Some top jobs and careers for students earning a Bachelor's degree with a major in education include:

Child Life Specialist. As a child life specialist, you'll work as a member of a pediatric health-care team that focuses on the emotional, social, and developmental needs of hospitalized children and adolescents while easing the anxiety and stress that comes from being hospitalized—and providing various types of support to the patients and their families. You'll most likely work in a special playroom in the hospital designed for the activities you'll develop, but you may also find yourself working in a child's hospital room or in specific programs within a school. You may also conduct informational tours for children who are expecting to be hospitalized so they are more familiar with the facility at the time they are admitted.

Curriculum Specialist. In this job (also known as instructional coordinator), you'll play a large role in improving the quality of education in the classroom by developing curricula, selecting textbooks and other materials, training teachers, suggesting new techniques and technologies, and assessing educational programs in terms of quality and adherence to regulations and standards. You'll research teaching methods and techniques and develop procedures to determine whether program goals are being met—including developing questionnaires and interviewing school staff. Curriculum specialists often specialize in specific subjects or grade/education levels.

Employee Development/Training Specialist. In this job, you'll conduct training and development programs for employees within an organization as a way of developing skills, enhancing productivity and quality of work, and building worker loyalty to the firm. You'll help all employees maintain and improve their job skills, and possibly prepare for jobs requiring greater skill, and you'll help supervisors improve their interpersonal skills to deal effectively with employees. You may set up individualized training plans to strengthen an employee's existing skills or teach new ones, as well as develop leadership or executive development programs. You may also lead programs to assist employees with job transitions as a result of mergers and acquisitions, as well as technological changes.

Guidance Counselor. As a high school guidance counselor, you'll provide social, educational, career, and personal assistance to a certain number of assigned students, with much of the advice focused on future career and educational choices, including counseling students about technical and trade schools, community colleges, and four-year colleges and universities. You'll be involved in vocational, aptitude, and achievement testing; helping students complete college applications; planning and leading workshops on topics such as anger management, alcohol and drug prevention, peer pressure, and study skills; assisting in dropout prevention programs; and responding to student crises and other problems.

Teacher, Adult Education. As an adult (literacy or remedial) education teacher, you'll instruct adults in reading, writing, speaking, science, history, or math to help prepare them for further education or so they can find employment. You may find yourself working with adult students who have major deficiencies in their skills or with students who wish to work toward their General Education Development (GED) certificate or other high school equivalency credential. Most of your students will typically be high school dropouts with different levels of skills and knowledge, typically with little or no study skills, or possibly with a learning disability. You'll assess each student's proficiencies and develop individualized education plans to help them achieve their goals.

Teacher, Elementary Education. In this job, you'll work in an elementary school typically instructing one class of children (age 5 to 13) in several subjects, including reading, math, geography, and science. In some schools, two or more teachers work as a team and are jointly responsible for all their students. If you specialize in a subject, such as music, art, or a foreign language, you may move from class to class and grade to grade. Part of your job as a teacher is to also serve as a counselor, role model, and disciplinarian, and regularly spend time outside of class communicating with parents, preparing lessons, grading papers, and improving your knowledge and skills.

Teacher, Secondary Education. As a secondary education teacher, you'll help students (in grades 6 through 12) delve more deeply into subjects introduced in elementary school and expose them to more information about the world. You'll be responsible for teaching a single subject area, such as English, math, art, music, social studies, science, or a foreign language, teaching a large number of students in multiple classes. You could also teach courses that focus on occupations or careers or teach field-specific skills in areas such as mechanics, health care, computer technology, and woodwork. Working as a secondary education teacher usually allows you to combine two passions—one for teaching and for the subject you are teaching.

Other Career Possibilities. Here are some other job and career paths for education majors:

Activities Coordinator	Grant Writer
Admissions Counselor	Journalist
Athletic Coach	Librarian
Camp Director	Media Specialist
Career Development Specialist	Peace Corps/Vista Worker
Child Psychologist	Student Affairs Administrator
Day Care Administrator	Teacher, English for Speakers of Other Languages (ESOL)
Educational Materials Sales	
Financial Aid Counselor	Vocational Rehab Counselor

Skills Needed/Developed

Students majoring in teacher education develop numerous valuable and transferable skills. The following are the most critical to graduates:

Organizational Skills. Perhaps one of the most valuable skills you'll learn for teaching, this skill deals with your ability to manage large amounts of information and demands through task analysis, time management, and goal-setting.

Interpersonal Communications. Because you'll be working directly with students, parents, and other teachers and administrators, you must be able to talk and listen in one-on-one and small-group situations.

The Professor Says

Other transferable skills you gain from these majors include:

◆ Evaluation

◆ Leadership

◆ Creativity

◆ Teamwork

Written and Oral Communications. Speaking and writing skills are essential when pursuing a career in education. You'll need the ability to clearly express yourself, whether talking with clients or creating written instructions or guidelines.

Observation. The ability to read and understand people's reactions is an important skill you'll need to learn for this career. Observation skills help you assess how your teaching, training, coaching, or therapy is being received (and performed).

Expected Growth

Job growth in the next decade for students who major in education is expected to be strong, and in some cases much faster than the average (18 to 25 percent) growth for all careers.

Child Life Specialists

Job growth for child life specialists is expected to be about as fast as the average (10 to 15 percent) for all careers over the next decade, but because it is a relatively new field, competition for jobs will remain strong.

Additional information can be found at Child Life Council (www.childlife.org).

Wondering what employers look for in a child life specialist? Here's a sample child life specialist job description:

> Under the general direction of the assistant director of child life/social services, performs the following functions for the hospital: assesses the developmental, social, and physical needs of assigned patients and provides appropriate interventions, such as preparations and therapeutic play; plans and implements individual, group, and special events programming; takes a leadership role in creating a child-centered environment; facilitates patient and parent adjustment to the health-care environment; maintains records as assigned; assumes responsibility and accountability for assigned administrative tasks; participates in continuing professional development opportunities; and participates in the orientation, development, and direction of hospital volunteers. Qualifications: 1. Bachelor's degree in child development, psychology, education, or closely related field, including coursework and knowledge of the specific needs and developmental levels of children and adolescents and impact of illness; 2. Requires completion of an approved child life internship or equivalent experience as a child life specialist; 3. Must successfully meet child life certification requirements within one year of hire; 4. Able to meet typical physical demands; 5. Experience with death and dying preferred.

Curriculum Specialists

Job growth for curriculum specialists is expected to be much faster (18 to 25 percent) than for all careers over the next decade.

Wondering what employers look for in a curriculum specialist? Here's a sample curriculum specialist job description:

> If you are passionate about the field of early childhood education or child development, enjoy on-going training, and you have a sincere desire to cultivate our next generation of children, we have a position for you! The curriculum specialist oversees program curriculum implementation plans and objectives. Your day consists of assessing children through observation, coordinating the planning of emergent curriculum, and acting as a role model for both children and staff. You will also interpret and articulate the mission and philosophy of our programs to other teachers and at community-sponsored events. As a mentor and coach, you will have the opportunity to facilitate training seminars on best practices, provide observation feedback to teachers, and work very closely with the site

supervisor/manager with the end goal of delivering an extraordinary, high-quality program for our children and parents. Our centers range in size, and serve infants, toddlers, preschool, and school-age children. Our teachers work with a low ratio classroom of up to 14 children.

Employee Development Specialists/Trainers

Job growth for employee development specialists is expected to be faster than the average (18 to 25 percent) for all careers over the next decade.

Sources of additional information:

◆ American Society for Training Development (www.astd.org)

◆ Society for Human Resource Management (www.shrm.org)

Wondering what employers look for in an employee development specialist? Here's a sample employee development specialist job description:

> We have an immediate opening for an employee development specialist for our San Francisco office. In this position, you will conduct a wide range of training courses for all staff levels, developing a sound understanding of your audience and adjusting delivery for maximum effectiveness. We will also rely on you to develop training initiatives on a district or regional basis, and work closely with clients on training needs, scheduling, and courses that support their specific initiatives. Expect to develop and design new training material, revamp our new employee training manual, and update central core programs to address the organization's needs. Job involves about 30 percent travel. This highly visible position requires a Bachelor's degree, some corporate training experience, certification in core course curriculum (or ability to obtain), and excellent project management, decision-making, facilitation, and communication skills. The ability to develop positive relationships with internal and external clients—particularly district leadership—is essential.

Guidance Counselors

Job growth for guidance counselors is expected to be faster than the average (18 to 25 percent) for all careers over the next decade.

Additional information can found at American School Counselor Association (www. schoolcounselor.org).

Teachers, Adult Education

Job growth is expected to be about as fast as the average (10 to 15 percent) over the next decade.

Additional information can be found at American Association for Adult & Continuing Education (www.aaace.org).

Teachers, Elementary Education

Demand for elementary education teachers is expected to remain strong—with growth expected to be about as fast as the average (10 to 15 percent) for all careers over the next decade.

Sources of additional information:

◆ American Federation of Teachers (www.aft.org)

◆ Association for Childhood Education International (www.acei.org)

◆ National Association for the Education of Young Children (www.naeyc.org)

Wondering what employers look for in an elementary education teacher? Here's a sample elementary school teacher job description:

> We are seeking an educator for our newest elementary school. Non-negotiable requirements are passion, focus, energy, organizational skills, an entrepreneurial spirit, and full devotion to teaching and developing young minds. Responsibilities include: collaborating with other teachers in preparing and organizing units and lessons; modeling strict behavior management strategies; tutoring at-risk students; instructing students individually and in groups; establishing clear objectives for all lessons, units, and projects; preparing, administering, and grading tests and assignments; meeting with parents or guardians; enforcing administration policies and rules; evaluating student performance and behavior; attending professional development meetings and workshops; and collaborating with other teachers and administrators in the development, evaluation, and revision of lessons, units, and programs. Additional requirements: teaching certification; strong organizational skills; excellent speaking, reading, writing, and math skills; commitment to educational progress of children; ability to excel at motivation and teaching; and time-management skills.

Teachers, Secondary Education

Demand for secondary education teachers is expected to remain strong—with growth expected to be about as fast as the average (10 to 15 percent) for all careers over the next decade.

A source of additional information can be found at American Federation of Teachers (www.aft.org).

Wondering what employers look for in a secondary education teacher? Here's a sample secondary school teacher job description:

> We are seeking secondary teachers in mathematics, English, social studies, Spanish, and science. Under the direction of the principal, you'll prepare curriculum and lesson plans; teach skills and knowledge of core and/or elective subject matter to secondary pupils using the course of study and other appropriate learning activities; serve as a resource and advisor to students and parents; participate in staff development and departmental meetings and activities; provide classroom management and student supervision; and promote the mission/goals of the school. You must have expertise in subject content area; ability to model and innovate best teaching and learning practices; knowledge of current strategies in project-based learning; experience working with diverse student population; experience in the application of technology in the classroom; Bachelor's degree or higher with valid teaching certificate; solid classroom management skills; strong communication skills; and ability to work well with a diverse group of people. All candidates must undergo a background check and medical testing.

A Day in the Life ... of an Elementary School Teacher	
6:30 A.M.	As my alarm wakes me for the start of another day, I'm reminded that while teaching is a very rewarding career, it is also a demanding one.
8:00 A.M.	Head to school, coffee in hand, planning to arrive about 30 minutes early to do some last-minute classroom prep for today's classes.
8:50 A.M.	First bell rings, the teaching day begins! I'll teach writing and math in these first two periods.
10:45 A.M.	With my students off for a short recess, it's time to return a parent's phone call.
11:00 A.M.	Class resumes with a focus this period on social studies.
12:00 P.M.	Lunch.
12:45 P.M.	Classes resume, but this period is my free period.
3:30 P.M.	School is officially over for the day, but I have a meeting with the other teachers on my 3rd grade team. Other days, I usually stay to meet with parents, complete lesson planning, finish some grading, or arrange my classroom.
6:00 P.M.	Dinner—a short chance to relax while I eat.
7:30 P.M.	Time to finish a bunch of paperwork, including official lesson plans, grading, and reports to parents. I work many nights and weekends, which definitely takes its toll, but I love the long winter and summer vacations.

Earnings Potential $

Education graduates on average earn $32,000—a lower annual salary than the average for all college graduates, which is currently around $38,000.

The following section provides some general guidelines of salaries to expect upon graduation. Remember, salaries vary by employer, industry, and region.

The Professor Says _____

Not sure about these career choices? These are just some of the career possibilities for a major in education. Remember that it is always important to learn more about prospective careers by researching online, talking with professors, conducting informational interviews, and job-shadowing.

Child Life Specialist. Median starting salary for a child life specialist is about $30,000.

Curriculum Specialist. The median salary for an entry-level curriculum specialist is $33,000.

Employee Development Specialist. Median annual salary for an entry-level employee development specialist is $41,000.

> **The Professor Says**
>
> Remember that you're not done once you pick your college major—in fact, it's just begun, because the next thing you need to do is gain work experience. Just about all "entry-level" jobs for college graduates require some work experience outside the classroom. Seek out internships, volunteer, and figure out other ways to gain the experience you need.

Guidance Counselor. Median annual salary of an entry-level guidance counselor varies by school system, but a rough estimate is about $35,000 to $40,000.

Teacher, Adult Education. Annual starting salary for an adult education teacher ranges from $30,000 to $36,000.

Teacher, Elementary Education. Annual starting salary for an elementary education teacher varies by state and school system, but is typically around $33,000.

Teacher, Secondary Education. Annual starting salary for a secondary education teacher varies by state and school system, but is typically around $34,000.

The Least You Need to Know

- Students who have a passion for education should be able to find a number of fast-growing and good-paying careers in education or industry upon graduation.

- If you have a desire to make an impact on the lives of children, then teaching is a career path for you.

- Job growth for many education-related careers will be fast or faster than the average for all careers over the next decade.

- Jobs in school systems will require a teaching certificate beyond your college degree.

23

Health Services: Nursing and Nutrition/Dietary Science

In This Chapter

◆ Discover careers that use your passion for health

◆ Use those helping skills in jobs that demand them

◆ Learn the classes nursing and nutrition/dietary science majors require

◆ Find key job and salary information

What do you do if you have always been interested in helping people with their health? Have you always been a health-food junkie? Have you always been the one who took care of friends' cuts and scrapes? Wondering about the types of careers for people like you?

This chapter reveals rewarding careers for students who major in one of the health services.

About the Majors

The health services include majors in nursing and nutrition/dietetics. By majoring in one of these areas, you'll gain a solid background and general knowledge about health and applied science that can be used in a variety of in-demand careers in a wide range of employment settings (i.e., hospitals, large medical practices, insurance companies, and home health companies).

Nursing

Nursing majors receive a general background in the sciences as well as a specific nursing curriculum leading to a Bachelor of Science degree in Nursing that is designed to meet the diverse health needs of clients in a variety of settings, as well as to coordinate health services, deliver humanistic nursing care, and engage in health assessment and health maintenance.

Nursing is a rather specialized major, especially at traditional four-year colleges, so you'll need to do your research to find a program that meets your interests and needs.

Typical courses include:

Nursing Competencies	Childbearing
Professional Foundations	Community Health Nursing
Health Assessment and Promotion	Complex Health Promotion
Nursing Research	Health Across the Lifespan
Advanced Nursing Competencies	Nursing Synthesis
Pharmacology	Nursing of Children and Families
Pathological Human Processes	Emerging Issues in Nursing Practice
Adult Health Issues	
Health-Care Systems and Policy	Culturally Congruent Health Care
Mental Health Issues	Nursing Leadership and Management
Clinical Decision-Making	

Nutrition and Dietetics

Nutrition and dietetics majors receive a general background in the science of nutrition and dietary science—in preparation for advanced nutrition education or employment—so that they can effectively serve in a profession that works to affect the eating behaviors and subsequent health and quality of life of a multicultural and diverse population. These majors add to the scientific investigation about food and health, and foster an appreciation of food's relationship to other sciences.

The Professor Says

If your career goal is to become a registered nurse, check to make certain that the university you want to attend will assist you with obtaining your R.N. designation. Schools should, upon the completion of your undergraduate degree program, send a statement of endorsement to the Board of Nursing in the state where you plan to practice nursing—and thus, where you'll take the National Council Licensure Examination for Registered Nurses (NCLEX-RN).

Nutrition and dietetics are pretty specialized majors (often housed in the same department), especially at traditional four-year colleges, so you'll need to do your research to find a program that meets your interests and needs. Typical courses include:

Careers in Food and Nutrition

Nutrition Science

Food Science

Advanced Food Science

Life Cycle Nutrition

Community Nutrition

Advanced Human Nutrition

Nutrition in Disease

Nutrition Counseling

Sports Nutrition

Medical Nutrition Therapy

Nutrient Metabolism

Food and the Consumer

Nutrition and Aging

Dietary Research

Diet Therapy

Issues in Dietetic Practice

Seminar in Dietetics

Mechanisms of Nutrient Action in the Body

Management of Food Service Systems

Food and Nutrition Policy Regulation and Law

Nutritional Issues in Gerontology

Multicultural Aspects of Food and Nutrition Patterns

Delivery Systems for Food and Nutrition Information

The Professor Says _____

If your career goal is to become a dietician, check to make certain that the university you want to attend for dietary science or nutrition is fully accredited, because once you complete your coursework and a dietetic internship program, you become eligible to take the national registration exam and become a registered dietitian—a path taken by most nutrition majors.

Background on Careers

Careers in one of the health services are among the most important and in demand of any professional careers in the country. Health service providers combine basic human care and a passion for wellness with some of the most innovative and highly developed medical technologies, thus helping build and maintain an awareness of our physical and mental well-being.

Graduates with one of these health services majors generally seek employment in administrative, therapeutic, teaching, research, or public health/public service positions in clinics, hospitals, schools, or other similar institutions, but can also seek employment in business and industry or in private practice.

Some top jobs and careers for students earning a Bachelor's degree with a major in the health services include:

Dietitian, Registered. As a registered dietitian, you'll apply the science of nutrition by utilizing your nutrition knowledge to promote health and/or treat disease in hospitals, clinics, community settings, private consulting practices, sports nutrition and corporate wellness programs, newspapers and magazines, food and nutrition-related businesses and industry, hotels and resorts, pharmaceutical companies, and more. You may conduct medical nutrition therapy for the treatment and control of a disease or condition, see a wide variety of patients, or specialize in a particular area of nutrition and dietetics.

Nurse-Midwife. In this job, you are very involved in the labor and delivery of your patients' babies, sometimes never leaving the mother during the entire labor process, typically delivering babies in hospitals or in homes. You may also provide both prenatal and postpartum care for both mothers and newborns. In addition, nurse-midwives now provide family planning and birth control counseling, and normal gynecological services such as physicals and breast exams, pap smears, and preventive health screening. In most states, nurse-midwives may prescribe medications. Some nurse midwives are Certified Nurse-Midwives, meaning they are registered nurses who are also certi-fied midwives.

Nurse, Registered. As a registered nurse, you'll work in hospitals, doctors' offices, schools, governmental agencies, nursing homes, and community health settings while performing a wide variety of tasks. You'll strive to promote good health, prevent dis-ease, and help patients cope with illness by providing advice and emotional support, and you'll be an advocate of health education and wellness for patients, families, and communities. When providing direct patient care, you'll observe, assess, and record patient symptoms, reactions, and progress. Nurses collaborate with physicians in per-forming treatments and examinations, administering medications, and providing direct patient care in convalescence and rehabilitation.

Patient Advocate. As a patient advocate (sometimes also referred to as patient ombudsman or patient representative), you'll be hired by a doctor's office, a hospital, or a private organization, where your responsibility will be to inform patients of their rights as a patient and assist in developing a patient-focused culture throughout the organization. You'll talk to patients on the phone and in the office, offering advice on physicians, pharmacies, and hospitals, as well as advice on how to work within the rules of managed-care organizations. The array of problems you'll help with range from billing issues to patients who are unhappy about prescribed treatments.

Physician Assistant. In this job, working as part of a health-care team, you'll take medical histories, perform physical exams, order and interpret lab tests and x-rays, diagnose and treat illnesses, assist in surgery, prescribe and dispense medication, and counsel patients. Like the physicians you'll serve, you can follow many career paths, including university hospital work, private practice, and jobs with Health Maintenance Organizations (HMOs). Basically, wherever there are doctors, there are physician assistants. You may also have managerial duties, such as ordering medical supplies or equipment and supervising technicians and assistants. In rural areas or inner cities, you may be the principal care provider for your patients.

Weight Reduction Specialist. In this job, you'll help people with their weight by assisting them in devising and carrying out a weight-loss plan using established dietary programs and positive reinforcement procedures. You'll conduct interviews with your clients to obtain information on weight development histories, eating habits, medical restrictions, and nutritional objectives; weigh and measure your clients using measur-ing instruments and entering data on client records; discuss eating habits with your clients to identify dispensable food items and to encourage increased consumption of high-nutrition, low-calorie food items, selecting an established diet program that matches your clients' goals and restrictions. You may also give clients weight-loss aids, such as calorie counters, or sell nutritional products to be used in conjunction with diet programs.

Other Career Possibilities. Here are some other job and career paths for nursing and nutrition/dietetics majors:

Clinical Specialist

Cookbook Editor

Critical Care Nurse

Emergency Room Nurse

Food and Drug Inspector

Food Science Researcher

Forensic Nurse

Health-Care Administrator

Health Educator

Menu Planner

Nurse Anesthetist

Nutritionist

Oncology Nurse

Pediatric Dietician

Pharmaceutical Sales Representative

Public Health Nurse

School Nurse

Test Kitchen Specialist

Women's Health Practitioner

The Professor Says

These majors are also a solid foundation for students considering continuing their education and going into careers that require additional degrees, such as:

◆ Dentistry

◆ Law

◆ Medicine

◆ Nurse Practitioner

◆ Teaching

◆ Veterinary Medicine

Skills Needed/Developed

Students majoring in the health services develop numerous valuable and transferable skills. The following are the most critical to graduates:

Analytical/Critical Thinking. This skill involves your ability to get to the heart of a problem or situation by breaking it down into smaller, more manageable parts, analyzing information, evaluating alternatives, and proposing a viable solution.

Listening. Before you can treat your patients, you need to be able to listen and hear what they are saying. Active listening is a vital skill for you to develop as a health services professional and involves not only following along with the speaker, but letting him or her know you are tracking the message.

Written and Oral Communications. Speaking and writing skills are essential when pursuing a career in health services. You'll need the ability to clearly express yourself, whether talking with patients or recording their information.

Multi-Tasking/Project Management. Because health services workers often work on multiple projects and patients with varying demands and deadlines, you must have strong project management skills, with the ability to organize, plan, and prioritize your work.

Teamwork. This skill involves your ability to work with other people—whether they are similar or different—and is one of the most important for any career, including the health services.

The Professor Says

Other transferable skills you gain from these majors include:

◆ Record keeping

◆ Leadership

◆ Organization

◆ Technical/computer

Expected Growth

Overall, job growth in the next decade for students majoring in the health services field is expected to be strong, and in some cases much faster than the average growth (25 percent or higher) for all careers.

Dietitians, Registered

Job growth for all dieticians and nutritionists is expected to be as fast as the average (10 to 15 percent) for all careers over the next decade.

A source of additional information can be found at American Dietetic Association (www.eatright.org).

Nurse-Midwives

Job growth for nurse-midwives is expected to be as fast as the average—or faster—(10 to 25 percent) for all careers over the next decade.

Sources of additional information:

◆ American College of Nurse-Midwives (www.midwife.org)

◆ Midwives Alliance of North America (www.mana.org)

Wondering what employers look for in a certified nurse-midwife? Here's a sample nurse-midwife job description:

> Work for our health center, which offers a full range of high-quality, primary health care, along with pharmacy assistance and linkage to other social service agencies. Some services include pediatrics and immunizations; medical care for pregnant women; internal medicine and family practice; physicals; and screenings for diseases such as cancer and diabetes. We are seeking a professional, team player who enjoys a degree of independence and the challenge of thinking through patient management. We are open to new graduates as well as experienced candidates. The salary range is $60–$90k depending on experience. Includes a full benefits package and bonus possibility. Spanish speaking preferred, but not mandatory. Candidates must have a Bachelor's degree in nursing or health-related field and C.N.M. certificate.

Nurses, Registered

Job growth for registered nurses is expected to be as fast as the average (10 to 15 percent) for all careers over the next decade, with some organizations citing a shortage of 800,000 nurses by 2020.

Sources of additional information:

◆ American Nurses Association (www.nursingworld.org)

◆ Discover Nursing (www.discovernursing.com)

◆ Minority Nurse (www.minoritynurse.com)

◆ National League for Nursing (www.nln.org)

◆ National Student Nurses' Association (www.nsna.org)

◆ Nurse.org (www.nurse.org)

◆ NurseZone.com (www.nursezone.com)

profiles

Pioneering Nurse Mary Elizabeth Carnegie

Mary Elizabeth Carnegie, D.P.A., R.N., F.A.A.N., is a member of the American Nurses Association Hall of Fame because of her passion for the field of nursing and her commitment to the advancement of black and other minority nurses. After graduating from the Lincoln Hospital School for Nurses and earning a degree in sociology from West Virginia State College, Carnegie became assistant director of nursing at Hampton University in Virginia, where she established the state's first nursing program for blacks—and where, years later, a research center was named in her honor. She has written, edited, and contributed chapters to nearly 20 books and is author of all three editions of the award-winning *The Path We Tread: Blacks in Nursing Worldwide, 1854–1994.* She served as dean and professor of the school of nursing at Florida A&M University and is a past president of the American Academy of Nursing. Dr. Carnegie has received eight honorary doctorates and countless awards for her efforts.

Patient Advocates

Some job growth is expected—about as fast as the average (10 to 15 percent) for all careers.

Sources of additional information:

◆ National Patient Advocate Foundation (www.npaf.org)

◆ Society for Healthcare Consumer Advocacy (www.shca-aha.org)

Wondering what employers look for in a patient advocate? Here's a sample patient advocate job description:

> We need a caring and attentive professional, motivated by an opportunity to make a meaningful difference in others' lives, to work with a great team in a fast-paced and collaborative office as we revolutionize the way health care is delivered! You will develop and nurture long-term relationships with our members throughout the country and be their liaison with the health-care community, and work with our research team to identify the best hospitals, physicians, alternative medicine practitioners, and the most appropriate health-care options in the world on behalf of our members. In this exciting role, you will also identify and facilitate access to the best wellness options. Ideal candidates will have a four-year college or nursing degree, fluency in spoken and written Spanish and English medical terminology, and outstanding interpersonal and written/verbal skills. Other skills that successful advocates possess are proficiency in computer

applications and Internet, ability to negotiate and get things done, passion for helping people/customer service, detail-oriented, good time-management skills, independent and resourceful, creative, can-do attitude, and strong work ethic.

A Day in the Life ... of a Registered Nurse	
6:00 A.M.	Get up, grab a shower, and drink a cup of coffee.
6:45 A.M.	Arrive on my floor of the hospital to check in with the night shift and see which patients I will be handling today. In a typical day, I may be assigned to anywhere from 3 to 10 or more patients, depending on staffing and acuteness of the patients.
7:00 A.M.	Walk the floor, visit with patients, and begin general care procedures. I'll check vitals and administer drugs on this round.
8:00 A.M.	Back to the nurse's station to complete paperwork. You would be amazed at how much of our work deals not with patient care but paperwork.
9:30 A.M.	With visiting hours about to start, I need to finish things up and be ready to deal with patients' families and friends.
10:00 A.M.	Time to deal with new orders from the doctors, plus we've been told to expect three new patients today.
11:30 A.M.	Lunchtime on the floor—for the patients as patient meals arrive.
12:30 P.M.	Another round on the floor, checking IV lines, medications, and other patient care.
1:00 P.M.	The rest of the day is fairly similar to the morning; some days are much more hectic than others. Most of us feel we work long hours with too few co-workers for not enough pay. But, on the other hand, we love what we do.
7:00 P.M.	My shift is over. The night shift has arrived, and after a short debriefing of the day, I am ready to head home.

Physician Assistants

Job growth is expected to be much faster than the average (25 percent or higher) over the next decade, and is expected to be one of the fastest growing of all occupations.

Sources of additional information:

◆ American Academy of Physicians Assistants (www.aapa.org)

◆ National Commission on the Certification of Physician Assistants (www.nccpa.net)

Weight Reduction Specialists

Demand for weight reduction specialists is expected to remain strong (and perhaps get stronger), and growth should be about as fast as the average (10 to 15 percent) for all careers over the next decade.

Earnings Potential $

Nutrition/dietetic graduates earn an average of $33,000—a lower annual salary than the average for all college graduates, which is currently around $38,000. Nursing graduates, however, at $45,000, make more than the average.

The following section provides some general guidelines of salaries to expect upon graduation. Remember, salaries vary by employer, industry, and region.

The Professor Says

There are many career possibilities for a major in the health services beyond the ones featured here. Remember that it is always important to learn more about prospective careers by researching online, talking with professors, conducting informational interviews, and job-shadowing.

Dietitian, Registered. Median starting salary for a registered dietitian is $40,000.

Nurse-Midwife. The median salary for a nurse-midwife ranges from $45,000 to $60,000.

Nurse, Registered. Median annual salary for entry-level registered nurses is $45,000.

Patient Advocate. Median annual salary of an entry-level patient advocate is about $45,000.

Physician Assistant. Annual starting salary for a physician assistant ranges from $56,000 to $65,000. Surgical physician assistants can earn more than $100,000.

Weight Reduction Specialist. Starting salary for a weight reduction specialist is about $40,000.

The Professor Says

Your next step after choosing your major? Gaining work experience. Just about all "entry-level" jobs for college graduates require some work experience outside the classroom. Seek out internships, volunteer, and figure out other ways to gain the experience you need.

The Least You Need to Know

◆ Students who major in one of the health services have numerous choices of helping careers with various types of organizations, including hospitals, doctor offices, health-care providers, and businesses.

◆ Many health services careers pay above the average for all jobs for college graduates.

◆ Job growth for many health service careers will be fast or faster than the average for all careers over the next decade.

◆ Many of the careers in the health services field require at least one certification in addition to your college education; some require additional education as well.

Chapter 24

Exercise Science and Recreation and Leisure Studies

In This Chapter

- ◆ Discover careers that use your passion for recreation
- ◆ Use those active life skills in jobs that demand them
- ◆ Learn the typical classes exercise science and recreation studies majors require
- ◆ Find out key job and salary information

What do you do if you have always been interested and involved in an active lifestyle? Played a lot of sports? Do you enjoy helping others become healthy and fit? Enjoy your local parks and recreational facilities?

This chapter reveals rewarding careers for students who major in exercise science or recreation and leisure studies.

About the Majors

These majors—in exercise science and recreation and leisure services—can lead to careers in a wide range of employment settings, including fitness and sports organizations, camps, resorts, municipal parks departments, health-care facilities, and business.

Exercise Science

Exercise science (also called integrative physiology and integrative health science) majors learn the biology of the human organism and how it responds to internal and external stimuli, including increased and decreased activity levels, environmental conditions, and disease processes. It involves the scientific disciplines that facilitate the measurable responses of human biological systems, including anatomy, biomechanics, neuroscience, physiology, biology, biochemistry, chemistry, mathematics, physics, and statistics. Students prepare for careers in exercise physiology, biomechanics, sport psychology, motor learning, and physical activity and fitness.

Exercise science is a somewhat specialized major, though you should find it at larger universities. Typical courses include:

- Biomechanics
- Human Physiology
- Skeletal Muscle Biology
- Sports and Exercise Physiology
- Motor Development and Control
- Foundations of Exercise and Sport Psychology
- Gross Anatomy for Exercise Science
- Biomechanics of Human Motion
- Human Growth and Motor Development
- Embryology and Connective Tissue Anatomy
- Cardiovascular Physiology Issues
- Advanced Biomechanical Movement
- Fitness Evaluation and Exercise Prescription
- Care and Maintenance of Sports Injuries

Recreation and Leisure Studies

Recreation and leisure studies majors take courses that emphasize life development and communication studies, the study of leisure, and management and leadership issues within the field. Majors learn how to plan, design, and evaluate recreation and leisure programs. There are typically two tracks: program management and therapeutic recreation. In program management, courses address the delivery of leisure services, such as special events/program planning and evaluation; the history and philosophy of leisure; leadership and management; risk analysis; and planning, designing, and operating facilities. In therapeutic recreation, courses focus on leisure and aging, and the clinical aspects and techniques and principles of therapeutic recreation.

Major Pitfalls

Interested in a career in physical or occupational therapy and wondering why they are not included in this chapter? In recent years, schools that offer physical or occupational therapy programs have been required to upgrade their programs from an undergraduate to a graduate level. Thus, students entering these programs must have already earned a Bachelor's degree. Upon completion, the students receive a Master's degree in physical or occupational therapy. Some of these schools are now offering a six-year degree program that includes both a Bachelor's and Master's degree.

Recreation and leisure studies is a fairly specialized major, so you'll need to do your research to find a program that meets your interests and needs. Typical courses include:

Foundations of Recreation, Parks, and Leisure Services

Leisure: Human Diversity and the Environment

Principles of Leadership

Special Problems in Recreation

Programming in Recreation, Parks, and Leisure Services

Diversity in Recreation, Parks, and Leisure Services

Foundations of Therapeutic Recreation

Therapeutic Activity Intervention and Aging

Management in Recreation, Sport, and Leisure Services

Evaluation of Leisure Services

Urban Recreation and Leisure Services

Legal Dimensions of Recreation, Parks, and Leisure Services

Planning, Designing, and Maintaining Recreation Areas

Fiscal Administration in Recreation and Leisure Services

Therapeutic Recreation Program Planning

Facilitation Techniques in Therapeutic Recreation

Principles and Resources of Nonprofit Management

Eco-Tourism and Ecology of Outdoor Recreation

The Professor Says _____

Many of the career paths in these fields require additional certifications and licenses beyond what you'll get while in college, so be certain to investigate exactly what you'll need for the career path you seek.

Background on Careers

Careers that arise from a major in exercise science or recreation and leisure studies are in demand because of the active lifestyle that Americans enjoy.

Some top jobs and careers for students earning a Bachelor's degree with a major in the health services include:

Athletic Trainer. As an athletic trainer, you'll work with clients ranging from professional athletes to industrial workers to help prevent and treat musculoskeletal injuries for people of all ages. Athletic trainers are often among the first health-care providers on the scene when injuries occur, and therefore you must be able to recognize, evaluate, and assess injuries and provide immediate care when needed—but you'll also be heavily involved in the rehabilitation and reconditioning of those injuries. Finally, you'll help prevent injuries by advising on the proper use of equipment and applying protective or injury-preventive devices such as tape, bandages, and braces.

Exercise Physiologist. In this job, you'll be involved with identifying physiological mechanisms underlying physical activity, comprehensively delivering treatment services concerned with the analysis, improvement, and maintenance of health and fitness, rehabilitation from heart disease and other chronic diseases and/or disabilities. You'll also professionally guide and counsel athletes and others interested in athletics, sports training, and human adaptability to acute and chronic exercise. You may work in the clinical area, education, administration, business, or research. You may have to be certified by the American Society of Exercise Physiologists (ASEP) to practice exercise physiology.

Fitness Instructor. In this job, you'll teach strengthening, endurance, aerobic, flexibility, and weight-training exercises, while promoting exercise as a healthy lifestyle choice. You are responsible for assessing the fitness level of clients, ensuring the safety of individuals, and teaching students to perform their exercises correctly. You must have excellent communication skills, a high degree of personal fitness and coordination, and should enjoy having clear rules, being organized, dealing with people, and designing new programs. In smaller facilities, you may also perform a variety of functions in addition to fitness instructing, such as tending the front desk, signing up new members, giving tours of the fitness center, writing newsletter articles, creating posters and flyers, and supervising the weight training and cardiovascular equipment areas.

Personal Trainer. As a personal trainer, you'll work in a variety of settings, such as gyms, health clubs, spas, and cruise ships, and assess the fitness levels and goals of your clients—and develop a fitness regimen to help them safely achieve them. As a trainer, you'll meet with your clients for an hour at each session and take them through workouts (weights, aerobics, and flexibility training) to help them reach their goals. You will monitor your clients' progress through methods such as body-fat testing and monitoring heart-rate levels, and give your clients advice about their lifestyle and general information about health and nutrition. Personal training could be the perfect career for you if you love motivating others to attain their goals and dreams.

Sports Administration Specialist. In this job, you'll work for an organization that manages a sports club, sporting event, or sports league. You'll assist management with organizing meetings, training, coaching, conferences, and other events, as well as consulting with clients, members, the community, and local sporting organizations. You may also be involved with dealing with local sports councils, regional committees, and national governing bodies. You'll also be involved with the promoting and marketing, producing promotional literature, reports and event materials, and handling media requests. In some cases, you may also assist in managing budgets, controlling finances allocated for community activities, and coordinating or raising corporate or local sponsorships.

Therapeutic Recreation Specialist. As a therapeutic recreation specialist (also referred to as a recreational therapist), you'll work with individuals who have mental, physical, or emotional disabilities—selecting activity modalities that are utilized to treat or maintain the physical, mental, and emotional well-being of consumers served. These interventions help individuals remediate the effects of illness or disability and achieve an optimal level of personal independence. The goals of interventions include improving physical, cognitive, and social functioning. You'll mostly work as a member of an interdisciplinary team, developing individual treatment plans and programs that are consistent with clients' needs, abilities, and interests. Many employers insist on hiring those individuals who have the NCTRC (National Council for Therapeutic Recreation Certification).

Other Career Possibilities. Here are some other job and career paths for exercise science and recreation and leisure studies majors:

Activities Specialist

Athletic Coach

Camp Director

Cruise Recreation Director

Early Childhood Motor Skills Instructor

Health Consultant

Health Information Specialist

Human Kinetics Specialist

Movement Education Specialist

Municipal Recreation Specialist

Recreation Director

Resort Recreation Director

Strength/Conditioning Coach

The Professor Says _____

These majors are also a solid foundation for students considering continuing their education and going into careers that require additional degrees, such as:

◆ Chiropractic Medicine

◆ Dentistry

◆ Optometry

◆ Occupational Therapy

◆ Physical Therapy

◆ Osteopathic Medicine

Skills Needed/Developed

Students majoring in exercise science or recreation and leisure studies develop numerous valuable and transferable skills. The following are the most critical to graduates:

Observation. The ability to read and understand people's reactions is an important skill you'll need to learn for this career. Observation skills help you assess how your training, coaching, or therapy is being received (and performed).

Interpersonal Communications. Because you'll be working directly with people, you must be able to talk and listen in one-on-one and small-group situations.

Written and Oral Communications.
Speaking and writing skills are essential
when pursuing a career in these fields.
You'll need the ability to clearly express
yourself, whether talking with clients or
creating written instructions or guidelines.

Investigation. Cataloging information,
observing and comparing people, data, and
things are essential skills you'll learn in
these majors.

The Professor Says _____

Other transferable skills
gained from these majors
include:

◆ Research

◆ Leadership

◆ Organization

◆ Teamwork

Expected Growth

Overall, job growth in the next decade for students who major in exercise science or
recreation and leisure studies is expected to be strong, and in some cases much faster
than the average (25 percent or higher) growth for all careers.

Athletic Trainers

Job growth for athletic trainers is expected to be much faster than the average (25 percent or higher) for all careers over the next decade.

A source of additional information can be found at National Athletic Trainers'
Association (www.nata.org).

Wondering what employers look for in an athletic trainer? Here's a sample athletic
trainer job description:

> Responsibilities include providing assistance with the provision of physical and
> occupational therapy services under the direction and supervision of the therapist
> for patient populations, including pediatric, adolescent, adult, and geriatric age
> groups. Provide athletic training for community events and company-sponsored
> health and wellness promotion programs. Utilize effective interpersonal skills.
> Qualifications: Bachelor's degree in athletic training, exercise science, or physi-
> cal education. National Athletic Training Association (NATA) Certification
> required. Experience in clinical- and/or collegiate-level care preferred. Must be
> able to lead/coordinate group activities. Must have highly developed interper-
> sonal skills.

Exercise Physiologists

Job growth for exercise physiologists is expected to be faster than the average (18 to 25 percent) for all careers over the next decade.

Wondering what employers look for in an exercise physiologist? Here's a sample exercise physiologist job description:

> Performs health coaching for our members with chronic diseases; conducts behavioral assessments to identify individual member knowledge, skills, and behavioral needs; coordinates specific health coaching as directed by nurse case manager to address objectives and goals as identified during assessment; implements coaching plan by using behavior change principles to identify member barriers and develop ways to overcome those barriers; coordinates with the nurse case manager to provide feedback on member goal attainment and clinical issues; monitors and evaluates the interventions and modifies as necessary; and performs other related duties as required. Requires a Bachelor's degree in the field of exercise physiology and relevant experience in health education, exercise instruction, or patient education, as appropriate. Must have the ability to work on multiple projects; strong organizational, problem-solving, and decision-making skills; and effective oral and written communication skills.

Fitness Instructors

Job growth for fitness instructors is expected to be much faster than the average (25 percent or higher) for all careers over the next decade.

Sources of additional information:

- ◆ IDEA Health & Fitness Association (www.ideafit.com)
- ◆ National Exercise Trainers Association (www.ndeita.com)

Personal Trainers

Job growth for personal trainers is expected to be much faster than the average (25 percent or higher) for all careers over the next decade.

Sources of additional information:

- ◆ Aerobics & Fitness Association of America (www.afaa.com)
- ◆ National Strength & Conditioning Association (www.nsca-lift.org)

Wondering what employers look for in a personal trainer? Here's a sample personal trainer job description:

> Our personal trainers have the ability to make fitness a way of life. At Quintessential Fitness, our fitness team helps get members involved with the benefits of health and fitness. With our 24/7/365 Program, our trainers provide personal, specialized fitness programs for their clients which include food intake, cardio respiratory training, supplementation, and resistance training. We are the industry leader in training and continuing education classes. We also offer National Certification Tuition Reimbursement. Prior experience is preferred, but not required; however, a love for fitness is a must! Also, you must be a true team player, one who has already learned the basics on the court, on the track, in the water, on the field, or on a team project. Want to get started? CPR Requirements: Must be valid. Accepted certifications: AFAA, ACSM, ACE, BSMI, Cooper, NCSF, NASM, NSCA, ISSA, NFPT. Accepted Bachelor's degrees: athletic training, exercise physiology, exercise science, human performance, kinesiology, nutrition, physical education, sports management.

Sports Administration Specialists

Job growth is expected to be faster than the average (18 to 25 percent) over the next decade.

Wondering what employers look for in a sports administration specialist? Here's a sample sports administration specialist job description:

> The youth sports health coordinator is responsible for Urban Youth Sports (UYS) program implementation and management, community organizing, and relationship and collaboration management. He/she is responsible for identifying community needs relating to youth physical activity and health and for developing and implementing appropriate sports and physical activity programming in collaboration with the UYS team. This person is responsible for attending community and task force meetings and other meetings to help us meet our youth sport-development goals. A core function of this position is to develop and foster relationships in the community centers, the community at large, and with parents and children of the surrounding neighborhoods. Bachelor's degree in related field required. Strong problem-solving, organizational, communication, technological, and interpersonal skills required. Must have ability to collaborate in the community; ability to coordinate programs; demonstrated experience working with a diverse team; excellent written communications; and strong time-management skills.

Therapeutic Recreation Specialists

Demand for therapeutic recreation specialists is expected to remain strong—but growth is expected to be slower than the average (under 8 percent) for all careers over the next decade.

Sources of additional information:

◆ American Therapeutic Recreation Association (www.atra-tr.org)

◆ National Council for Recreation Therapeutic Certification (www.nctrc.org)

◆ Therapeutic Recreation Resources (www.recreationtherapy.com)

Wondering what employers look for in a therapeutic recreation specialist? Here's a sample therapeutic recreation specialist job description:

You will be responsible for providing therapeutic activities, including creative arts, leisure education, special events, and experiential education groups such as dance movement and music therapy. You'll also be responsible for patient assessment, treatment planning, and documentation as part of an interdisciplinary team. You must be compassionate, caring, and nurturing, along with being organized, creative, and energetic, and enjoy working with youth. We are looking for exceptional individuals who want to provide hope to the children in our care. If clinical excellence is your desire, we would love to hear from you. New grads are encouraged to apply. Education: Bachelor's degree from an accredited college or university in therapeutic recreation, recreation science, or related field. Experience: related experience, with knowledge of psychiatric patient care techniques with understanding of mental illness preferred. Licensure: Must be eligible for CTRS and obtain certification within one year. Must maintain a valid driver's license. Additional Requirements: CPR certification. May be required to work overtime and weekend hours. We offer excellent benefits.

Fitness Superstar Denise Austin

For 25 years, Denise Austin, named "America's favorite fitness expert," has been working to promote people's health and fitness—on television, through videos and DVDs, and in books. She started gymnastics at the age of 12 and earned an athletic scholarship to the University of Arizona, graduating with a degree in exercise physiology. She began teaching aerobic exercise classes in the Los Angeles area, earning her own local television program two years later. Her career took off from there. Her television program, *Denise Austin's Daily Workout*, is the longest-running fitness show on television. Austin has produced more than 50 exercise videos, including her most recent, *Denise Austin's Personal Training System*. She has authored 10 books on fitness, including her most recent book, *Tone Your Tummy Type: Flatten Your Belly and Shrink Your Waist in 4 Weeks*. She is a member of the President's Council on Physical Fitness and Sports (PCPFS), an organization that strives to promote, encourage, and motivate Americans of all ages to become physically active and participate in sports.

Earnings Potential $

Exercise science and recreation and leisure studies graduates earn at least $30,000—a lower annual salary than the average for all college graduates, which is currently around $38,000.

The following section provides some general guidelines of salaries to expect upon graduation. Remember, salaries vary by employer, industry, and region.

Athletic Trainer. Median starting salary for an athletic trainer is about $32,000.

Exercise Physiologist. The median salary for an entry-level exercise physiologist is $33,000.

Fitness Instructor. Median annual salary for an entry-level fitness instructor ranges from $25,000 to $30,000.

The Professor Says _____

Your next step? Pick several careers that most fit your interests with a major in exercise science or recreation and leisure studies and dig more deeply into them. Remember that it is always important to learn more about prospective careers by researching online, talking with professors, conducting informational interviews, and job-shadowing.

Personal Trainer. Median annual salary of an entry-level personal trainer varies—partly on the number of clients and the hourly rate charged for services—but a rough estimate is about $25,000 to $30,000.

Sports Administration Specialist. Annual starting salary for a sports administration specialist is $38,000.

Therapeutic Recreation Specialist. Starting salary for a therapeutic recreation specialist is about $37,000.

The Professor Says

Your next step after choosing your major? Gaining work experience. Just about all "entry-level" jobs for college graduates require some work experience outside the classroom. Seek out internships, volunteer, and figure out other ways to gain the experience you need.

The Least You Need to Know

◆ Students who have a passion for health and wellness should be able to find a number of fast-growing and good-paying careers upon graduation.

◆ Many health services careers pay close to, or just below, the average for all jobs for college graduates.

◆ Job growth for many exercise science and recreation and leisure studies careers will be fast or faster than the average for all careers over the next decade.

◆ Some of the careers in exercise science and recreation and leisure studies fields require at least one certification in addition to your college education; some require additional education as well.

25

Health Sciences: Pre-Med and Pre-Pharmacy

In This Chapter

◆ Discover careers that use your passion for medicine

◆ Use those medical skills in jobs that demand them

◆ Learn the classes pre-med and pre-pharmacy majors require

◆ Find out key job and salary information

What do you do if you have always been interested in being a doctor? If you've always dreamed of saving lives? Have you always thought about discovering the next wonder drug? Want to be the local pharmacist?

This chapter reveals rewarding careers for students majoring in one of the health sciences—pre-med or pre-pharmacy.

About the Majors

The health sciences include majors in pre-med and pre-pharmacy (and some colleges actually have a major called health sciences), preparing you for a future professional career in medicine. By majoring in one of these areas, you'll gain a solid background and general knowledge about math and applied science that can be used in a variety of in-demand careers in a wide range of employment settings (i.e., hospitals, pharmaceutical companies, large medical practices, insurance companies, and more) whether you attend graduate school or not.

Pre-Med

Pre-med majors take a set of courses, commonly referred to as the pre-med curriculum, to meet the admission requirements of medical schools. The pre-med curriculum consists of general chemistry, organic chemistry, biology, and physics. An increasing number of schools also require biochemistry. Some schools require calculus or some other math option, and a few require two years of biology.

Pre-med is a fairly common major, especially at traditional four-year colleges and universities, but you'll want to check to see whether it's a major or simply a program.

Typical courses include:

General Chemistry

Biological Principles

General Physics

Organic Chemistry

Elective courses include:

Genetics

Biochemistry

Embryology

Human Physiology

Human Anatomy

Microbiology

The Professor Says

So, what major should you choose if considering medical school? According to the Association of American Medical Colleges, as a pre-medical student, you may select any major you choose, provided that you complete the pre-med curriculum. You can choose to major in pre-med; you can choose a major from one of the sciences; you can choose a major in which the material comes easily to you so that you'll graduate with a high grade point average; or you can choose a major based on your passions.

Pre-Pharmacy

Pre-pharmacy majors typically receive a foundation of coursework in mathematics and the basic sciences (chemistry, biology, physics). In fact, like pre-med, some pre-pharmacy programs are also encouraging additional courses in biology and anatomy. One thing to watch for as you look at programs: some pre-pharmacy programs are only two- or three-year programs and not full-degree programs.

Pre-pharmacy—as a major—is a rather specialized major, especially at traditional four-year colleges, so you'll need to do your research to find a program that meets your interests and needs. In many situations, it might be best to investigate undergraduate programs at the university where you want to attend pharmacy school.

Typical courses include:

General Chemistry

Biological Principles

General Physics

Organic Chemistry

Elective courses include:

Cellular and Molecular Biology

Biochemistry

Human Anatomy

Microbiology

Human Physiology

Genetics

 Major Pitfalls

Because medical and pharmacy schools have their own requirements for admission, it's best to start planning as early as possible, developing a list of which programs you hope to apply to/attend so that you can be certain to take all the courses they require as prerequisites while you are still in college.

Background on Careers

Careers in medicine will always be in demand, and whether or not you go on to attend medical or pharmacy school and become a doctor or pharmacist, plenty of other options are still available to you with an undergraduate degree in these areas.

Graduates of these health sciences programs typically start their careers in medical, pharmaceutical, or research positions with clinics, hospitals, medical practices, pharmacies, or other similar institutions, but can also seek employment in business and industry.

Following is a list of some top jobs and careers for students earning a Bachelor's degree with a major in the health sciences:

Health (Information) Services Specialist. As a health services specialist, you'll work for a medical practice providing a variety of services, such as reviewing medical records for completeness and accuracy; preparing statistical, case, and other types of reports; preparing materials and forms and gathering all pertinent information and data for admissions and discharges; assisting in the development of medical records policies and procedures; reviewing existing policies and procedures to ensure compliance with federal and state laws and agency rules, regulations, and policies; ensuring the security and confidentiality of patient medical records; and sometimes handling patient concerns and complaints.

Medical Laboratory Technician. In this job (also referred to as a Medical Technologist), you'll conduct a full range of tests to help detect, diagnose, and treat diseases. After the tests are run, you'll record, evaluate, and send results back to physicians or medical researchers for review. This job is typically a critical first job for many science graduates, one in which you'll be honing your research skills while providing key laboratory support, such as inspecting, cleaning, testing, calibrating, adjusting, and maintaining lab equipment, before advancing to higher-level positions within the laboratory, academic institution, or hospital. You may work in research, quality control, or a manufacturing environment. Some technicians run all types of tests while others specialize.

Pharmaceutical Chemist. As a pharmaceutical chemist, you'll help develop and evaluate new medications that prevent, cure, and relieve symptoms of disease and improve analytical techniques for monitoring the levels of drugs in the body. Pharmaceutical chemists use both sophisticated instruments and simple experimental procedures to study the safety and reliability of existing and experimental drugs and chemicals that are present in drug samples or blood or tissue samples taken from humans or animals that have been treated with a drug. You'll typically work in teams of professionals during the development and testing of new drugs.

Pharmaceutical Technician. As a pharmacy technician, you'll help licensed pharmacists provide medication and other health-care products to patients in a variety of settings, including retail pharmacies, hospitals, nursing homes, and assisted-living facilities. You'll typically perform routine tasks such as collecting key information from patients (as well as handling their general questions and complaints), preparing prescribed medication for patients (often by retrieving, counting, pouring, weighing, measuring, and sometimes mixing medications and preparing labels and instructions), establishing and maintaining patient profiles, preparing insurance claim forms, and stocking and taking inventory of prescription and over-the-counter medications.

Pharmaceutical Sales Representative. As a pharmaceutical sales representative, you'll combine your love of medicine with a passion for sales and work in a highly competitive and sometimes frustrating profession making sales calls and presentations to medical facilities (doctors offices, hospitals, pharmacies, nursing homes, and assisted-living facilities) in an attempt to educate and persuade the staff to begin (or continue) prescribing your company's medications. You'll spend much of your day on the road, attempting to call on prospective customers to introduce products and/or increase sales-level volume from existing customers; provide the technical expertise to explain products and answer technical questions; and maintain accurate records of all sales activity.

Physician Assistant. In this job, working as part of a health-care team, you'll take medical histories, perform physical exams, order and interpret lab tests and x-rays, diagnose and treat illnesses, assist in surgery, prescribe and dispense medication, and counsel patients. Like the physicians you'll serve, physician assistants (PAs) can follow many career paths, including university hospital work, private practice, and jobs with Health Maintenance Organizations (HMOs). Basically, wherever there are doctors, there are physician assistants. You may also have managerial duties, such as ordering medical supplies or equipment and supervising technicians and assistants. In rural areas or inner cities, you may be the principal care provider for your patients.

Other Career Possibilities. Here are some other job and career paths for pre-med and pre-pharmacy majors:

Anesthesiologist	Nuclear Medicine Technologist
Audiologist	Pharmacologist
Drug Information Specialist	Phlebotomist
Forensic Scientist/Criminalist	Physical Therapist
Geriatric Care Manager	Psychiatrist
Health Promotion and Awareness Coordinator	Radiopharmacist
	Respiratory Therapist
Hospital Administrator	Surgeon
Medical Devices Sales Representative	

Skills Needed/Developed

Students majoring in the health sciences develop numerous valuable and transferable skills. The following are the most critical to graduates:

Analytical/Critical Thinking. This skill involves your ability to get to the heart of a problem or situation by breaking it down into smaller, more manageable parts, analyzing information, evaluating alternatives, and proposing viable solutions.

Problem-Solving. One of the most important skills for any scientist, this skill involves your ability to identify complex problems, review existing conditions and restrictions, and develop and evaluate alternative solutions to the problem.

Scientific Method. Like all science majors, you'll possess an understanding of the scientific method, which involves the formulation of a hypothesis concerning some phenomena, experimentation to demonstrate the truth or fallacy of the hypothesis, and a conclusion that validates or modifies the hypothesis.

The Professor Says

Other transferable skills you gain from these majors include:

- Teamwork
- Leadership
- Organization
- Synthesizing information

Written and Oral Communications. Speaking and writing skills are essential when pursuing a career in health sciences. You'll need the ability to clearly express yourself, whether talking with patients or other medical professionals.

Technical/Computer Skills. Because many of the jobs in the health sciences require using computers and specific software applications, you'll acquire key technical and computer skills.

Expected Growth

Overall, job growth is expected to be strong in the next decade for students who major in the health sciences field. In some cases, growth will be much faster than the average (25 percent or higher) for all careers.

Physicians

Job growth for all physicians and surgeons is expected to be faster than the average (18 to 25 percent) for all careers over the next decade.

Sources of additional information:

◆ American Board of Medical Specialties (www.abms.org)

◆ American College of Physicians (www.acponline.org)

◆ American College of Surgeons (www.facs.org)

◆ American Medical Association (www.ama-assn.org)

◆ Association of American Medical Colleges (www.aamc.org)

profiles

AIDS Researcher Ruth Ruprecht

Ruth Ruprecht, M.D., Ph.D., is a professor of medicine at Harvard Medical School and the Dana-Farber Cancer Institute whose ground-breaking research led to the discovery that pregnant women infected with HIV could safely take antiretroviral drugs to protect their babies from the disease. After studying chemistry at Zurich University, Switzerland, she earned a Ph.D., in human genetics from Columbia University and an M.D. from the University of Miami School of Medicine. Dr. Ruprecht completed her residency training in internal medicine at the University of California, followed by a fellowship in hematology-oncology at Memorial Sloan-Kettering Cancer Center. She later joined the Dana-Farber Cancer Institute. Dr. Ruprecht directs a multi-institutional AIDS research program that involves collaborators in the United States, Europe, China, and Africa. She is the recipient of a National Institutes of Health (NIH) Merit Award and the (Massachusetts) Governor's Award in Recognition of Outstanding Contributions to AIDS Research, and has published numerous papers in medical journals.

Pharmacists

Job growth for pharmacists is expected to be faster than the average (18 to 25 percent) for all careers over the next decade.

Sources of additional information:

◆ American Association of Colleges of Pharmacy (www.aacp.org)

◆ American Pharmacists Association (www.aphanet.org)

The Professor Says _____

There are all types of pharmacists, including:

- ◆ Community (Chain-Store) Pharmacist
- ◆ Independent (Retailer) Community Pharmacist
- ◆ Hospital and Institutional Pharmacist
- ◆ Managed-Care Pharmacist
- ◆ Consulting Pharmacist
- ◆ Academic Pharmacist
- ◆ Pharmaceutical Corporation Pharmacist
- ◆ Government Pharmacist

Health (Information) Services Specialists

Job growth for health services specialists is expected to be much faster than the average (25 percent or higher) for all careers over the next decade.

Medical Laboratory Technicians

Job growth for medical laboratory technicians is expected to be faster than the average (18 to 25 percent) for all careers over the next decade.

Sources of additional information:

- ◆ American Medical Technologists (www.amt1.com)
- ◆ American Society of Clinical Pathology (www.ascp.org)

Wondering what employers look for in a medical laboratory technician? Here's a sample medical technician job description:

> We need a medical technologist who can evaluate test results for gross errors prior to release; verify, transcribe, and transmit results per protocol; refer questionable or designated review results; follow critical-result and call-result policies; assure proper instrument function prior to release of test data; perform calibration and maintenance procedures; troubleshoot instrument malfunctions; communicate patient information to physician, office staff, and hospital employees; act as clinical laboratory information resource to all customer groups; and accurately transcribe and verbalize patient data. Bachelor of Science degree in medical technology or biology or related field is required.

Pharmaceutical Chemists

Job growth for pharmaceutical chemists is expected to be faster than the average (18 to 25 percent) for all careers over the next decade as the pharmaceutical industry continues to increase spending on new drug development and clinical trials.

A source of additional information can be found at American Association of Pharmaceutical Scientists (www.aapspharmaceutica.com).

Pharmaceutical Technicians

Job growth for pharmaceutical technicians is expected to be much faster than the average (25 percent or higher) for all careers over the next decade.

A source of additional information can be found at National Pharmacy Technician Association (www.pharmacytechnician.org).

Wondering what employers look for in a pharmaceutical technician? Here's a sample pharmaceutical technician job description:

> We're looking for a pharmacy technician with excellent communication skills to complement our Medicaid team. This office-based role offers a Monday through Friday schedule and a nice change of pace from the hospital or retail setting. The primary responsibilities of this position include serving as the key point of contact for providers in assisting with the administration of pharmacy benefits; processing prior notification requests and coordinating evaluation of requests by clinical pharmacists and medical directors; assisting with the administration of pharmacy benefits; researching appeals and complaints; and interfacing with pharmacists, providers, and medical directors to gather and provide information regarding prescriptions and previous cases. Strong communication and customer service skills are key, and general computer proficiency is also needed. Prefer someone who is a Certified Pharmacy Technician—or has ability to quickly obtain certification.

Pharmaceutical Sales Representatives

Demand for pharmaceutical sales representatives is expected to remain very strong— and growth should be faster than the average (18 to 25 percent) for all careers over the next decade.

Wondering what employers look for in a pharmaceutical sales representative? Here's a sample pharmaceutical sales representative job description:

> As a sales representative in the pharmaceutical sales industry you will meet or exceed product sales objectives for an assigned portfolio of products. You will be responsible for providing health-care professionals with all relevant information that promotes quality health-care decisions. The following represents your key responsibilities to achieve this objective: jointly create call plan and resource strategies with district management; successfully implement the call plan, and deploy resource strategies as developed with district management to maximize sales results; continuously prospect for appropriate new customers and develop business relationships with the "highest value" customers; customize the delivery of product to align with customer needs; prepare for and actively participate in all required sales conferences and training classes at local and/or remote locations; undertake a program of performance and career development to continually strive to improve knowledge, skills, and capabilities. This position requires a Bachelor's degree. Prior pharmaceutical or health-care selling experience is preferred. A demonstrated ability to work independently and manage time effectively is required. Must have effective interpersonal, organizational, and communication skills. Demonstrated creativity to accomplish sales goals is required. An understanding of market strategy, tactical mix, and financial management is required.

Physician Assistants

Job growth is expected to be much faster than the average (25 percent or higher) over the next decade, and is expected to be one of the fastest-growing of all occupations.

Sources of additional information:

◆ American Academy of Physicians Assistants (www.aapa.org)

◆ National Commission on the Certification of Physician Assistants (www.nccpa. net)

Earnings Potential $

It may be a bit misleading to talk about earnings potential here since both pre-med and pre-pharmacy are majors designed for continued studies, not careers. Students who have a major in the sciences, though, generally earn a starting salary higher than the average for all college graduates.

The following section provides some general guidelines of salaries to expect upon graduation. Remember, salaries vary by employer, industry, and region.

Physician. Median starting salary for a primary care physician in the first year of practice is about $120,000; for a surgeon, it's about $170,000.

Pharmacist. The median salary for a first-year pharmacist ranges from $82,000 to $88,000, depending on the type of employer.

Health Services Specialist. Median annual salary for an entry-level health services specialist ranges from $35,000 to $40,000.

Medical Laboratory Technician. Median annual salary of an entry-level medical laboratory technician is about $32,000.

The Professor Says

Not sure about these career choices? These are just some of the career possibilities for a major in pre-med and pre-pharmacy. Remember that it is always important to learn more about prospective careers by researching online, talking with professors, conducting informational interviews, and job-shadowing.

Pharmaceutical Chemist. The median annual salary of an entry-level pharmaceutical chemist is $40,000.

Pharmaceutical Technician. Starting salary for a pharmaceutical technician is about $25,000.

Pharmaceutical Sales Representative. Beginning salaries for pharmaceutical sales representatives vary widely since total compensation is based on commission and salary, though most first-year salespeople earn between $50,000 and $80,000.

Physician Assistant. Annual starting salary for a physician assistant ranges from $56,000 to $65,000. Surgical physician assistants can earn more than $100,000.

The Professor Says

Remember that you're not done once you pick your college major—in fact, it's just begun, because the next thing you need to do is gain work experience. Just about all "entry-level" jobs for college graduates require some work experience outside the classroom. Seek out internships, volunteer, and figure out other ways to gain the experience you need.

The Least You Need to Know

◆ Pre-med and pre-pharmacy students are well-positioned for attaining well-paying jobs upon completion of graduate studies.

◆ Students who major in one of the health sciences and choose not to attend graduate school can find rewarding careers with various types of organizations, including hospitals, doctor offices, health-care providers, and pharmaceutical companies.

◆ Many health sciences careers pay above the average for all jobs for college graduates.

◆ Job growth for many health science careers will be fast or faster than the average for all careers over the next decade.

Part 6

Careers in the Social Sciences Using a Major in ...

This part spotlights a wide variety of career paths you could follow if you major in one of the social sciences, including history, psychology, and sociology, as well as criminology and pre-law.

Social science majors study the human aspects of the world around us and typically find careers related to understanding human behavior or finding ways to improve the lives of people. Whether you want to help create laws and legislation or use them to take people to court, create computer systems or websites to enable people to live better lives, or counsel people who are less fortunate than you, a major in one of these fields may be just right for you.

"What if I majored in anthropology?"

Chapter **26**

History and Political Science

In This Chapter

- ◆ Discover careers that use your passion for history
- ◆ Use those persuasion skills in jobs that demand them
- ◆ Learn the typical classes that history and political science majors require
- ◆ Find key job and salary information

What do you do if you love researching and learning about the past? What can you do with your life if you enjoy analyzing long-past events, wars that have been won or lost ages ago, or the rise and fall of civilizations, societies, families, politicians, governments, and political parties? Do you enjoy attending political events and reading about the political process? How can you make a living based on your passion for history or political science?

This chapter reveals rewarding careers for students majoring in history or political science.

About the Majors

History and political science majors share a number of common traits, interests, and skills. Both majors focus on the study of people and events, but what can you expect from these majors if you choose to study one or both of them?

History Majors

History majors and historians examine, analyze, and seek to interpret the facts, figures, artifacts, and timelines of the past. They possess a natural curiosity and use multiple sources of information to uncover records of the day, including government reports, institutional records, media accounts, personal stories, photographs, films, art, and any other information source. Some historians specialize in a particular time, place, or person (or group of people). Historians don't simply study past events; they seek out, record, and analyze political, social, economic, and cultural events, as well as peoples' lives and achievements, to gain a true understanding of the past.

Most colleges and universities offer just one general history track, though often students can specialize in American history or world history. Typical courses include:

The Study of History

Contemporary Civilization

Early World Civilization

American History

Slavery and the Civil War

The American Revolution

World History

European History

World Wars

American Diplomacy

Modern Europe

Modern Russia

Modern Middle East

Modern Asia

History of Communism

History of Capitalism

Medieval Europe

History of the Holocaust

Women and History

History of the American Indian

The Renaissance and the Reformation

History of Ancient Civilizations

Development of American Foreign Relations

The Crusades and Holy Wars

Political Science Majors

Political science majors examine world events and public affairs through multiple viewpoints and attempt to put them in perspective. They study the workings of various governments and governmental agencies, including the history and development of governments, the rise and fall of political parties, rulers, and organizations, the traditions and laws of ruling bodies, and the inner workings of power brokers and lobbyists. Political scientists review both the formal and informal traditions, rules, and culture of ruling bodies, as well as research public opinion, analyze polling and election data, review public documents and records, and meet with government officials.

Many colleges allow political science majors to specialize in a certain area, such as U.S. politics, international politics, law and justice, and public policy. Typical courses include:

American Government

Introduction to Politics

Comparative Politics

International Relations

World Affairs

Law and Society

Public Administration

Western Political Thought

Environmental Politics

Gender Politics

American Judicial System

State and Local Government

Constitutional Law

International Law

Latin American Politics

Asian Politics

The American Presidency

Press and Politics

National Security and World Relations

Political Theory and Methodology

Political Parties and Elections

American Political Thought

Politics of the Developing World

Political Science Research Methods

Background on Careers

Of course, you could easily become a teacher or professor of history or political science at the secondary school or college level (although additional education and certifications are typically required) as some majors do, but what about other career paths for people who do not want to teach? Historians and political scientists also work in government, archives, libraries, museums, historical societies, historic preservation societies and other nonprofit organizations, think tanks, publishing houses, political parties, law firms, and large corporations.

Some top jobs and careers for students earning a Bachelor's degree with a major in history or political science include:

Archivist/Curator/Museum Technician. As an archivist, you'll acquire, organize, analyze, and maintain records and documents, art collections, buildings, and other historical objects; verify authenticity and significance of the historical material, and develop plans to ensure the long-term preservations of collections for researchers and the public. You may also conduct tours and give lectures on historical topics. Archivists work for libraries, museums, governments, corporations, colleges and universities, historical sites, and any other organizations that require the preservation of important materials.

Legislative Analyst/Aide. In this job, you carry out research, writing, and liaison functions for an elected official, such as a state or federal senator or congressional representative or a municipal officeholder. You also communicate with the elected official's constituents. You might also work for a lobbyist or nonprofit organization, and can play a major role in shaping political discussions and legislative direction by recommending alternative solutions to current problems.

Librarian Technician/Library Aide. As a library technician, you'll administer school, community, or corporate library facilities, typically in one of two areas: technical and user services. Technical services deal with acquiring and preparing materials. User services deal directly with library users. Librarians, more aptly called information professionals, deal with documents in a variety of mediums and from a wide variety of sources.

Lobbyist/Public Policy Specialist. Politicians are certainly not alone when developing and voting on key laws and legislation. Behind the scenes in governmental bodies across the United States, scores of lobbyists labor to protect and promote the interests of the groups they represent. Typically, as a lobbyist, you represent specific businesses or industires, but more recently political organizations have hired lobbyists to help influence positions on moral and cultural issues.

A Day in the Life ... of a Lobbyist

8:00 A.M.	I arrive early to catch the major headlines in key media outlets and review the agenda for today.
9:30 A.M.	Our staff meeting covers key agenda items, legislative imperatives, and key contacts.
10:00 A.M.	I walk up to the statehouse to meet with several key legislators and their staff.
12:00 P.M.	Lunch with several key legislators that support client's position, discussing expectations of hearings that will follow this afternoon. Meals are important opportunities to make contacts and promote the cause I represent for my clients.
1:30 P.M.	Attend hearings on a key issue important to the folks who pay my salary.
3:30 P.M.	Stepping out of the hearings for a moment, I call to get a research assistant working on a key point that arises in the hearing unexpectedly.
4:30 P.M.	With the hearings adjourned for the day, it's back to the office to meet with the research assistant, analyze the information, and prepare a position paper.
5:30 P.M.	E-mail the position paper to the legislators who support the position of my client so that they have it first thing in the morning.
6:00 P.M.	Rush home to change for a business dinner.
7:30 P.M.	Dinner with key members of the agricultural co-op to bring them up to speed on current legislative issues and make sure they are happy with my services.

Politician/Political Campaign Aide. Some politicians attend law school first, but as a recent college graduate, you can certainly run for local office in your municipality, county, or even state. Politicians play a major role in shaping the political, social, and cultural landscape of the people they represent. And if you don't want to be the politician yourself, you can become a key member of the campaign support staff.

Protocol Specialist/Foreign Service Agent. The federal government hires history and political science majors to help

The Professor Says

Some of the more lucrative and prestigious career paths that history and political science majors follow require additional education at the graduate level. These careers include:

- College Professor (Doctorate required)
- Lawyer (Juris Doctorate)
- Think Tank Fellow (Master's degree or higher)

understand the history, politics, and culture of foreign countries. As a foreign service agent or protocol specialist (also referred to as a diplomat), you'll work at various locations around the world (including in the United States) promoting the interests of the U.S. government and businesses. Numerous governmental agencies need workers to provide critical insight and context for potential policy decisions.

Sales Analyst. By drawing on a keen understanding of culture, history, and people, history and political science graduates evaluate consumer and cultural cycles and predict market swings. Using your research skills, you can help corporations enhance their success by studying short-term and medium-term sales histories, developing sales forecasts, and making recommendations for market strategy shifts.

Other Career Possibilities. Some other job and career paths for history and political science majors include:

Community Relations Assistant	Military Officer
FBI/CIA Agent	Museum Curator
Genealogist	Peace Corps/VISTA Worker
Government Worker/Civil Servant	Public Opinion Interviewer
Historical Preservationist	Research Assistant
International Relations Specialist	Teacher, Social Studies
Labor Relations Specialist	Writer/Editor/Foreign Correspondent

Skills Needed/Developed

Students majoring in history and political science develop numerous valuable and transferable skills. The following are the most critical to graduates:

Research Proficiency. Just about all jobs and careers in political science and history require the aptitude to uncover information and solutions to complex issues. This skill includes the ability to understand and interpret information from one situation and apply it to the current situation.

Oral and Written Communication. Speaking, listening, and writing skills are essential to political science and history careers. Political science majors, especially, learn the power of persuasive speech and debating techniques. Many jobs and careers require writing comprehensive documents and position papers, as well as reports and memos.

Interpersonal (Persuasive) Communications. This skill involves the ability to listen, respond, interact, and communicate successfully, and includes accurately interpreting verbal and nonverbal messages, giving feedback, communicating effectively as a team member, and using cultural and social sensitivity.

Analytical/Critical Thinking. You must develop the ability to get to the heart of a problem or situation by breaking it down into smaller, more manageable parts, analyzing information, evaluating alternatives, and proposing viable solutions.

The Professor Says

Other transferable skills gained from these majors include:

◆ Teamwork

◆ Leadership

◆ Time management

◆ Technical/computer

Record Keeping. An eye for detail and a natural ability for organization are critical skills for political science and history majors. Many of the jobs and careers for history and political science majors require accurate recording and accessing critical information and artifacts.

Expected Growth

Overall, job growth in the next decade for students who major in history or political science is expected to be average (10 to 15 percent) at best, and in some cases slower than the average growth for all careers.

Historians

Job growth for historians is expected to be slower than the average (under 8 percent) for all careers over the next decade.

Sources of additional information:

◆ American Historical Association (www.historians.org)

◆ Organization of American Historians (www.oah.org)

Political Scientists

Job growth for political scientists is expected to be slower than the average (under 8 percent) for all careers over the next decade.

Sources of additional information:

◆ The American Political Science Association (www.apsanet.org)

◆ International Political Science Association (www.ipsa.ca)

Historian Doris Kearns Goodwin

Doris Kearns Goodwin is a Pulitzer Prize–winning author and presidential historian. She graduated Phi Beta Kappa from Colby College. While in college, she undertook summer internships at the U.S. Congress and the State Department. She won a Woodrow Wilson Fellowship and earned a Ph.D. in Government at Harvard University. She worked with President Lyndon Johnson and later assisted the former president with preparing his memoirs. Some of her books include: *Lyndon Johnson and The American Dream*; *The Fitzgeralds and The Kennedys*; *No Ordinary Time: Franklin and Eleanor Roosevelt: The Home Front in World War II* (Pulitzer Prize for history in 1995); and *Team of Rivals: The Political Genius of Abraham Lincoln*.

Archivists/Curators/Museum Technicians

Some job growth is expected—about as fast as the average for all careers (10 to 15 percent)–but expect strong competition for available jobs, because qualified applicants generally outnumber job openings.

Sources of additional information:

◆ Society of American Archivists (www.archivists.org)

◆ Academy of Certified Archivists (www.certifiedarchivists.org)

Legislative Analysts/Aides

Job growth is expected to be about the same as average (10 to 15 percent) over the next decade, but opportunities will always be available for sharp graduates in both political parties at the local, state, and national levels.

Sources of additional information:

◆ Democratic National Committee (www.democrats.org)

◆ Republican National Committee (www.rnc.org)

Wondering what employers look for in a legislative aide? Here's a sample legislative aide job description:

> This position represents the university to state government. Research, review, and provide information regarding legislation and budgets in the areas of higher education, employment, agriculture, environment, labor, and other topics affecting the university. Prepare written materials and set up meetings as appropriate. Assist with modifying, advancing, or opposing legislation. Respond to requests for information. Develop and maintain databases. Strong interpersonal, communication (written and oral), and organization skills are required. Ability to manage multiple priorities is important.

Librarian Technicians/Library Aides

The combination of a large number of retirements and the increase in the use of digital information should spur moderate to high job growth (15 to 19 percent) over the next decade, especially in specialized libraries.

Sources of additional information:

- American Library Association (www.ala.org)
- Special Libraries Association (www.sla.org)

Lobbyists

The lobbying industry is highly competitive, but expectations are that jobs will continue to grow as more organizations seek to influence legislative agendas.

A source of additional information can be found at the American League of Lobbyists (www.alldc.org).

Politicians/Legislators

About 66,000 legislators worked in federal, state, and local governments in 2004, with job growth expected to be slower than average (under 8 percent) over the next decade.

Sources of additional information:

- Democratic National Committee (www.democrats.org)
- Republican National Committee (www.rnc.org)

Senator Joseph Maxwell "Max" Cleland

Joseph Maxwell "Max" Cleland graduated with a history degree from Stetson University in 1964. While attending college, Cleland was also a member of ROTC, so upon graduation he served in the U.S. Army for three years before being seriously wounded in Vietnam. He started his political career as a state senator in 1971, serving in that capacity until 1975, when he was hired as a consultant to the U.S. Senate Committee on Veterans Affairs. In 1977, President Jimmy Carter appointed him to lead the U.S. Veterans Administration—the youngest director ever, and the first Vietnam veteran to do so. In 1982, Cleland was elected as Georgia's secretary of state, a position he held for 14 years before winning a seat as U.S. senator for Georgia.

Protocol Specialists/Foreign Service Agents/Officers

Job growth is expected to be better than average (18 to 25 percent) as older diplomats retire and diplomatic opportunities around the world increase.

Sources of additional information:

◆ American Foreign Service Association (www.afsa.org)

◆ Association for Diplomatic Studies and Training (adst.org)

Sales Analysts

Job growth is expected to be faster than average (18 to 25 percent) over the next decade as the need for competitive information and viable forecasting becomes critical in the marketplace.

Sources of additional information:

◆ American Marketing Association (www.marketingpower.com)

◆ Business Marketing Association (www.marketing.org)

Wondering what employers look for in a sales analyst? Here's a sample sales analyst job description:

This position involves supporting the senior marketer in every phase of the strategic sales process. Sales analysts are called on to track current market, industry, and company activity; develop economic forecasts and research; present information and prepare client presentation materials; and coordinate with professionals throughout the organization, including senior management, group heads, product specialists, and fellow analysts. Candidates must demonstrate quantitative skills, strategic and creative thinking, and distinguished written and oral communications skills. Must work effectively as an individual and as part of a team.

The Professor Says

There are many career possibilities for a major in history or political science beyond the ones featured here. Remember that it is always important to learn more about prospective careers by going online, talking with professors, conducting informational interviews, and job-shadowing.

Earnings Potential $

History and political science graduates earn a slightly lower annual salary than the average for all college graduates, which is currently around $38,000. More specifically, history majors earned an average annual salary of $33,000, while political science majors earned an average yearly salary of $32,000.

The following provides some general guidelines of salaries to expect upon graduation. Remember, salaries vary by employer, industry, and region.

Archivist/Curator/Museum Technician. Median annual salary of an archivist ranges from $36,000 to $41,000.

Legislative Analyst/Aide. Beginning salaries can range from as low as $15,000 for lower-level political offices and nonprofit organizations to more than $30,000.

Librarian Technician/Library Aide. Median annual earnings of library technicians vary, depending on the type of library:

    College and university libraries: $28,940

    Federal government libraries: $39,647

    Local government libraries: $23,560

    Elementary and secondary school libraries: $22,510

The Professor Says

Your next step after choosing your major? Gaining work experience. Just about all "entry-level" jobs for college graduates require some work experience outside the classroom. Seek out internships, volunteer, and figure out other ways to gain the experience you need.

Lobbyist. Median annual salary of a lobbyist ranges from $49,000 to more than $90,000.

Politician/Legislator. Median annual salaries range somewhat broadly from little or next to nothing for local political office to much higher for national elected positions. The middle half of all legislators earned between $13,080 and $37,380 in 2004.

Protocol Specialist/Foreign Service Agent/ Officer. Starting salary for a foreign service agent is about $40,000.

Sales Analyst. Salaries for entry-level positions are typically in the $35,000 to $40,000 range.

The Least You Need to Know

◆ Political science or history majors have numerous choices of careers in all types of organizations, including education, business, and government.

◆ You can major in political science or history and obtain a well-paying job upon graduation.

◆ While job growth will be moderate at best, history and political science graduates should still be able to find good jobs.

◆ As a political science or history major, you'll learn valuable skills that are in demand in a number of career fields.

Chapter 27

Mathematics and Computer Science

In This Chapter

- ◆ Discover jobs that draw on a passion for using numbers
- ◆ Use your analytical skills in careers that demand them
- ◆ Use your computational skills in careers that demand them
- ◆ Learn the typical classes that math and computer science majors require
- ◆ Find out what kinds of jobs and salaries to expect

What do you do for a career if you love math and mathematical models and equations? If spending hours on your computer designing programs excites you? What if you spend more time at your computer than anything else? Consider yourself a geek—and proud of it? Have pi memorized to at least 15 decimal places?

This chapter reveals rewarding careers for students majoring in math or computer science.

About the Majors

These two majors—often housed in the same academic department—depend on abstract thinking and strong analytical and decision-making skills. The study of mathematics gives students a solid foundation for a variety of careers using the theoretical and applied skills developed. Math and computer science work together in the design and development of computer programming languages, networks, systems, and hardware.

Mathematics

Math majors learn a body of knowledge centered on concepts such as quantity, structure, space, and change, preparing them for professional careers in statistics, actuarial sciences, business and industry, economics, mathematical modeling, cryptography, teaching, and more.

Mathematics is a common major at any college or university. Typical courses include:

Basic College Mathematics	Multivariate Calculus
Elementary Functions	Linear Algebra
History of Mathematics	Calculus for Life Sciences
Vector Analysis	Logic and Proof
Math Concepts for Teachers	Differential Equations
Calculus	Number Theory
Mathematical Game Theory	Operations Research
Chaos and Fractals	Graph Theory
Mathematical Modeling	Probability
Geometry	Statistics
Advanced Calculus	Abstract Algebra
Advanced Geometry	Complex Analysis
Business Calculus	Actuarial Mathematics
Cryptology	Algebraic Structures

Computer Science

Computer science is the study of theoretical and applied aspects of computer technology and usage. These majors learn computer architecture and languages, but more than that, get a solid foundation in math and statistics so that their careers are not restricted to any specific technology. Within some majors, you may specialize in management information systems (MIS), computer science, information technology, and digital communications (web design and e-marketing).

Computer science is a fairly common major, especially at larger colleges and universities. Typical courses include:

Computers and Information Technology

Web Design and Programming

Computer Science

Programming Language Basics

Computer Architecture

Operating Systems

Software Development

Programming in C

Programming in C and C++

Programming in UNIX

Internet Programming

Writing in Computer Science

Computer Organization

Multinational Finance

History of Computing

Ethics in Computer Science

Computer Graphics

Systems Engineering

Compiler Design

Database Systems Design

Artificial Intelligence

Multimedia Techniques

Analysis of Algorithms

Computer System Security

Introduction to Robotics

Software Engineering

Gaming Programming

Background on Careers

Mathematics graduates gain the quantitative skills and abstract thinking abilities for a career in a wide variety of fields. While you could certainly teach math to middle and high school students, you can also land jobs in the private sector as an actuary, air traffic controller, business consultant, inventory control specialist, risk analyst, or transportation planner.

Computer science graduates enter a world that is dependent on computers and where career possibilities range from database management, computer infrastructure, information technology, computer engineering to web administration. You may work in academia, government, or industry—because just about every organization has a need for computer scientists.

Some top jobs and careers for students earning a Bachelor's degree with a major in math or computer science include:

Actuary. In this job, you'll conduct analyses, pricing, and risk assessment to estimate financial outcomes; apply knowledge of mathematics, probability, statistics, principles of finance and business to calculations in life, health, and casualty insurance, annuities, and pensions; and develop probability tables regarding fire, natural disasters, death, unemployment, etc., based on analysis of statistical data and other pertinent information.

Computer Programmer. As a computer programmer, you'll write detailed code (commands) that instruct computers to perform tasks, such as finding specific information, analyzing it, and choosing equipment for the process. While you may develop your own programs, you will probably work with established programs, updating, modifying, and expanding their functions to meet the needs of the organization. Some of the current programming languages you may use in this job include: Java, XML, C, C++, Perl, Visual Basic, ASP, and SQL.

Cryptographer. Literally, cryptographer means "code-writer." You'll investigate ways to keep information secret, or ways to break the code of messages. You may work for the governmental or military organizations, but there is also demand in industry to develop new methods for keeping e-mail and online payments private and secure, blocking pirates from stealing cable programming, and protecting financial information from ATMs.

Financial Analyst. As a financial analyst, you'll increase company profitability through asset management and cost savings. You will help businesses make investment and acquisition choices based on reviewing detailed economic research, evaluating the data and identifying patterns, as well as using statistics and other analyses. You'll also develop a number of financial reports, including financial forecasts, profit-and-loss statements, and expense and income statements.

Operations Research Analyst. In this job, you'll take a scientific approach to analyzing problems and making decisions using analytical and numerical techniques. You'll develop and manipulate mathematical and computer models of organizational systems, such as supply chain, production, and transportation and distribution. You'll help management find better and more effective ways to allocate an organization's resources—capital, materials, equipment, and people—by developing multiple solutions to specific problems or processes.

Purchasing Agent/Specialist. As a purchasing agent, you are typically employed by medium to large organizations, evaluating organizational requirements and developing purchasing specifications, while assisting in the purchasing of general and specialized equipment, materials, and business services. You'll review purchasing proposals, consult with suppliers and obtain price quotes, set contract terms and conditions, award contracts to vendors offering the best overall deal, monitor the delivery schedule, and work with suppliers to correct any problems.

Statistician. As a statistician, you'll work closely with people in other fields to design the collection of data, analyze the data, and draw conclusions from data based on mathematical and computational studies of data and chance—using computers as a tool for analyzing complex data sets and solving mathematical problems. You may work in medicine, government, education, agriculture, or business, using statistical techniques to predict election results, population growth, or the behavior of financial instruments; establish insurance or quality control standards; and determine new drug effectiveness through clinical trials.

Web Administrator. In this job, you'll design, develop, manage, maintain, update, and troubleshoot an organization's web systems—its internal system (Intranet), external system (Internet), and e-mail system—as well as related database systems. Because you'll work with just about every department in the organization, a strong background in business is recommended for people considering this career.

Other Career Possibilities. Some other job and career paths for math and computer science majors include:

Air Traffic Controller	Information Specialist
Biometrician/Biostatistician	Market Research Analyst
Compensation/Benefits Administrator	Mathematics Editor/Writer
Computer Facilities Manager	Quality Assurance Analyst
Data Processing Manager	Risk Analyst
Database Manager	Robotics Programmer
Demographer	Software Developer
External Auditor	Systems Analyst
	Underwriter

Skills Needed/Developed

Students majoring in mathematics or computer science develop numerous valuable and transferable skills. The following are the most critical to graduates:

Abstract Reasoning. This is the ability to identify patterns from seemingly unrelated items and make predictions based on those patterns. Some feel this skill is the engine that helps drive problem-solving skills.

The Professor Says

Other transferable skills gained from these majors include:

- Multi-tasking
- Research and planning
- Communications
- Organizational
- Gathering information

Critical Thinking. This ability uses logic and reasoning and applies them to complex situations creating a better understanding of a situation and underlying issues.

Detail-Oriented. These majors require an extreme need for attention to detail and the ability to collect and manage all sorts of information.

Problem-Solving. This skill involves your ability to identify complex problems, review existing conditions and restrictions, and develop and evaluate alternative solutions to the problem.

Decision-Making. Somewhat related to problem-solving, decision-making is your ability to select one course of action from several possible alternatives.

Expected Growth

Graduates with a solid foundation in math and computer science will always be in demand because of the fundamental elements of these majors.

Math Majors

Job growth for mathematicians is expected to decline over the next decade because of a reduction in the number of jobs with the specific title of "mathematician."

Sources of additional information:

- American Mathematical Society (www.ams.org)
- Association for Women in Mathematics (www.awm-math.org)

◆ Mathematical Association of America (www.maa.org)

◆ Society for Industrial and Applied Math (www.siam.org)

Computer Science Majors

Job growth for computer scientists is expected to be much faster than the average (25 percent or higher) for all careers over the next decade.

Sources of additional information:

◆ American Society For Women in Computing (www.awc-hq.org)

◆ American Society for Information Science & Technology (www.asis.org)

◆ Association for Computing Machinery (www.acm.org)

◆ Computing Research Association (www.cra.org)

profiles

Microsoft CEO Steven Ballmer

Steve Ballmer is the chief executive officer of Microsoft Corporation, one of the world's leading manufacturers of software for personal and business computing applications. He is known both for his leadership skills and his passion for the company. Ballmer earned a Bachelor's degree (with honors) in both math and economics from Harvard University. After a short stint as a brand manager with Procter & Gamble, he enrolled in the Standford University Graduate School of Business to pursue his M.B.A., but dropped out of Stanford a year into his studies when Microsoft founder Bill Gates (a friend from Harvard days) persuaded him to work at the company. In the past 20 years, Ballmer has headed several divisions, been promoted to president, and finally to CEO when Gates relinquished the title. Ballmer is currently the longest-serving employee of Microsoft after Gates.

Actuaries

Employment is expected to grow faster than the average (18 to 25 percent) for all jobs over the next decade.

Sources of additional information:

- ◆ American Academy of Actuaries (www.actuary.org)
- ◆ International Actuarial Association (www.actuaries.org)
- ◆ Society of Actuaries (www.soa.org)

Computer Programmers

Employment is expected to grow about as fast as the average (10 to 15 percent) for all jobs over the next decade.

Sources of additional information:

- ◆ The Programmers Guild (www.programmersguild.org)
- ◆ USENIX, the Advanced Computing Systems Association (www.usenix.org)

Cryptographers

Some job growth is expected—about as fast as the average (10 to 15 percent) for all careers—but there will be strong demand for those graduates with top skills.

Financial Analysts

Job growth is expected to be faster than the average (18 to 25 percent) for all jobs over the next decade.

Wondering what employers look for in a financial analyst? Here's a sample financial analyst job description:

> You'll be part of a team that is responsible for analyzing changes in production, raw materials, manufacturing methods, pricing, or services provided, in order to determine their effects on costs. You will give a prognosis for projects to be undertaken based on past and present financial performance. In order to do this, you must take into account factors like cost of raw materials, labor, transportation, and other overhead. You will maintain and improve integrity of standard and current costs for the products we produce. You will assist the company in understanding known and hidden costs, such that an accurate cost standard can be achieved. You will also assist in developing manufacturing budgets. You will

assist every other layer of management in understanding reports and the processes that drive them. Additionally, you will represent the finance department on capital project teams by providing financial and cost information.

Operations Research Analysts

Job growth is expected to be slower than average (under 8 percent) over the next decade, though job opportunities should still be strong as organizations continue to focus on increasing efficiency and productivity.

Wondering what employers look for in an operations research analyst? Here's a sample operations research analyst job description:

> We are currently seeking an operations research analyst to develop and use analytic models to help clients make sound business decisions. As an operations research analyst, you will: develop advanced statistical models; use sophisticated optimization techniques; design custom analysis tools; leverage basic programming skills to gain insight from client data; collaborate with clients to develop and implement innovative solutions; take initiative on both client engagements and internal projects; communicate results and discuss issues with project teams and clients; and gain immediate responsibility for project deliverables. Beyond a strong academic record (GPA of 3.5/4.0 or higher), we seek individuals with the following: detail orientation, analytic problem-solving skills, organization and planning skills, and communication skills.

Purchasing Agents/Specialists

Job growth is expected to be slower than average (under 8 percent) for all jobs over the next decade.

Wondering what employers look for in a purchasing agent? Here's a sample purchasing agent job description:

> We have an immediate need for a purchasing specialist to join the purchasing department. The position's responsibilities include: coordinate activities involved with procuring of goods and services (materials, equipment, tools, parts, service agreements, etc.); negotiate discounts, volume purchasing discounts, OEM pricing, delivery schedules; develop negotiation strategies and prepare routine contract documents in accordance with corporate policies around terms and conditions; maintain accurate and accessible records (e.g., price and vendor histories);

prepare specialized responses for proposals, bids, and contract modifications; evaluate unique contract requirements to ensure compliance with legal requirements and corporate policies; and work with purchasing team, vendors, and customers to resolve contract issues and disputes. Must possess excellent analytical and negotiation skills, computer and spreadsheet skills, as well as excellent communication (verbal, written, presentation) and organizational skills.

Statisticians

Job growth is expected to be slower than average (under 8 percent) over the next decade, mainly because of a decline in the use of the "statistician" job title. Job opportunities should remain good.

A source of additional information can be found at the American Statistical Association (www.amstat.org).

Web Administrators

Employment is expected to grow about as fast as the average (10 to 15 percent) for all jobs over the next decade; however, as the web continues to expand, jobs should be plentiful.

A source of additional information can be found at the Web Design & Developers Association (www.wdda.org).

Wondering what employers look for in a web administrator? Here's a sample web administrator job description:

> This entry-level position is perfect for someone passionate about electronic commerce and marketing. Responsibilities include, but are not limited to, managing, developing, monitoring, and updating information and maintaining the company's portals. Implement HTML modifications on current pages; assist with the flow of information. Perform backups and ensure user accessibility to the sites. Monitor site traffic and help scale site capacity to meet traffic-demands performance. Improve the company's efficiency and maintain the look and feel for the site. Responsible for the company's Internet and Intranet. College degree in computer science with some focus in marketing is desired. Must have working knowledge of HTML, JavaScript, SQL, Flash, and Adobe Photoshop. You should have the ability to manage multiple projects and priorities simultaneously.

Mathematician John F. Nash Jr.

John F. Nash Jr., a brilliant mathematician who developed a theory about an equilibrium point in game theory that eventually led to being awarded a Nobel Prize in Economics, lived a troubled life because he began suffering from schizophrenia at the peak of his career. In his senior year in high school, Nash won a coveted Westinghouse Scholarship. He earned his Bachelor's and Master's degrees in math from Carnegie Institute of Technology (now Carnegie Mellon University), and has a Ph.D., in math from Princeton University. Dr. Nash, who established the mathematical principles of game theory—known as the Nash Equilibrium—attempting to explain the dynamics of actions among competitors, was a professor of math at MIT and has an informal relationship with Princeton University. His life was immortalized in the film *A Beautiful Mind*.

Earnings Potential $

Both math and computer science majors earn more than the average annual salary for all college graduates, which is currently around $38,000. Math graduates average about $45,000, while computer science graduates average about $46,000.

The following provides some general guidelines of salaries to expect upon graduation. Remember, salaries vary by employer, industry, and region.

Actuary. Median annual salary of an entry-level actuary is approximately $51,000.

Computer Programmer. Beginning salary for a computer programmer is about $47,000.

Cryptographer. Median annual earnings of an entry-level cryptographer range from $40,000 to $51,000.

Financial Analyst. The median annual salary of a financial analyst is about $45,000.

Operations Research Analyst. The median annual salary of an entry-level operations research analyst is $48,000.

Purchasing Agent/Specialist. The average salary for an entry-level purchasing agent is between $41,000 and $51,000 a year.

The Professor Says

Your next step? Pick several careers that most fit your interests with a major in math or computer science and dig more deeply into them. Remember that it is always important to learn more about prospective careers by going online, talking with professors, conducting informational interviews, and job-shadowing.

Statistician. The median annual salary for an entry-level statistician is $41,000.

Web Administrator. The median annual salary for a typical entry-level web administrator is $49,000.

> **The Professor Says** _____
>
> Remember that you're not done once you pick your college major—in fact, it's just begun, because the next thing you need to do is gain work experience. Just about all "entry-level" jobs for college graduates require some work experience outside the classroom. Seek out internships, volunteer, and figure out other ways to gain the experience you need.

The Least You Need to Know

◆ Students with a passion for math or a gift for computer science will find jobs upon graduation as the skills they develop are in demand.

◆ While some of the traditional job titles for math majors are in decline, there will still be plenty of jobs for graduates—just with different job titles.

◆ Plenty of entry-level math and computer science jobs are available with just an undergraduate degree.

◆ A majority of the career paths for math and computer science majors pay higher than the average for all college majors.

Chapter 28

Psychology, Sociology, and Social Work

In This Chapter

- ◆ Discover jobs that draw on a passion for people
- ◆ Use your analytical skills in careers that demand them
- ◆ Learn the classes psychology, sociology, and social work majors require
- ◆ Find out what kind of jobs and salaries to expect

What do you do for a career if you have a passion for understanding why people act as they do? Always wondered why people sometimes view the same issue completely differently? Interested in broader social groups or communities? Have a desire to help people?

This chapter reveals rewarding careers for students majoring in psychology, sociology, or social work.

About the Majors

These three majors all deal with understanding and helping people—whether as individuals or in groups and communities.

Psychology

Psychology majors learn about human and animal behavior. The major is broad and diverse, and devoted to understanding, predicting, and controlling behavior. It encompasses such areas as mental ability, individual differences, abnormal psychology, human perception, learning and memory, and attitudes and social behavior.

Psychology is a common major that you should be able to find at any college or university. Typical courses include:

Introduction to Psychology	Biological Psychology
Personality	Clinical Psychology
History of Psychology	Childhood Behavioral Disorders
Abnormal Psychology	Cultural Psychology
Psychological Testing	Introduction to Counseling
Cognitive Psychology	Psychology of Women
Abnormal Psychology	Psychological Testing and Assessment
Child Psychology	
Human Sexuality	Introduction to Individual Differences
Behavioral Statistics	
Social Psychology	Industrial and Organizational Psychology
Health Psychology	

Sociology

Sociology majors study social life, social change, and the social causes and consequences of human behavior. Sociologists investigate the structure of groups, organizations, and societies, and how people interact within these contexts. Since all human behavior is social, the subject matter of sociology ranges from the intimate family to entire populations, including an examination of such things as the divisions of race, gender, and social class.

Sociology is a fairly common major, especially for larger colleges and universities. Typical courses include:

Introduction to Sociology	Popular Culture
Sociology of Families	Sociology of Deviance
Sociology of Religion	Social Psychology
Sociology of Education	Social Work
Sociology of Emotions	Correctional Institutions
Sociology of Law	Criminal Justice
Sociology of Health and Illness	Contemporary Social Theory
Sociology of Addictions	American Social Changes
Community Action/Organization	Race, Nationality, and Immigration
Sociology of Sports	Work, Occupations, Professions
Gender and Society	
Social Inequity	Population, Society, and Environment
Modern Organizations	Social Theory and Critical Thinking
Aging and Society	
Social and Cultural Change	Quantitative Methods of Social Research
Urban Sociology	

Social Work

Social work majors learn about human behavior and the social environment, social research, social policy and social service institutions, and social work methods. Social work encompasses a large variety of services and fields of practice, and as a major you'll learn how social work deals with meeting the needs that society defines as problems or concerns.

You can often find one or two courses on social work (as part of a sociology major) at most colleges and universities, but it is a fairly specialized major, so you'll typically only find it at much larger colleges and universities.

Typical courses include:

Introduction to Social Work and Human Services

Social Policy and Human Service Programs

Probation and Parole

Child Welfare: Policies and Services

Juvenile Delinquency

Social Work with Families

Aging and the Aged

Death and Bereavement

Social Welfare

Alcoholism and Other Drug Abuse

Generalist Social Work Practice with Organizations

Generalist Social Work Practice with Individuals

Methods of Social Work Research

Human Behavior and the Social Environment

Social Welfare and Criminal Justice in the United States

Background on Careers

Psychology graduates gain the skill of understanding the behavior of individuals—knowledge that you can apply to nearly every setting in which you may find yourself. The education you obtain with a major in psychology prepares you for a variety of careers related to human behavior within the corporate and not-for-profit sectors (such as in human resources or marketing). A major in psychology may also lead to graduate study and a career in clinical, experimental, developmental, or other specialization in psychology.

Major Pitfalls

An undergraduate degree in psychology will not enable you to practice psychology. Therapy and counseling are done by professional psychologists and require a Master's (M.A.) or higher, which means that until you go to graduate school and complete two to six years of study, you will not be qualified to perform the kind of work that may have attracted you to the field of psychology.

Sociology graduates gain the skills to address challenging social science and human services issues, preparing you for a wide variety of careers. The education you receive as a sociology major helps you understand how social systems work and patterns of behavior, and prepares you for a variety of careers using that understanding of people and systems, including social work, social services, human resources, teaching, and more—as well as for graduate school.

As a social work graduate, you learn the skills to deal with diverse populations, preparing you for a career in social work, social services, and other fields of human service working in a variety of areas, including mental health, health services, family services, substance abuse, child welfare, school social work, local, state, and Federal government, corrections, homelessness outreach and services, domestic violence treatment and prevention, hospice services, job training, and many others. The major also prepares you for graduate work in the field.

Major Pitfalls

An undergraduate degree in social work allows you to begin a career in the field, but if you want to provide therapy to clients, be a clinician, or simply advance to more rewarding careers, you'll need to consider a Master's degree (Master of Social Work) or Doctoral degree (Doctorate in Social Work).

More specifically, here are some top jobs and careers for students who earn a Bachelor's degree with a major in psychology, sociology, or social work:

Child Welfare Worker. In this job, you'll be responsible for protecting the lives and well-being of children—making a critical difference at a key moment in their lives—primarily by supporting and strengthening their families. You'll investigate reported cases of abuse and neglect, and provide services to the children and their families when needed. In cases where families can't or won't protect their children, you may recommend foster care, or, in cases where parents are no longer able to parent, work with the courts to find adoptive homes for children.

Community Health Worker. As a community health worker—sometimes also referred to as a health agent, health promoter, village health worker, and community health aide—you'll provide outreach, education, referral and follow-up, case management, advocacy, and home visiting services to members of the community who need it the most, typically the poor and under-privileged. You may be involved with providing pre- and postnatal advice, offering childcare education and assistance, and assisting in disease screening, monitoring, follow-up, and prevention techniques.

Community Relations Representative. In this job you'll work for a governmental agency or nonprofit organization helping children, teens, and adults make the best decisions about education, job skills, nutrition, and health—by motivating and encouraging them to set goals and accomplish the things they need to do to move forward with a healthy and rewarding life. You'll help people believe in themselves, even through difficult situations, giving hope, direction, and the promise of an exciting future to people who need it most.

Guidance Counselor. As a school guidance counselor, you'll provide social, educational, career, and personal assistance to a certain number of assigned students, with much of the advice focused on future career and educational choices, including counseling students about technical and trade schools, community colleges, and four-year colleges and universities. You'll be involved in vocational, aptitude, and achievement testing; helping students complete college applications; planning and leading workshops on topics such as anger management, alcohol and drug prevention, peer pressure, and study skills; assisting in dropout-prevention programs; and responding to student crises and other problems.

Housing/Student Life Coordinator. In this job, you'll work for a college or university, assisting the administration with student housing services or student activities—promoting the adjustment and well-being of students. You may handle issues such as placing students in residential facilities, counseling on roommate issues, dealing with disciplinary issues, supervising student organizations, organizing new student orientation, developing student programs on a variety of topics, planning off-campus trips and events, and organizing student recognition/awards programs. You'll typically also be responsible for supervising and training a student support staff.

Probation Officer. As a probation officer, you'll supervise a certain number of offenders on probation or parole through personal contact with the offenders and their families—through office visits as well as meeting in offenders' homes and at their places of employment or therapy. You'll also spend time working for the courts, where you'll investigate the backgrounds of the accused, write pre-sentence reports, and recommend sentences. You may be required to testify in court as to your findings and recommendations. You'll typically specialize in either adults or juveniles; however, in small, usually rural, jurisdictions you may counsel both adults and juveniles.

Resident Treatment Worker. In this job, you'll perform basic para-professional therapeutic work in the care or treatment of residents at a residential institution for the elderly, emotionally abused or disturbed, mentally retarded, or mentally ill—providing direct care, support, treatment, and training. You'll help maintain a safe and healthy environment, give routine care, respond to crisis situations, develop educational and developmental programs, supervise recreational activities, encourage social interactions, provide counseling for residents and their families, and assist in the oversight of all residents.

Youth Counselor. As a youth counselor, you'll be responsible for providing programs for low-income youth and counseling for individuals to identify and solve complex personal and family problems. You may be involved with maintaining a caseload of youths who have complex personal and family problems; investigating and analyzing their personal, family, and social problems; referring them to appropriate agencies and programs needed; recording their personal history, problems, and the particular actions recommended or taken; working with their family and friends to advise of problems and gain their support; and preparing reports for determination of their eligibility, treatment plan, and monthly progress.

Other Career Possibilities. Some other job and career paths for psychology, sociology, and social work majors include:

Admissions Counselor	Psychiatric Social Worker
Behavioral Therapist	Psychiatrist
Career Counselor	Psychologist
Clinical Social Worker	School Psychologist
Corporate Foundation Specialist	School Social Worker
Court-Appointed Special Advocate	Social Service Aide
	Social Work Researcher
Human Factors Engineer	Substance Abuse Counselor
Human Resources Assistant	
Market Research Analyst	Therapist
	Vocational Rehabilitation
Marriage Counselor	Counselor

Skills Needed/Developed

Students majoring in psychology, sociology, and social work develop numerous valuable and transferable skills, but those included here are the most critical to graduates:

Communications (in writing, visually, and verbally). Speaking, writing, and listening skills are essential to a counseling career, as you must be able to listen to the needs of clients, ask questions as appropriate, and respond with suggestions and recommendations.

The Professor Says

Other transferable skills you gain from these majors include:

◆ Research
◆ Teamwork
◆ Organizational
◆ Interpersonal communications

Problem-Solving. This skill involves your ability to identify complex problems, review existing conditions and restrictions, and develop and evaluate alternative solutions to the problem.

Decision-Making. Somewhat related to problem-solving, decision-making is your ability to select one course of action from several possible alternatives.

Critical Thinking. This skill involves your ability to use logic and reasoning and apply them to complex situations so that you can better understand the situation and underlying issues.

Expected Growth

Graduates with a solid foundation in psychology, sociology, and social work will always be in demand because of the unique insights you gain about people and their behaviors—and the ability to use those skills in a variety of careers.

Psychology Majors

Job growth for psychologists and psychology graduates is expected to be faster than the average (18 to 25 percent) for all careers over the next decade.

Sources of additional information:

◆ American Counseling Association (www.counseling.org)

◆ American Psychological Association (www.apa.org)

◆ Association for Psychological Science (www.psychologicalscience.org)

◆ Association for Women in Psychology (www.awpsych.org)

Psychologist Judith Rich Harris

Judith Rich Harris is a developmental psychologist and author whose research has focused on the development of children, specifically examining how personalities develop. She graduated magna cum laude from Brandeis and was awarded the Lila Pearlman Prize in psychology. She then went on to Harvard University, where she earned a Master's degree in psychology. She has written two books. Her first book, *The Nurture Assumption*, makes the argument that parents play a much smaller role in influencing their child's social development; instead, it is the influence of the child's peers that has the largest impact. In her most recent book, *No Two Alike*, Harris tackles the question of why even identical twins raised in the same household can have very different personalities. In 1998, she received the George A. Miller Award from the American Psychological Association for her article entitled "Where Is the Child's Environment? A Group Socialization Theory of Development."

Sociology

Demand for sociologists and sociology graduates is expected to remain strong over the next decade.

Sources of additional information:

- ◆ American Sociological Association (www.asanet.org)
- ◆ Association for Applied & Clinical Sociology (www.aacsnet.org)

Social Work

Job growth for social workers and social work graduates is expected to be faster than the average (18 to 25 percent) for all careers over the next decade.

Sources of additional information:

- ◆ National Association of Social Workers (www.socialworkers.org)
- ◆ Clinical Social Work Association (www.cswf.org)

Social Work Educator Barbara White

Barbara White is dean of the School of Social Work at the University of Texas at Austin, where she also holds the Centennial Professorship in Leadership. She earned Bachelor's degrees from Florida A&M and Florida State universities before completing a Master's degree in social work and a Ph.D., degree in political science, both from Florida State University. Dr. White is the former president of the National Association of Social Workers (NASW). She has authored articles and book chapters on issues dealing with cultural diversity, women, domestic violence, and social work education. She has received numerous awards over the years, including the Presidential Award for Leadership in Social Work Education from the NASW, and was inducted into the National Women of Achievement's African American Women's Hall of Fame.

Child Welfare Workers

Employment is expected to grow faster than the average (18 to 25 percent) for all jobs over the next decade.

Wondering what employers look for in a child welfare worker? Here's a sample child welfare worker job description:

> Our children need you! Are you a social worker or a social work student preparing to graduate from school? We are looking for caring, compassionate, and committed social workers and caseworkers to join our team of child welfare professionals. These positions provide services to individuals or families in cases involving suspected child or adult abuse or neglect, out-of-home placement, guardianship, emergency protective orders, or adoption. This is a challenging career. You will work with our most vulnerable children and families to provide a safe, secure, and healthy home environment. We need social workers and caseworkers like you, but more than that, our children need you, too. Help a child, change the future. Vacancies are located in several of our local departments of social services throughout the state.

Community Health Workers

Employment is expected to grow about as fast as the average (10 to 15 percent) for all jobs over the next decade.

Wondering what employers look for in a community health worker? Here's a sample community health worker job description:

> We are seeking a candidate who has the ability to interact with a variety of people within the community and local organizations, including schools, community centers, and housing complexes. Must have ability to work closely and compassionately with vulnerable populations on sensitive topics, including reproduction and sexually transmitted diseases. Must coordinate multiple duties, work independently, and be a team member. Should possess excellent public speaking, organizational, and teaching and communication skills. Ability to speak, read, and write English and Spanish required. Grant-funded position.

Community Relations Representatives

Employment is expected to grow about as fast as the average (10 to 15 percent) for all jobs over the next decade.

Guidance Counselors

Job growth for guidance counselors is expected to be faster than the average (18 to 25 percent) for all careers over the next decade.

A source of additional information can be found at the American School Counselor Association (www.schoolcounselor.org).

Housing/Student Life Coordinators

Employment is expected to grow as fast as the average (10 to 15 percent) for all jobs over the next decade.

A source of additional information can be found at the National Association of Student Personnel Administrators (www.naspa.org).

Probation Officers

Employment is expected to grow about as fast as the average (10 to 15 percent) for all jobs over the next decade.

A source of additional information can be found at the American Probation and Parole Association (www.appa-net.org).

Wondering what employers look for in a probation officer? Here's a sample probation officer job description:

> This mission-critical position will conduct pre-sentence investigations and pre-bail investigations and supervise pre-trial defendants, and post-conviction offenders. The jobholder is responsible for supervising misdemeanor cases, providing court attendance/testimony, completing documentation of adult nonviolent offender progress, and ensuring compliance with state standards. Office and field visits required. Education and Professional Work Experience: a minimum of a baccalaureate degree is required in one of the following academic disciplines: psychology, sociology/social work, counseling, or criminology. Leadership skills, analytical ability, good judgment, investigative skills, and a high degree of integrity are critical to be successful in the job. Strong verbal and writing skills are required. Competent computer skills are necessary.

Residential Treatment Workers

Employment is expected to grow faster than the average (18 to 25 percent) for all jobs over the next decade.

Wondering what employers look for in a youth counselor? Here's a sample youth counselor job description:

> We are a progressive residential treatment facility serving a co-ed population of adolescents aged 10 to 21 years that is seeking enthusiastic individuals to assist in the care and treatment of the students we serve. Our campus offers a variety of educational and recreational resources, including a computer lab, farm program, pool, and comprehensive gymnasium. Enjoy coming to a job where you will provide adolescents with role modeling and mentoring and where you will apply a positive behavioral approach to help improve behavior. A four-year degree in counseling, human services, or psychology is required. Organizational skills, excellent communication skills (oral and written), and the ability to follow directions are a must. Excellent starting salary and outstanding benefit package (health coverage, life insurance, 401K, direct deposit, holiday pay, paid time off, free meals, and a one-of-a-kind working environment) are included.

Youth Counselors

Employment is expected to grow faster than the average (18 to 25 percent) for all jobs over the next decade.

Wondering what employers look for in a youth counselor? Here's a sample youth counselor job description:

> We offer innovative programs addressing the issues of substance abuse, sexual offenses or behaviors with adolescent males and females between the ages of 13 and 17. Your duties as a youth counselor include establishing a therapeutic alliance with each resident and ensuring the environment remains safe and the facility culture remains positive; directing improvements to resident's social skills through role modeling and positive reinforcement; guiding youth in establishing boundaries, effective conflict resolution and self-management tasks; engaging the residents in creative and therapeutic activities; and occasionally escorting residents outside of the facility on recreational outings. To apply, you must have an undergraduate degree in a human services, sociology, or health-related field, and have working knowledge of therapeutic relationships, behavior management, and crisis intervention.

The Professor Says _____

Not sure about these career choices? These are just some of the career possibilities for a major in psychology, sociology, or social work. Remember that it is always important to learn more about prospective careers by going online, talking with professors, conducting informational interviews, and job-shadowing.

Earnings Potential $

Psychology, sociology, and social work majors all earn less than the average annual salary for all college graduates, which is currently around $38,000. Psychology graduates average about $30,000, sociology graduates about $31,000, and social work graduates about $28,000.

The following section provides some general guidelines of salaries to expect upon graduation. Remember, salaries vary by employer, industry, and region.

Child Welfare Worker. Median annual salary of an entry-level child welfare worker is approximately $27,000.

Community Health Worker. Beginning salary for a community health worker is about $32,000.

Community Relations Representative. Median annual earnings of an entry-level community relations representative are about $31,000.

Guidance Counselor. Median annual salary of an entry-level guidance counselor varies by school system, but a rough estimate is about $35,000 to $40,000.

Housing/Student Life Coordinator. The median annual salary of an entry-level housing/student life coordinator is about $35,000. Some positions include an on-campus apartment, while others pay much less but are designed for graduate students (who receive a free education and an annual graduate assistantship stipend).

> **The Professor Says**
>
> Your next step after choosing your major? Gaining work experience. Just about all "entry-level" jobs for college graduates require some work experience outside the classroom. Seek out internships, volunteer, and figure out other ways to gain the experience you need.

Probation Officer. The average salary for an entry-level probation officer ranges from $22,000 to $28,000 at the state level, and averages about $28,000 at the federal level.

Residential Treatment Worker. The median annual salary for an entry-level residential treatment worker is about $28,000.

Youth Counselor. The median annual salary for an entry-level youth counselor varies and averages about $28,000 without room and board, and about $22,000 with room and board.

The Least You Need to Know

- Students who have a passion for counseling and a desire to help people should be able to find jobs upon graduation as the skills they develop are in demand.

- Most of the jobs in psychology, sociology, and social work should continue to grow as fast or faster than other jobs.

- While there are plenty of entry-level jobs requiring just an undergraduate degree in psychology, sociology, and social work, there are better-paying and more-rewarding careers with advanced degrees.

- A majority of the entry-level career paths for these majors pay much less than the average for all college majors.

Chapter 29

Criminology or Pre-Law

In This Chapter

- ◆ Discover careers that use your passion for the law
- ◆ Use those reasoning skills in jobs that demand them
- ◆ Learn the classes criminology and pre-law majors require
- ◆ Find out key job and salary information

What do you do if you have always been fascinated (or frustrated) by the law? Crime and legal show junkie? Have you always wanted to be a lawyer or judge? Wondering about other careers for people like you?

This chapter reveals rewarding careers for students who major in criminology and pre-law.

About the Majors

Criminology (sometimes called criminal justice) and pre-law majors share an obvious interest in all things legal and illegal, but what can you expect from these majors if you choose to study one or both of them?

Criminology

Criminology majors receive a general background in the causes of crime and the agencies of criminal justice. Majors study crime, law, and punishment from several different perspectives, attempting to gain a basic understanding of the nature and causes of crime, deviant behavior, policing and private security, the courts and legal system, and the correctional system.

Most colleges and universities offer a few courses in criminology (often in the sociology department), but a much smaller number actually offer a major. Typical courses include:

The Justice System	Criminal Rights and Procedures
Criminology	Law Enforcement Systems
Sociology of Law	Juvenile Justice System
Community and Crime	The Correctional System
Juvenile Delinquency	Criminal Investigation
Theories of Social Structure	Celebrated Trials
Criminal Justice Policy	Ethics, Law, and Society
Social Deviance	Crime Prevention
Social Research Methods	Dispute Management
Theories of Criminal Behavior	Patterns of Criminal Behavior
Criminal Law	

Pre-Law Majors

Pre-law isn't so much a major as it is a preparatory program for declaring and examining your interest in attending law school. Typically, a faculty committee advises students on appropriate majors and extracurricular activities, as well as offering special programs, such as law school recruitment fairs, mock trials, courthouse field trips, lectures from visiting legal scholars and law professors, and law school admission prep workshops.

Many colleges, especially those that have a law school, offer a pre-law program. Most law schools actually prefer students with a broad academic background, rather than one focused on the law.

So, how do you choose a major if you know you want to attend law school? You have a couple of options. First, you can choose a major that relates to the type of law you think you'll want to practice—so major in criminology if you want to help convict or defend accused criminals, or major in business if you want to go into corporate law. Second, you can choose a major in which the material comes easily to you so that you'll graduate with a high grade point average. Third, you could choose a major based on your passions, because literally any major is acceptable to law school.

Some typical academic majors for pre-law students include:

English	Communications
Criminology	Business
Philosophy	Sociology
Political Science	Psychology
History	Science

Background on Careers

Criminology and pre-law majors are fairly career-focused, so while you may not know exactly what you want to do—or what type of lawyer you want to be—you do know you want to have a career involving the law and legal system.

The Professor Says _____

There are many different types of lawyers, including those that specialize in:

Administrative Law	Immigration Law
Civil Law	Intellectual Property Law
Communications/Media Law	International Law
Constitutional Law	Labor/Employment Law
Corporate Law	Medical/Malpractice Law
Criminal Law	Personal Injury Law
Divorce and Family Law	Real Estate Law
Entertainment Law	Securities Law
Environmental Law	Tax Law

Some top jobs and careers for students earning a Bachelor's degree with a major in criminology and pre-law include:

Attorney, Corporate. As a corporate attorney (sometimes referred to as in-house counsel), you'll be part of the legal department of a large organization, providing analysis and counsel on legal and policy issues on such things as proposed new products, intellectual property (brands) protection, mergers and acquisitions, financial offerings, financial structuring, securities offerings, nondisclosure agreements, non-compete clauses, outsourcing agreements, and business strategic planning. You may also prepare legal pleadings and motions, as well as represent the company or its officials in various legal proceedings.

Attorney, Private Practice. In this job, you'll practice law either in your own firm or as an associate with a firm that employs other lawyers. In this position, you may be a trial lawyer—representing clients in both civil and criminal litigation where your goal is to convince a jury or judge to believe your client's position based on facts and persuasive arguments—or engaged in office practice—which involves preparing contracts, deeds, wills, and other legal documents for clients. If you work for yourself or a smaller firm, you may have to be a generalist to have enough clients to make a living, but in larger firms, most attorneys specialize in an area of law, such as contracts, labor law, tax law, trademark law, and the like.

Criminologist. As a criminologist, you'll typically be employed by a law enforcement agency (local, state, or federal) to analyze the behavior and methods of criminals— sometimes from a distance by studying case files, and sometimes by going to crime scenes, attending autopsies, and questioning potential suspects—for a variety of reasons: to increase the chances of criminals being apprehended; to predict patterns and motives for behaviors in certain demographic groups; and to assess the responsiveness of crime to various methods of law enforcement. Some criminologists work in private practice, providing consulting services for law enforcement agencies.

Customs Inspector. In this job, you'll enforce the laws governing imports and exports by inspecting cargo, baggage, and articles worn or carried by people, vessels, vehicles, trains, and aircraft entering or leaving the United States, seizing prohibited or smuggled articles, intercepting contraband, and apprehending, searching, detaining, and arresting violators of U.S. laws. You'll also question suspicious persons to clarify irregularities and explain laws and regulations to tourists or others unfamiliar with customs statutes and procedures. You may also examine, count, weigh, gauge, measure, and sample commercial and noncommercial cargoes entering and leaving the United States.

Federal Bureau of Investigations (FBI) Special Agent. As an FBI agent, you'll serve as one of the federal government's principal investigators, responsible for investigating violations of more than 200 categories of federal law and conducting sensitive national security investigations, including investigating people suspected of violating federal laws such as terrorists, serial killers, kidnappers, bank robbers, drug traffickers, organized crime bosses, corrupt politicians, extortionists, bombers, and perpetrators of mail fraud and civil rights violations. Agents may conduct surveillance, monitor court-authorized wiretaps, examine business records, investigate white-collar crime, or participate in sensitive undercover assignments.

Mediator. In this job, you'll help people resolve disputes without going to court through "assisted negotiation" by meeting with all parties to the dispute, listening to the problems, attempting to find common ground, discussing options to resolve the dispute, and helping the parties come to some sort of agreement. You'll need excellent reasoning, problem-solving, and peace-making abilities as well an ability to be impartial because you have an equal and balanced responsibility to assist each mediating party and cannot favor the interests of any one party over another, nor should you favor a particular result in the mediation. Your role is to ensure that parties reach agreements in a voluntary and informed manner.

Paralegal. As a paralegal, also known as a legal assistant, you'll assist one or more lawyers by interviewing clients, conducting legal research, and developing first drafts of legal documents. You may also help prepare the legal arguments, draft pleadings, and motions to be filed with the court, obtain affidavits, and assist attorneys during trials. Paralegals also organize and track files of all important case documents and make them available and easily accessible to attorneys. You may also assist in preparing tax returns and planning estates. Some paralegals coordinate the activities of other law office employees and maintain financial office records. Paralegals are prohibited from the practice of law, such as setting legal fees, giving legal advice, and presenting cases in court.

Other Career Possibilities. Here are some other job and career paths for criminology and pre-law majors:

Claims Adjudicator	Deputy Sheriff
Correction Officer/Administrator	Drug Enforcement Agent
Court Administrator	Evidence Technician
Criminal Prosecutor, Assistant	Legal Affairs Writer/Reporter
District Attorney, Assistant	Litigation Manager

Lobbyist   Postal Inspector/Investigator

Pre-Trial Services Officer   Probation/Parole Officer

Polygraph Examiner   Secret Service Officer

Skills Needed/Developed

Students majoring in criminology or who have a pre-law career focus develop numerous valuable and transferable skills. The following are the most critical to graduates:

Analytical/Critical Thinking. This skill involves your ability to get to the heart of a problem or situation by breaking it down into smaller, more manageable parts, analyzing information, evaluating alternatives, and proposing a viable solution.

Written and Oral Communications. Speaking and writing skills are essential when pursuing a career in criminology or the law. You'll need the ability to clearly express yourself as many jobs and careers require writing comprehensive legal documents, as well as detailed reports and memos.

The Professor Says

Other transferable skills you gain from these majors include:

◆ Record keeping

◆ Leadership

◆ Time management

◆ Technical/computer

Organizational Skills. This skill deals with your ability to manage large amounts of information and demands through task analysis, time management, and goal-setting.

Research Proficiency. Just about all jobs and careers you'll find in criminology and the law require an aptitude to uncover information and solutions to complex issues, including your ability to understand and interpret information from one situation and apply it to the current situation.

Teamwork. This skill involves your ability to work with other people—whether they are similar or different—and is one of the most important for any career.

Expected Growth

Overall, job growth in the next decade for students who major in criminology or pre-law is expected to be strong, and in some cases much faster than the average (18 to 25 percent) for all careers.

Attorneys

Job growth for all attorneys and lawyers is expected to be as fast as the average (10 to 15 percent) for all careers over the next decade, but be prepared for a lot of competition, as many students graduate annually from law school.

Sources of additional information:

- American Bar Association (www.abanet.org)
- American Health Lawyers Association (www.healthlawyers.org)
- American Immigration Lawyers Association (www.aila.org)
- International Municipal Lawyers Association (www.imla.org)
- National Association of Criminal Defense Lawyers (www.criminaljustice.org)
- National District Attorneys Association (www.ndaa.org)
- National Employment Lawyers Association (www.nela.org)
- National Lawyers Association (www.nla.org)

profiles

Former Justice Sandra Day O'Connor

Sandra Day O'Connor is the first woman to serve as a Supreme Court justice. She attended Stanford University for both her undergraduate and law degrees, earning a Bachelor's degree in economics with honors, and ranked third in her graduating law school class while also serving as an editor of the *Stanford Law Review*. Most of her legal career was in government law, first as a deputy attorney, and later as Arizona's assistant attorney general. She was appointed by the governor of Arizona to a vacant seat in the Arizona Senate, and retained that seat for several years, becoming the majority leader—the first woman to hold that post in a state senate. She then ran successfully for election as a judge on the Maricopa County Superior Court. She later won appointment to Arizona's Court of Appeals. President Ronald Reagan, fulfilling a promise to appoint the first woman to the Supreme Court, did so in nominating O'Connor. She was approved by the Senate with 91 votes. She served for 24 years before retiring from the court in 2006.

Attorneys, Corporate

Job growth for attorneys is expected to be as fast as the average (10 to 15 percent) for all careers over the next decade.

Attorneys, Private Practice

Job growth for attorneys is expected to be as fast as the average (10 to 15 percent) for all careers over the next decade.

The Professor Says _____

All these careers are fine, but you want to be a judge and preside in a courtroom? There are about 30,000 judges in the United States—including municipal, county, state, and national judges—and the vast majority of them worked as lawyers before being appointed or elected a judge.

Criminologists

Job growth is expected to be about as fast as the average (10 to 15 percent) for all careers.

A source of additional information can be found at the American Society of Criminology (www.asc41.com).

profiles

Attorney-at-Law Steve Sands

Steve Sands is managing partner of Sands, White & Sands, P.A., a private law practice that specializes in medical negligence, personal injury, wrongful death, nursing home negligence and abuse, whistleblower qui tam actions, and pharmaceutical litigation. Sands is a Phi Beta Kappa scholar who graduated with honors from Tufts University before earning his J.D., also with honors, from the University of Florida Law School, where he was a member of the Law Review. He practiced commercial litigation with the Orlando-based law firm of Akerman, Senterfitt & Eidson before joining Florida's State Attorney's Office in Jacksonville. He returned to private practice, joining the law office of Larry Sands, P.A., which was later renamed Sands, White & Sands, P.A. Sands is a member of the Florida Bar, Academy of Florida Trial Lawyers, Association of Trial Lawyers of America, and the Volusia County Bar Association.

Customs Inspectors

Job growth is expected to be about as fast as the average (10 to 15 percent) over the next decade.

FBI Special Agents

Job growth for FBI agents (and other law enforcement careers) is expected to be as fast as the average (10 to 15 percent) for all careers over the next decade.

Sources of additional information:

◆ Federal Bureau of Investigation Jobs (www.fbijobs.gov)

◆ Federal Law Enforcement Officers Association (www.fleoa.org)

Wondering what the FBI is looking for in an entry-level agent? Here's what the FBI says about job opportunities:

> The FBI has a critical need to hire new special agents. These vital roles help the agency continue to meet the challenge of global terrorism and homeland security. In working for the FBI, you will have a daily impact on the nation's security and the quality of life for all U.S. citizens. A career with the FBI will provide you with a challenging, compelling, and rewarding experience. To become an FBI special agent, you must be a U.S. citizen or a citizen of the Northern Mariana Islands. You must be at least 23 years of age, but younger than 37 upon your appointment as a special agent. You must possess a four-year degree from a college or university accredited by one of the regional or national institutional associations recognized by the U.S. Secretary of Education. You must have at least three years of professional work experience. You must also possess a valid driver's license and be completely available for assignment anywhere in the FBI's jurisdiction. All applicants for the special agent position must first qualify under one of five special agent entry programs. These programs, most of which include certification or proof of competency, include: accounting, computer science/ information technology, foreign language, the law, and diversified.

Mediators

Job growth for mediators is expected to be as fast as the average (10 to 15 percent) for all careers over the next decade.

Sources of additional information:

◆ American Arbitration Association (www.adr.org)

◆ Association for Conflict Resolution (www.acrnet.org)

◆ Professional Mediation Association (www.promediation.com)

Wondering what employers look for in a mediator? Here's a sample mediator job description:

> Employment relations board mediator functions as a liaison between employers and employees (or their representatives), investigating areas of conflict and providing helpful assistance as a neutral party to keep the conflict from becoming a labor dispute. You'll mediate labor disputes arising from the collective bargaining process; interpret collective bargaining agreements for related disputes; and suggest alternatives and modifications. You'll also provide additional factual data to assist the parties in reaching consensual agreement, and assist union and management in co-operative efforts through facilitation and training. Requires a Bachelor's degree in industrial relations, business administration, law, or related fields; some experience in collective bargaining negotiations or the mediation of collective bargaining impasses; and a valid driver's license with a good driving record.

Paralegals

Job growth for paralegals is expected to be much faster than the average (25 percent or higher) for all careers over the next decade.

Sources of additional information:

◆ Legal Assistant Today (www.legalassistanttoday.com)

◆ National Association of Legal Assistants (www.nala.org)

◆ National Federation of Paralegal Associations (www.paralegals.org)

Wondering what employers look for in a paralegal? Here's a sample paralegal job description:

> We're looking for a paralegal who can work well within a fast-paced legal environment of an exciting consumer electronics company. The position will report to the General Counsel or Corporate Counsel and provides some administrative and other support to the in-house legal staff. The ideal candidate will play

a central role in keeping the business operations/activities organized, on track, and moving forward. Candidate must have exceptional communication skills, the ability to manage multiple tasks efficiently, and excellent judgment. You should be comfortable juggling tasks from the mundane to the more-strategic and able to work productively in a fast-paced, team-oriented environment with a smile and a sense of humor. Specific duties include dealing with intellectual property matters; being first point of contact for employees and outside counsel on all patent, trademark, and copyright matters; coordinating preparation of patent and trademark documents with outside counsel; maintaining patent and trademark databases, and updating legal department on monthly basis; presenting monthly trademark updates to marketing via e-mail and updating list on corporate intranet; monitoring third-party trademark usage, investigating potentially infringing marks, and reporting findings to attorneys; and reviewing marketing collateral and product packaging for proper patent and trademark usage.

Earnings Potential $

At $31,000, criminology graduates earn a lower annual salary than the average for all college graduates, which is currently around $38,000. Because pre-law majors can graduate with a variety of different majors, you might want to check other chapters with those majors.

The following section provides you with some general guidelines of salaries to expect upon graduation. Remember, salaries vary by employer, industry, and region.

Attorney, Corporate. Median starting salary for a corporate lawyer is $50,000.

Attorney, Private Practice. The median salary for a first-year associate ranges from $67,500 in small firms to $125,000 in larger firms.

The Professor Says

Your next step after choosing your major? Gaining work experience. Just about all "entry-level" jobs for college graduates require some work experience outside the classroom. Seek out internships, volunteer, and figure out other ways to gain the experience you need.

Criminologist. Median annual salary for an entry-level criminologist ranges from $29,000 to $32,000.

Customs Inspector. Median annual salary of a customs inspector is about $35,000—with as much as $30,000 in additional overtime pay.

FBI Special Agent. Median annual starting salary for a FBI special agent is $48,000.

Mediator. Starting salary for a mediator varies because many mediators work independently, but overall the median starting salary is about $35,000.

Paralegal. Salary for an entry-level paralegal position typically ranges from $30,000 to $40,000, depending on the size and type of firm.

The Professor Says

There are many career possibilities for a major in criminology and criminal justice, as well as pre-law, beyond the ones featured here. Remember that it is always important to learn more about prospective careers by researching online, talking with professors, conducting informational interviews, and job-shadowing.

The Least You Need to Know

◆ Students who major in criminology or are considering law school have numerous choices of careers with various types of organizations, including nonprofits, businesses, and the government.

◆ Careers for graduates with just a Bachelor's degree in criminology pay below the average for all jobs for college graduates.

◆ Job growth for many legal and criminology careers will be fast or faster than the average for all careers over the next decade.

◆ The more lucrative careers in this field require a graduate degree.

Additional Resources

These are big life decisions you are making. While this book is a comprehensive review of college majors and real careers, there are some other resources out there that can also assist you in making some of these big choices.

Included here are some of the best web-based resources and books for choosing your major and career, choosing a college, having success in college, and gaining experience in your career choice(s).

Choosing Your Major and Career

There are a number of good resources in print and online that can help you—in addition to this book, of course—with choosing a major or career.

Web Resources

- Choosing a College Major: How to Chart Your Ideal Career Path (www.quintcareers.com/choosing_major.html)

- Choosing a College Major (www.ecampustours.com/careers/majors/)

- Choosing a Major in College (www.collegeview.com/articles/CV/careers/selecting_major.html)

- Choosing Your College Major (www.collegeboard.com/student/csearch/majors_careers/468.html)

- Choosing Your Major (www.jobweb.com/Resources/Library/Careers_In/Choosing_Your_Major_122_01.htm)

- Choosing Your Major (www.collegeanswer.com/selecting/content/sel_id_majors.jsp)

- How to Choose a Major and Investigate Careers (www.washington.edu/students/ugrad/advising/majchoos.html)

- I Have to Pick a Major—Now What? (content.monstertrak.monster.com/resources/archive/careerfields/pickamajor/)

- Major Resource Kits (www.udel.edu/CSC/mrk.html)

- Taking the Mystery out of Majors (www.princetonreview.com/college/research/articles/majors/choosemajor.asp)

- What Can I do with a Major in …? (www.quintcareers.com/majors/)

Books

Andrews, Linda Landis. *How to Choose a College Major*. New York: McGraw-Hill, 2006.

The College Board Book of Majors. New York: College Board, 2006.

The College Career Bible. New York: Vault, 2006.

Guide to College Majors: Everything You Need to Know to Choose the Right Major. New York: Princeton Review, 2007.

Lederman, Ellen. *College Majors: A Complete Guide from Accounting to Zoology*. Jefferson, NC: McFarland & Company, 2007.

Nadler, Burton. *The Everything College Major Test Book: 10 Tests to Help You Choose the Major That is Right for You*. Avon, MA: Adams Publishing, 2006.

Tieger, Paul D., and Barbara Barron-Tieger. *Do What You Are: Discover the Perfect Career for You Through the Secrets of Personality Type*. New York: Little, Brown & Company, 2007.

Choosing Your Ideal College

While it is not part of the scope of this book, choosing where you are going to college is also an extremely important decision. Here are some good places for you to seek some guidance.

Web Resources

- AllAboutCollege.com (www.allaboutcollege.com)
- Choosing a College That's Right for You (www.quintcareers.com/choosing_a_college.html)
- College Guides for Top Colleges (www.collegeprowler.com)
- College Planning (www.ecampustours.com/collegeplanning)
- College Search (apps.collegeboard.com/search/index.jsp)
- CollegeSource Online (www.collegesource.org)
- Find a College (www.collegeboard.com/student/csearch/index.html)
- GoCollege (www.gocollege.com)
- Go to College—College Planning Resources (www.quintcareers.com/college_planning.html)
- Next Step Magazine: College Planning (www.nextstepmagazine.com)
- Peterson's College Planner (www.petersons.com)
- The Princeton Review (www.princetonreview.com)
- USNews.com: America's Best Colleges (www.usnews.com/usnews/edu/college/rankings/rankindex_brief.php)

Books

America's Best Value Colleges. New York: Princeton Review, 2006.

The Best 361 Colleges. New York: Princeton Review, 2006.

The College Board College Handbook 2008. New York: College Board, 2007.

College Navigator: Find a School to Match Any Interest from Archery to Zoology. New York: Princeton Review, 2007.

Fiske, Edward B. *Fiske Guide to Colleges 2007*. Naperville, IL: Sourcebooks, 2006.

Goldman, Jordan, and Colleen Buyers. *Students' Guide to Colleges: The Definitive Guide to America's Top 100 Schools*. New York: Penguin, 2005.

Peterson's 440 Colleges for Top Students 2008. New York: Peterson's, 2007.

Peterson's Four-Year Colleges 2008. New York: Thompson Peterson's, 2007.

Pope, Loren. *Colleges that Change Lives: 40 Schools You Should Know About Even If You're Not a Straight-A Student*. New York: Penguin, 2006.

Rahimi, Joey, Kelly Carey, Meghan Dowdell, Matt Hamman, Omid Gohari, and Luke Skurman. *The Big Book of Colleges 2007*. Pittsburgh: College Prowler, 2006.

Rugg, Federick E. *Rugg's Recommendations on the Colleges*. Fallbrook, CA: Rugg's Recommendations, 2006.

U.S. News Ultimate College Guide 2007. Naperville, IL: Sourcebooks, 2006.

Zmirak, John, ed. *All-American Colleges: Top Schools for Conservatives, Old-Fashioned Liberals, and People of Faith*. Wilmington, DE: Intercollegiate Studies Institute, 2006.

———. *Choosing the Right College: The Whole Truth About America's Top Schools*. Wilmington, DE: Intercollegiate Studies Institute, 2007.

College Success

College, like life, is a journey. While choosing a college and a major are important parts, you also need to succeed once you get there. Here are some resources to help you do just that.

Web Resources

◆ 10 Tips for Getting Good (or Better) Grades (www.quintcareers.com/getting_better_grades.html)

- 88 Surefire Tips for Succeeding in College (oedb.org/library/college-basics/88-surefire-tips)

- Keys to College Success (www.rong-chang.com/collsucc.htm)

- Your First Year of College: 25 Tips to Help You Survive and Thrive Your Freshman Year and Beyond (www.quintcareers.com/first-year_success.html)

Books

Arrington, Zach. *Confessions of a College Freshman: A Survival Guide for Dorm Life, Biology Lab, the Cafeteria, and Other First-Year Adventures*. Elgin, IL: RiverOak Publishing, 2001.

Combs, Patrick. *Major in Success: Make College Easier, Fire Up Your Dreams, and Get a Very Cool Job*. Berkeley, CA: Ten Speed Press, 2003.

Gibbs, George. *College Daze: Easing the Transition from High School to College*. Alexandria, VA: Octameron Associates, 2006.

How to Get Straight A's in College: Hundreds of Student-Tested Tips. Atlanta: Hundreds of Heads Books, 2007.

How to Survive Your Freshman Year. Atlanta: Hundreds of Heads Books, 2006.

Johnston, Julie, and Mary Kay Shanley. *Survival Secrets of College Students*. Hauppauge NY: Barron's, 2007.

Newport, Cal. *How to Win at College: Surprising Secrets from the Country's Top Students*. New York: Broadway, 2005.

Nist-olejnik, Sherrie, and Jodi Patrick Holschuh. *College Rules! How to Study, Survive, and Succeed in College*. Berkeley, CA: Ten Speed Press, 2007.

———. *College Success Strategies: Becoming an Effective Learner*. New York: Longman Publishing Group, 2005.

Rozakis, Laurie. *The Complete Idiot's Guide to College Survival*. Indianapolis: Alpha Books, 2001.

Help with Gaining Experience in Your Career Choice

Don't forget the advice in this book about gaining experience in your prospective career; you need to make certain that the career you think you want is really the one for you. Here are some resources for tips on job-shadowing, internships, volunteering, and other hands-on experiences.

Web Resources

◆ Get That Internship—And Excel in It! (www.quintcareers.com/internship_tutorial/)

◆ How to Find Your Ideal Internship (www.quintcareers.com/finding_ideal_internship.html)

◆ Informational Interviewing: A Powerful Tool for College Students (www.quintcareers.com/student_informational_interviewing.html)

◆ Internship Resources for College Students (www.quintcareers.com/grad_internships.html)

◆ Job Shadowing (www.jobshadow.org)

◆ Making the Most of Your Internship(s) (www.quintcareers.com/internship_success.html)

◆ Researching Companies and Careers Through Job Shadowing (www.quintcareers.com/job_shadowing.html)

◆ Volunteering and Nonprofit Career Resources (www.quintcareers.com/volunteering.html)

Books

Bravo, Dario, and Carol Whitely. *The Internship Advantage: Get Real-World Job Experience to Launch Your Career*. Upper Saddle River, NJ: Prentice-Hall Press, 2005.

Fedorko, Jamie, and Dwight Allott. *The Intern Files: How to Get, Keep, and Make the Most of Your Internship*. New York: Simon Spotlight Entertainment, 2006.

Hamadeh, Samer, and Mark Oldman. *Vault Guide to Top Internships*. New York: Vault, 2007.

Landes, Michael. *The Backdoor Guide to Short-Term Job Adventures: Internships, Summer Jobs, Season Work, Volunteer Vacations, and Transitions Abroad*. Berkeley, CA: Ten Speed Press, 2005.

Liang, Jengyee. *Hello Real World! A Student's Approach to Great Internships, Co-ops, and Entry Level Positions*. Charleston, SC: BookSurge Publishing, 2006.

Oldman, Mark, and Samer Hamadeh. *Best 109 Internships*. New York: Princeton Review, 2003.

Index